Seeing the Unseeable

Data, Design, Art

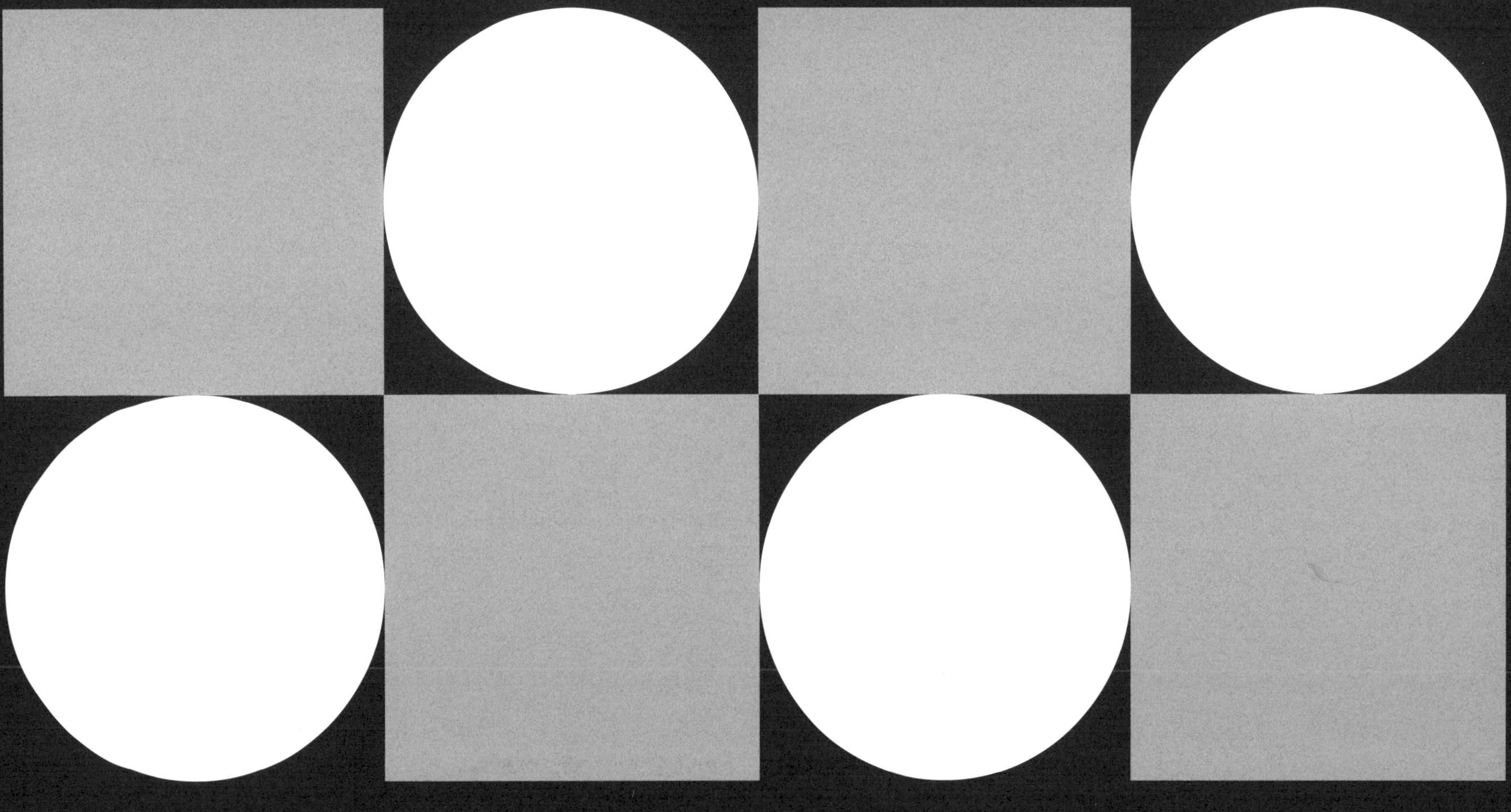

Seeing the Unseeable

Data, Design, Art

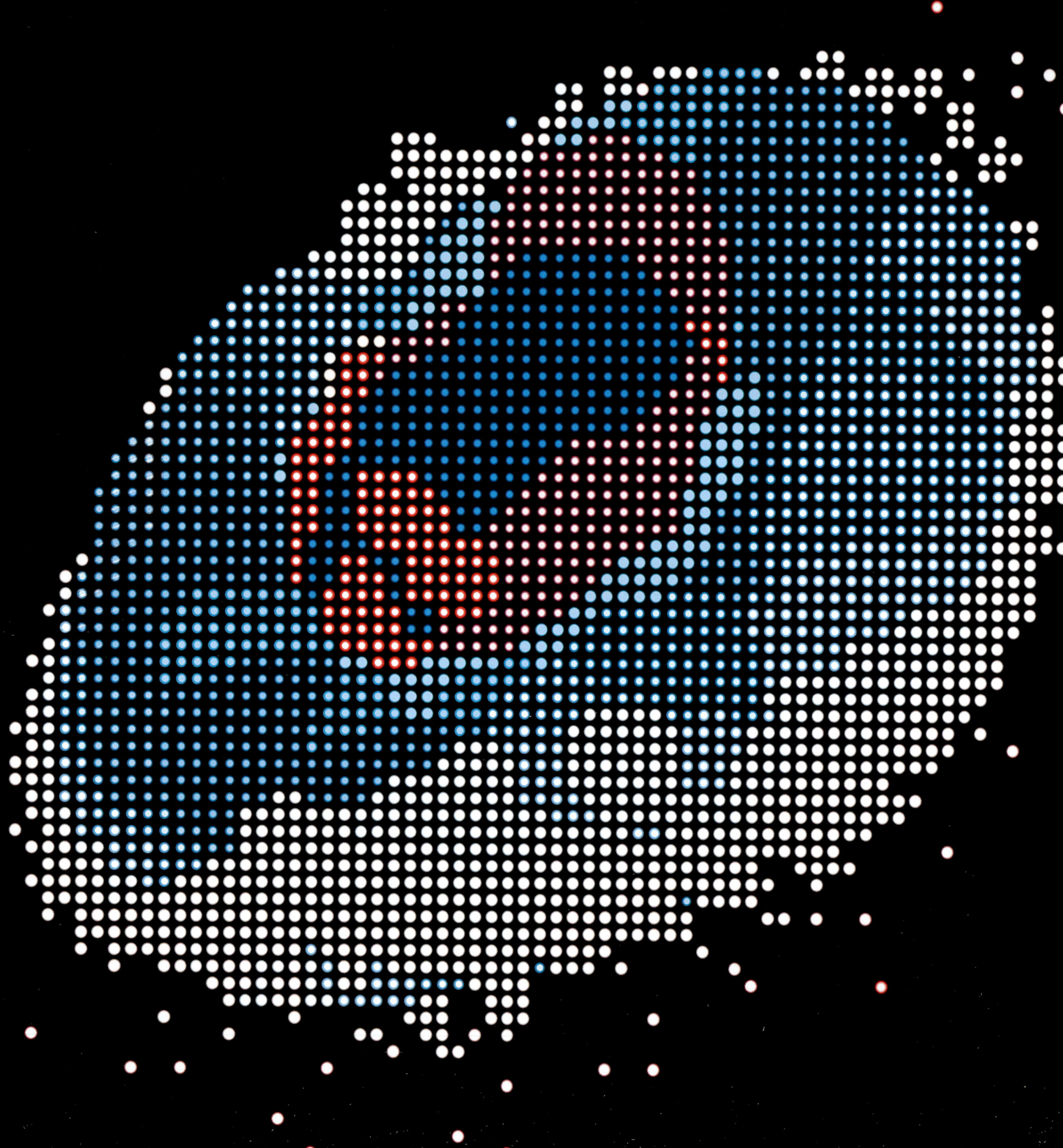

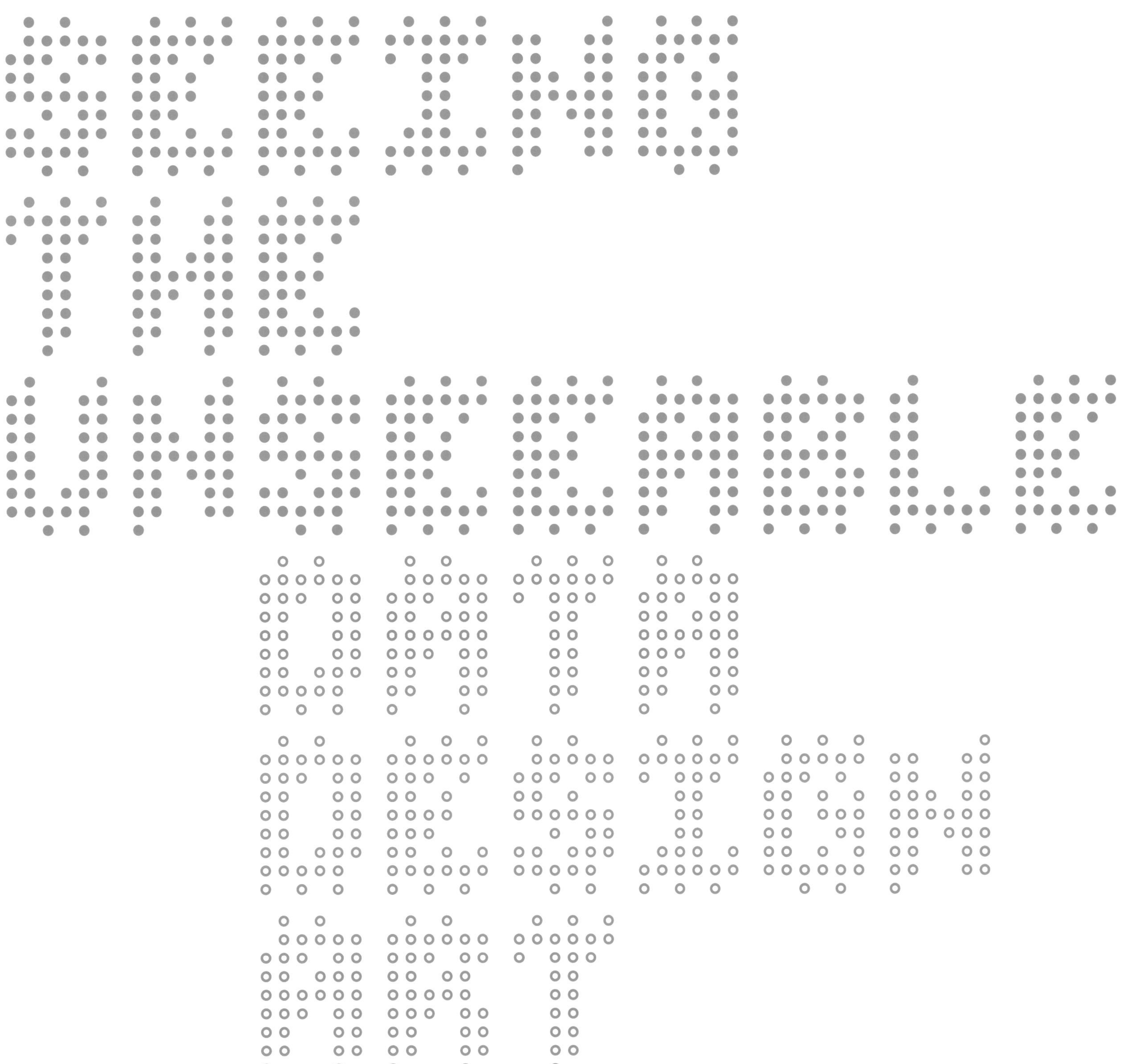

ArtCenter
College
of Design

HIRMER

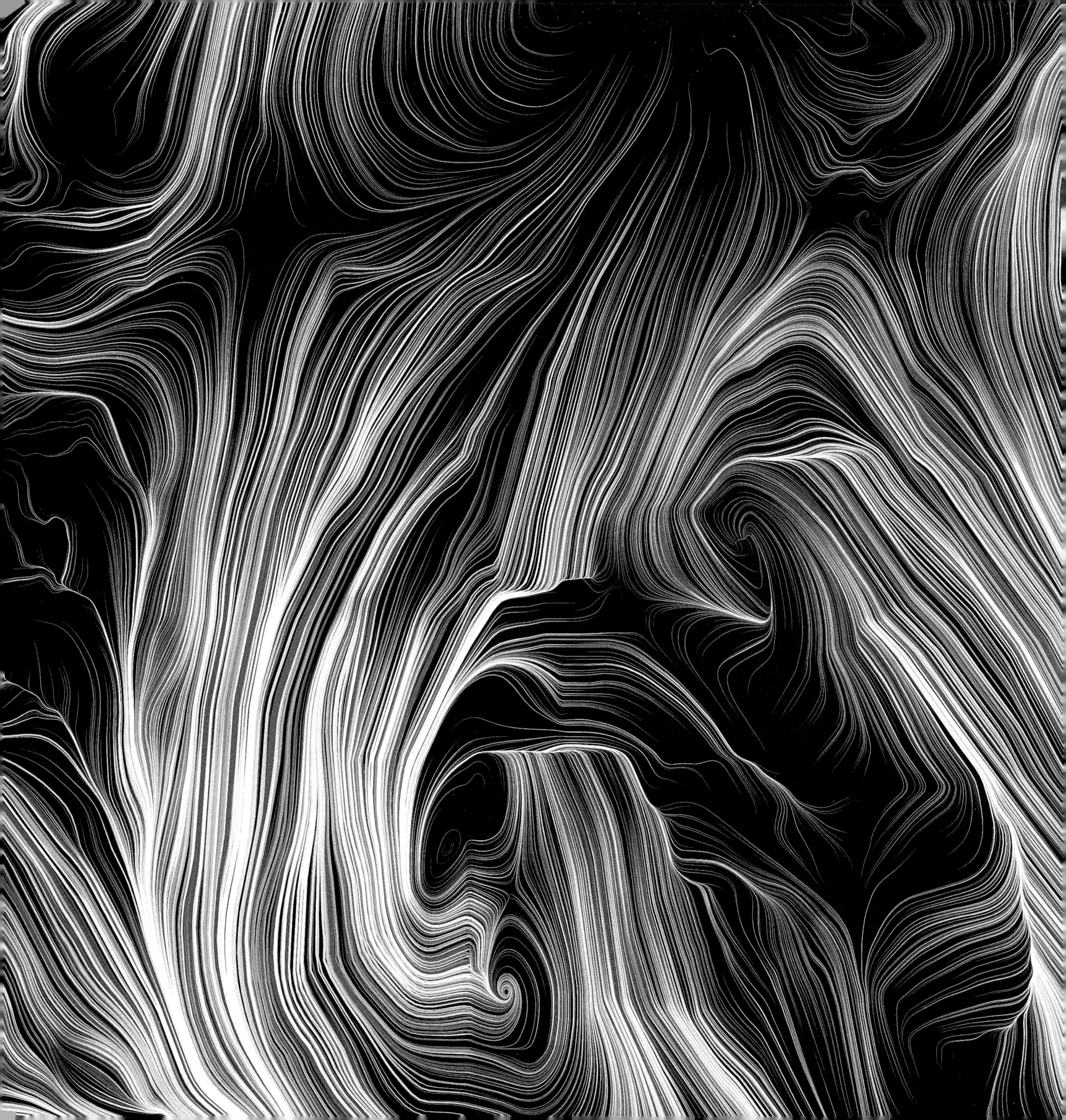

Contents

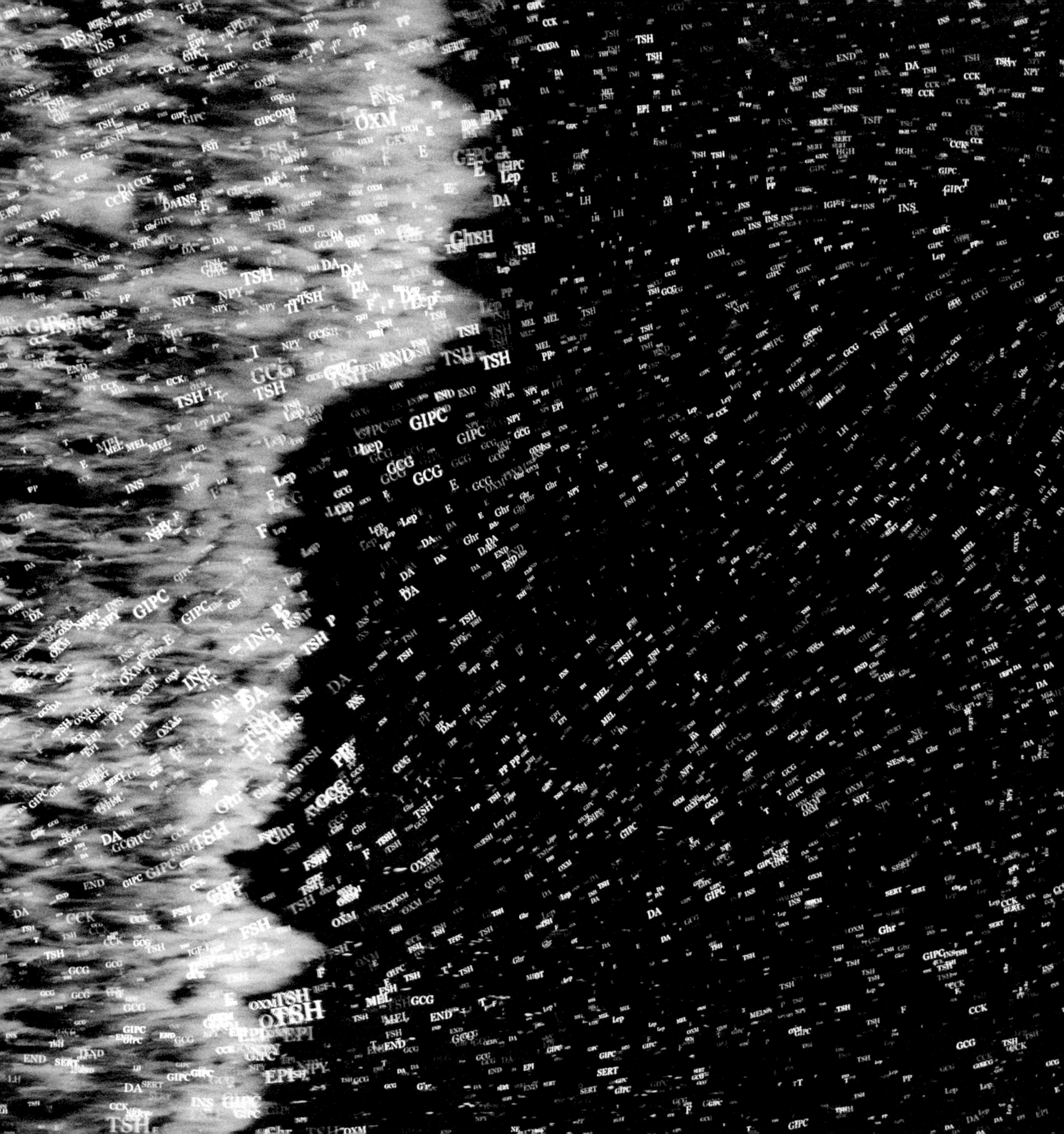

Foreword

In the wake of Big Data, or at least since the coining of the term in 1989,[1] the technological means and capacity to gather and mine data have advanced as rapidly as the ways to comprehend and utilize these incessantly multiplying depositories of information. Data visualization, the practice of representing vast magnitudes of information with the aim of making them understandable and engaging, is a field of study and practice that has been evolving. In its early and most basic form, data visualization is a method of design stemming from mapping and statistics. Due to advancements in machine learning and its potential for storage and processing, today it is considered indispensable to organizations ranging from business and government to healthcare and beyond. Correspondingly, data visualization has become an increasingly influential force in art and design, so much so that it has transformed visual literacy in the global cultural landscape.

This publication, *Seeing the Unseeable: Data, Design, Art*, emerged from an exhibition of the same title exploring data and data visualization in contemporary art and design. Featuring sixteen contemporary artists and designers (including collaboratives), it presents works from the past two decades that occupy the intersection between the practice of communicating quantitative information and the realization of new forms of expression. Representing an array of media, the exhibition and publication expose some of the most urgent and culturally relevant discussions surrounding the collection, manipulation, and critique of data in our current era, an extremely powerful dynamic that remains largely unseen in the public domain. Embracing forms ranging from the digital to the analog, and genres from art to design and craft, this project reveals persuasive contemporary viewpoints emerging from the rise of Big Data and its relationship to the extended debate between man and machine. More significantly, the exhibition and publication aim to provide compelling and alternative perspectives of how the manipulation of data may affect our daily lives.

The impetus for *Seeing the Unseeable* lies as much in the history of exhibitions at ArtCenter College of Design as in the Getty PST ART initiative *Art & Science Collide*, launched in 2020 through a series of grants and resulting in seventy exhibitions throughout Southern California in fall 2024. This project is the most recent in a distinguished profile of art–science exhibitions at ArtCenter's Alyce de Roulet Williamson Gallery, developed over a forty-year period by its founding director, Stephen Nowlin, often in collaboration with institutions including the California Institute of Technology, Jet Propulsion Laboratory, Huntington Library, and other science-related nonprofits and organizations in the "city of science" that is Pasadena. This endeavor debuts at an opportune moment for the college, with its mission "Learn to create. Influence change." This mission is dynamically reaffirmed and reignited by College President Karen Hofmann, an intrepid advocate of culture for our campus and surrounding communities. This project would not have been possible without the support of countless other individuals at ArtCenter College of Design and at the Getty. Our deepest appreciation is extended to the people that make both institutions invaluable.

The research for *Seeing the Unseeable* began in the early days of the Covid-19 pandemic, after a sequence of exploratory meetings with ArtCenter principals including deans Maggie Hendrie and Jane McFadden, followed by the formation of an advisory committee in fall 2020. Crucial to the formation of the project was a series of remote meetings with our advisory committee, a carefully selected group of artists, designers, and data scientists who so generously gave us their time and advice: Yoon Chung Han, Santiago Lombeyda, Pietro Perona, George Djorgovski, Maggie Hendrie, Dan Goods, Michael Greene, and Jane McFadden. Through a series of remote roundtable discussions from 2021

1 Possibly the first use of the term Big Data in the way it is used today was by Erik Larson, in a 1989 article for *Harper's Magazine* speculating on the origin of the junk mail he receives. He writes: "The keepers of big data say they are doing it for the consumer's benefit. But data have a way of being used for purposes other than originally intended." Quoted in Bernard Marr, "Fourth Industrial Revolution: A brief history of big data everyone should read," World Economic Forum, February 25, 2015, https://www.weforum.org/stories/2015/02/a-brief-history-of-big-data-everyone-should-read/.

to 2023, we learned from such figures as curator Paola Antonelli and artists/designers Laurie Frick, Golan Levin, Giorgia Lupi, Linnéa Gabriella Spransy, Fernanda Viégas, Martin Wattenberg, and others. Coupled with discussions among exhibition curators and advisory committee members, the findings provided bounteous food for thought. Attending with us were select stakeholders in the Southern California art–science field, who also contributed and provided additional avenues of consideration surrounding data, science, data visualization, design, and art: David Familian, Robert Kett, Hillary Mushkin, Sheila Pinkel, Arden Stern, and Margaret Wertheim. Further investigations and discussions with artists and designers ensued, as did travel to studios, exhibitions, and meetings outside of Los Angeles, including the phenomenal Eyeo Festival 2022 in Minneapolis, where Hyesoo Christina Valentine and I were introduced to more wise people in the field than we can recount, such as the ever-helpful Jason Forrest as well as other notables including Jer Thorpe and Alberto Cairo.

Throughout the production phase of the project, we became indelibly reliant upon our highly astute and patient editor, Jane Hyun. At ArtCenter we would like to acknowledge our project polymath, Francie Wong; our creative problem solver, Marco Rios; and our attentive coordinator, Erik Trammel. In the final stages of the project, conversations with the book's designer, Brad Bartlett, provided stimulation and enlightenment. Heidrun Mumper-Drumm capably consulted and co-organized our participation in the PST ART Climate Impact Program, a new benchmark in exhibition management for sustainable practices that we look forward to maintaining in future projects. We owe a debt of gratitude to the exhibition lenders, whose consideration was often boundless. And finally, to our extraordinary artists and designers featured in the exhibition, we are eternally thankful and remain in awe of their work. Our highest praise is reserved for them.

While several data-related exhibitions have preceded *Seeing the Unseeable*, none have addressed the field of data visualization specifically nor have been accompanied by significant essays or catalogues. Certainly, no exhibition or publication has brought the work of the emerging and established artists, designers, and data visualization practitioners herein together in a single project. With a focus on art and design produced from 2000 to the present, *Seeing the Unseeable* adds currency to the lineages of art and design in genres such as the digital, conceptual, and generative. With less emphasis on advanced technologies newly employed by artists, or the visual novelty of technology, this effort focuses more on how its use in recent art and design manifests issues around cultural impact and ontological change.

During our research and discussions over the past four years, I, along with co-curators Stephen Nowlin and Hyesoo Christina Valentine, have been faced with a plethora of questions, issues, and sometimes obstacles that often generated additional queries and hurdles. While we have still to find many of the answers and resolve the breadth of matters that we set out to tackle, these questions linger in subtle and gratifying ways. They provoke. As the project lives on, it is our deep desire that viewers and readers are, in turn, able to share the curiosity, the consideration, and the astonishment that we have experienced in the making of this exhibition and publication.

Julie Joyce
Director, ArtCenter Galleries
Vice President, Exhibitions

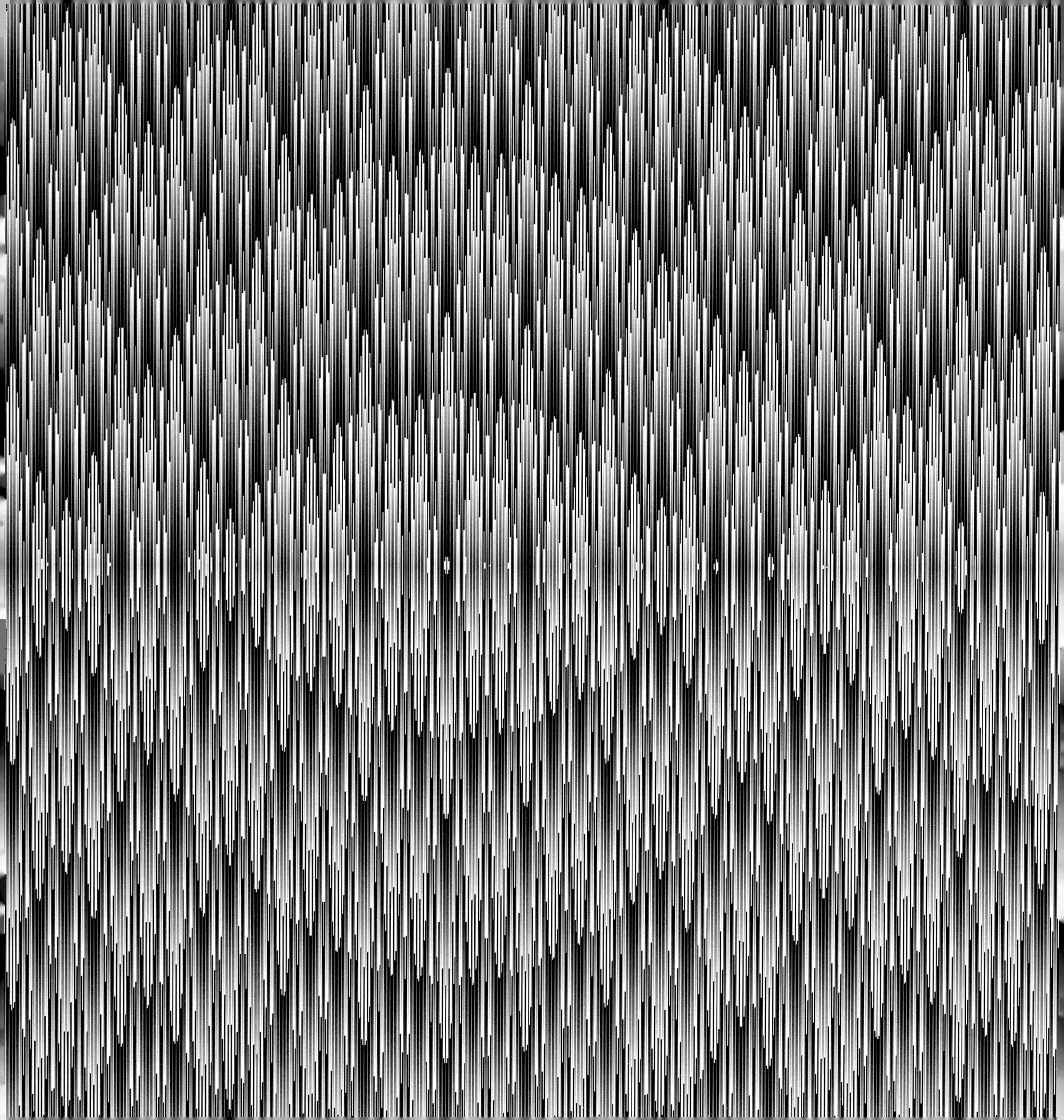

Conceived as a response to Big Data's outsized role in modern life, *Seeing the Unseeable* highlights works from the twenty-first century occupying the intersection of quantitative information and innovative forms of expression.

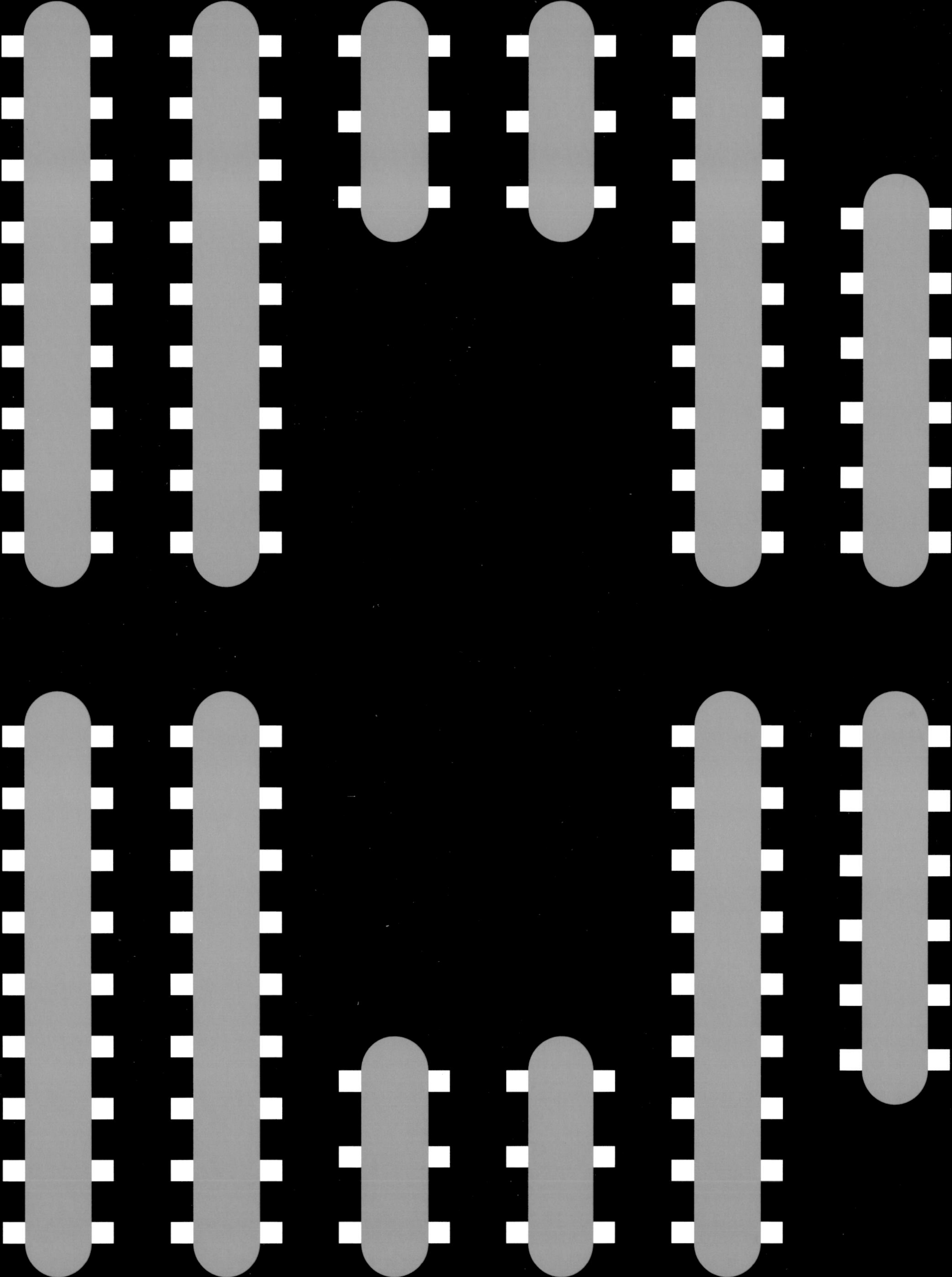

The hidden architectures that shape the visible today no longer consist of muscles and nerves, but of data and networks.

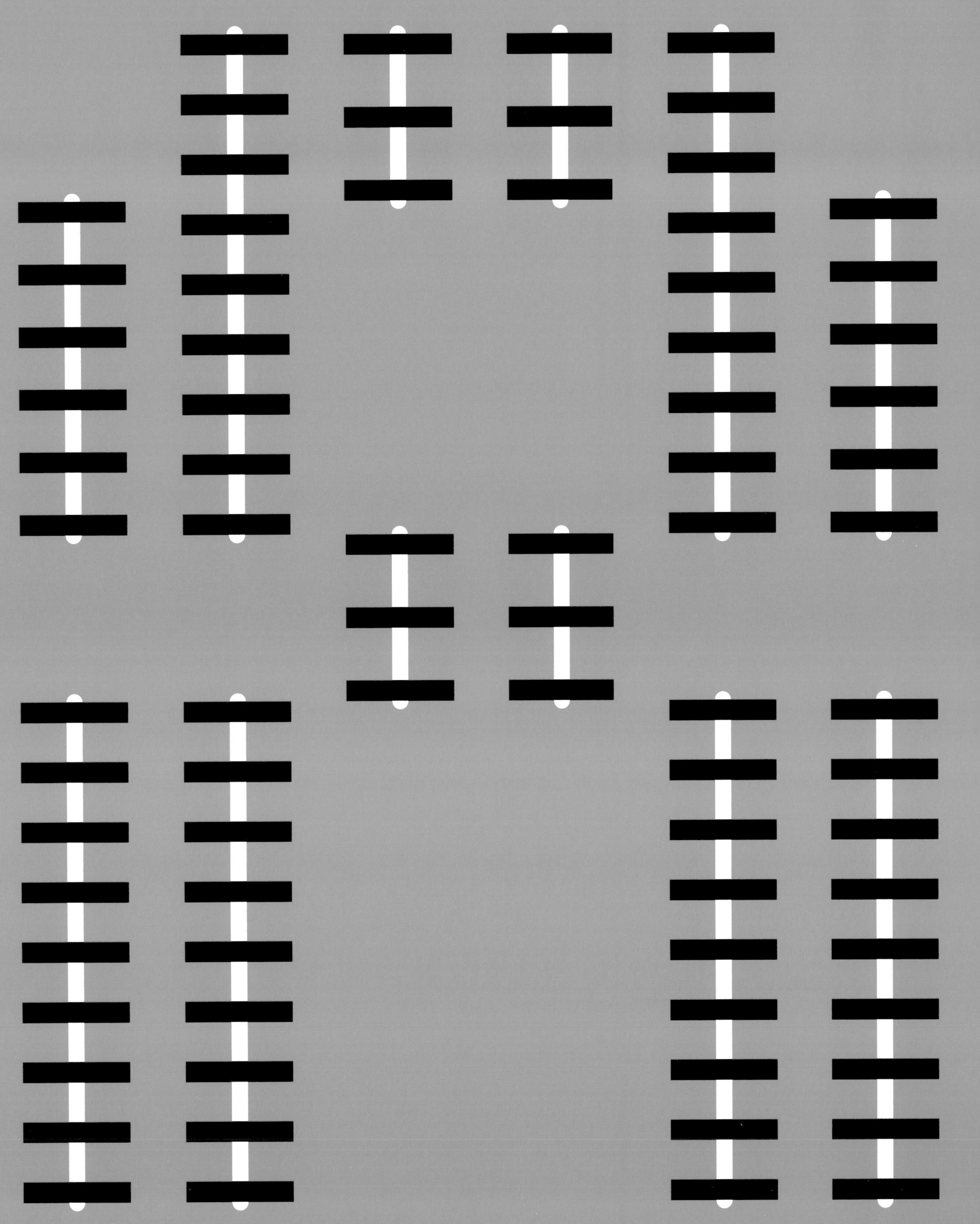

We're drowning (not waving) in a sea of data—with data, data everywhere, but not a drop of information.

HITO STEYERL

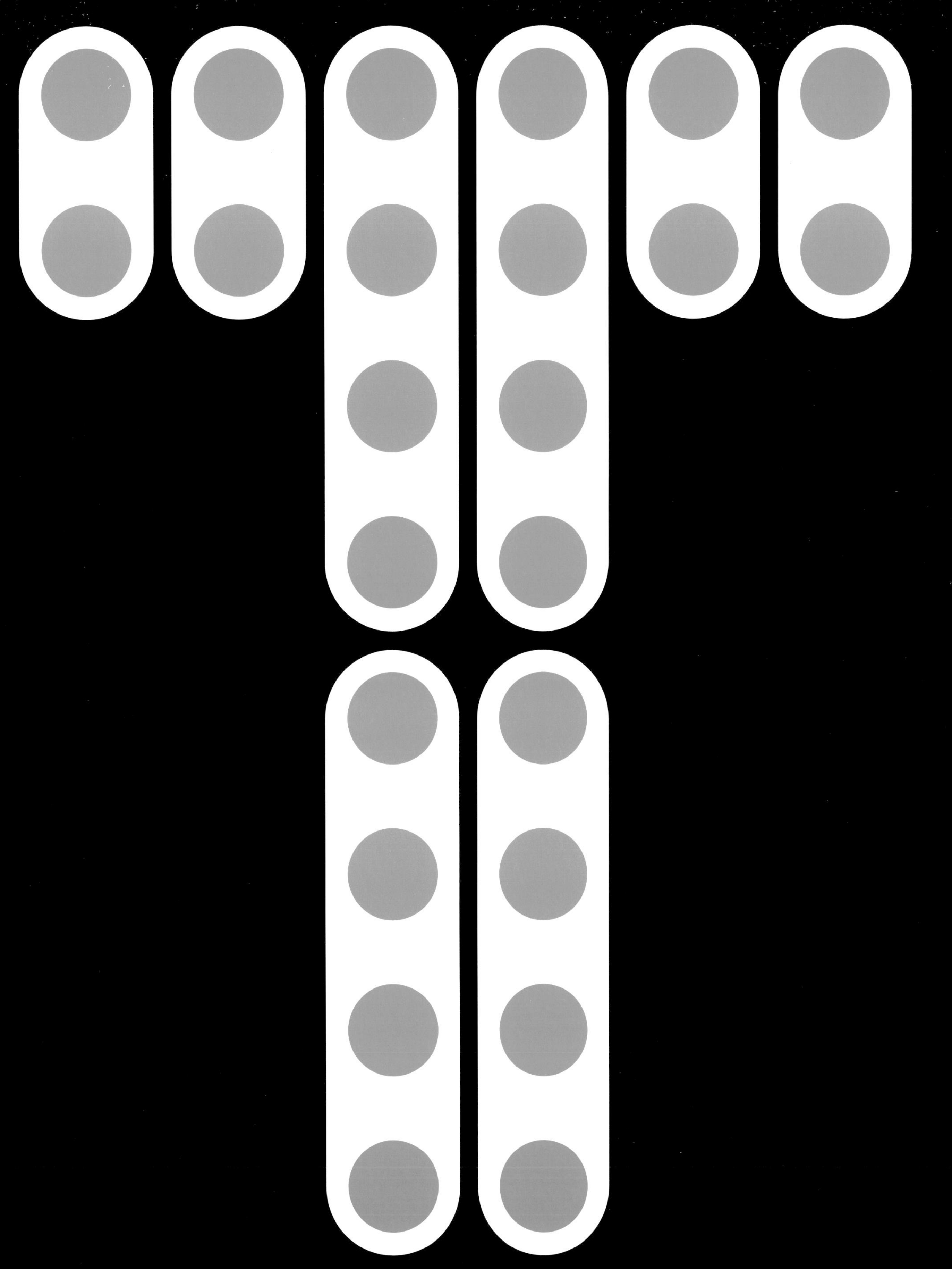

Seeing is superseded by calculating probabilities. Vision loses importance and is replaced by filtering, decrypting, and pattern recognition.

HITO STEYERL

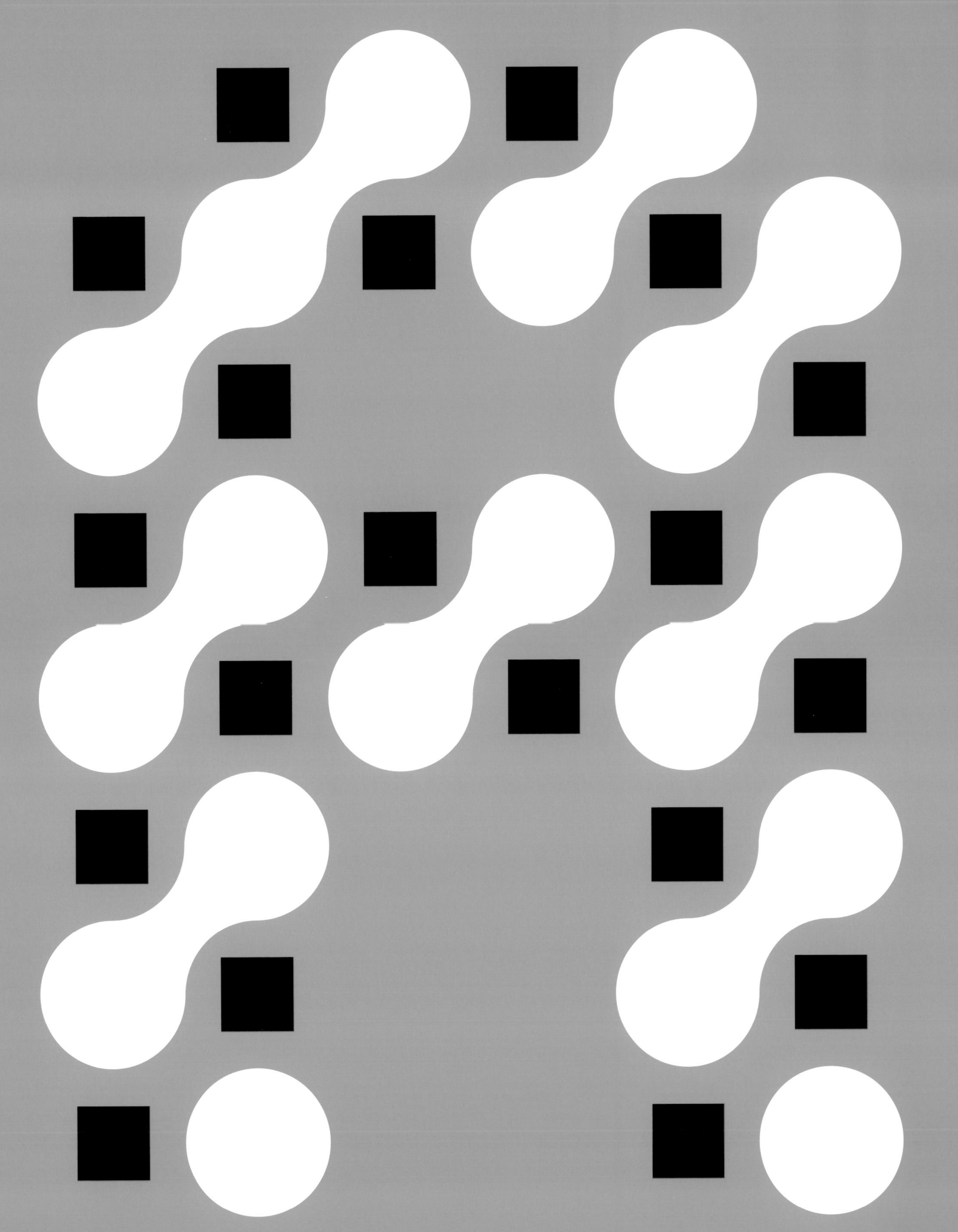

Introduction

The Cultural Ubiquity of Data

The once-uncharted, quotidian actions of our lives are now defined in data. From Apple Watches, Fitbits, and smartphones tracking the hours we sleep and steps we take, to multinational corporations scraping data on our digital consumption, every moment is available for harvest. We may not be able to see the mechanism working, but data algorithms can certainly be felt through the advertisements and content driven to us on our social media and entertainment feeds. So, it's no surprise that the term "data" is seen, heard, and spoken of daily in a variety of contexts, and data visualization has casually slipped into our visual vernacular in popular culture.[1]

This growing normalization and familiarity of data has loosened the term from its functional definition and opened it up for examination and experimentation. Given how ubiquitous data is in our lives, this is a timely moment to present an exhibition exploring the response of artists and designers to this subject. *Seeing the Unseeable* offers a spectrum of work that delves into the use and interpretation of data for scientific research and as a creative medium to prompt pertinent questions and issues surrounding data: What comprises data? How does it influence us? What are the societal implications? This exhibition calls attention to our complex relationship to data by creative individuals who are deeply interested in the outcomes, effects, and imaginings of this aspect of our digital age.

In essence, data is quite an abstract concept: a set of information that translates and represents our world for study. In many ways, the artists and designers featured in *Seeing the Unseeable* push the boundaries of data visualization design as

1 In movie franchises such as *Ironman* and *Mission Impossible*, data visualization has been used as visual plot points. In both series, data visualization is used to represent characters. In *Avengers: Age of Ultron* (2015), the AI character J.A.R.V.I.S. is visually introduced as a layered network map. The AI character known as the Entity is similarly represented in *Mission: Impossible – Dead Reckoning Part One* and *Part Two* (2023 and 2024). The visual representation is less about actual information than the semblance of large, aggregated data that forms the AI characters: more a signifier of information rather than actual data.

an art form, marking a turning point in what has been termed the fourth Industrial Revolution.[2] A primary feature of the works presented is the use of data as an artistic medium, such as Refik Anadol's digital paintings (*California Landscapes*, 2023), comprising over 150 million images of California national parks sifted through a customized algorithm, and Sarah Morris's household paint on canvas works (*Sound Graph* series, 2018–20) that translate audio recordings into sound graphs. Others are more straightforwardly invested in scientific research, as in Data to Discovery's data visualization models (*3DDNA* and *GRVN*, 2016–24) and Semiconductor art collaborative's colorful exploration of the lives of young stars (*Spectral Constellations*, 2022).

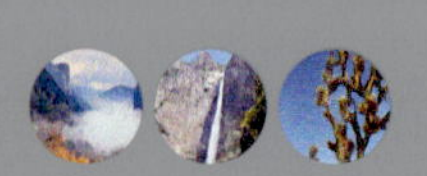
→ 32–33, 103–5

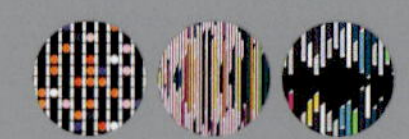
→ 44–45, 131–33

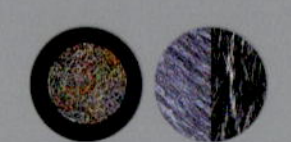
→ 31, 107–9

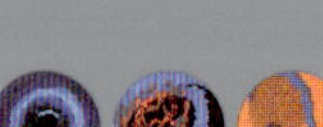
→ 2, 42–43, 72–73, 139–41

Seeing the Unseeable broadly focuses on three facets of creative approaches to data. The first, Data Humanism, highlights the visualization of data that aims to personalize and reaffirm the human experience behind data's reductiveness. For designer Giorgia Lupi and visual artist Ehren Shorday, this means experimenting with ways to convey human complexity through design. Their series *Incroci (Crossings)* (2022) features "data portraits" of one hundred individuals, each marking five significant moments in their subjects' lives beginning at birth to 2020, the year of the global Covid-19 pandemic shutdown. At once informative and intimate, this project represents a hybrid of design and art as it profoundly and simultaneously affirms the individual and community. Mika Tajima takes this further in her work *Archive of Feelings* (2023). The NFT videos articulate the emotional state of an entire city by translating data-scraped emotive terms posted on X (formerly Twitter), at midnight on New

→ 38–39, 123–25

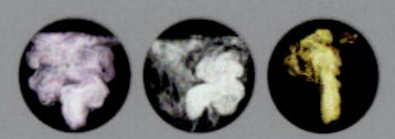
→ 50–51, 151–53

2 Klaus Schwab, founder and executive chairman of the World Economic Forum, coined the term in his book *The Fourth Industrial Revolution* (2016).

Year's Eve 2023, into a sensually undulating column of digital smoke. The work encapsulates the ineffable sentiments of hope and regret into a visual representation shifting in color and shape.

Artists Laurie Frick and Rafael Lozano-Hemmer also explore the human behind tracked biometric data and intimate details, engendering feelings of tenderness in representing our shared condition of living. Frick delves into the personal in her diptych → 40, 111–13 *Moodjam Intense* and *Moodjam Mild* (both 2024). Through a color-coding system the artist devised, reclaimed countertop tile samples of various colors are used to represent the artist's meticulous recording of her own physiological data. Lozano- → 6, 8, 31, 119–21 Hemmer's digital work *Hormonium (Text Stream 8)* (2022) is a literal body clock. Seemingly a video of crashing ocean waves, the work illustrates the ebb and flow of hormones (represented by their abbreviated names released in the retreating waves) tracked in real time over a ninety-year lifespan.

Another theme in the exhibition is Invisible Data, which addresses the intangibility of data and features those investigating the socio-political act of making data invisible. In works → 52–53, 115–17 such as George Legrady's *Phantom Waves Series* (2020–21) and Linnéa Gabriella Spransy's *Prime Mover* paintings (2019– → 34, 36–37, 86, 147–49 23), images are created out of numbers, the core elements of data. Both artists show numbers in a kind of pure form, beyond functioning as mere representations or translations of a subject. → 41, 135–37 Researcher and artist Mimi Ọnụọha's *Library of Missing Data Sets* (2016–21) calls attention to data bias through a series of filing cabinets filled with empty folders labeled with subjects that are overlooked or deliberately ignored.

Finally, data as an artistic medium can be seen in **Data Environments,** a range of works in the exhibition that creatively engage in conversations about our natural environment including climate change—a topic that is inundated with data to the point of paralysis. Iñigo Manglano-Ovalle's suspended, silvery cloud sculptures such as *Storm Prototype* (2006) are derived from storm data gathered by climatologists. The works are both physical and metaphorical in meaning, as actual storms parallel the migration of climate refugees. Evocative as a delicate line drawing, Fernanda Viégas and Martin Wattenberg's live-streamed digital *Wind Map* (2012) elegantly traces wind currents across the United States in real time and is considered an icon in the field of data design.[3] As wind speed and direction can be seen over specific regions in both macro and micro scales, the work personalizes the impact of the winds as they shift and grow in response to climate change. A more abstract representation of weather in the work of Hyojung Seo prompts a reconsideration of weather patterns as Singapore's wind data is visualized in undulating lines of sheet music and spiny circular forms that resemble sea urchins. While derived by data, the movement and composition of the playful work personifies the winds over Singapore as chimerical entities.

In works by such artists as Christine Wertheim, Margaret Wertheim, and Peggy Weil, data is approached as being embedded in nature. Selections from the Wertheims' crochet coral reefs drive home the devastation of coral ecosystems due to pollution, as the sculptural works are crocheted from the very plastic that is at the heart of the issue. Weil's photo installation

→ 34–35, 86, 127–29

→ 4, 49, 155–57

→ 30, 143–45

→ 46–48, 90, 98, 163–65

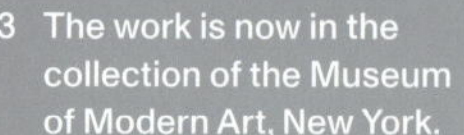

3 The work is now in the collection of the Museum of Modern Art, New York.

of archived ice cores taken from the Greenland Ice Sheet offers

→ 27–28, 159–61

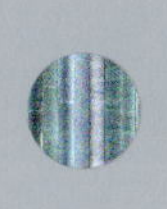

a walk back through time, as the cores are a de facto index of Earth's geological and atmospheric history.

These three thematic strands present some of the various ways data is being navigated from a philosophical approach and a position of critical analysis and creative application. And far from being limited to one approach to understanding, the works in *Seeing the Unseeable* interrelate and intersect, creating new and engaging pathways and ideas. While we have yet to know how this emergent and at times invasive practice of translating our lived experiences into data will affect us as a society, the artists in *Seeing the Unseeable* present countervailing propositions on how to navigate through and alongside technology and its byproducts. Throughout modern history, artists have been at the forefront of engaging with the technologies of their moment, their findings eventually distilling into the collective consciousness. At the heart of this project are the deeply thoughtful and visionary investigations by these artists and designers, whose work and ideas will continue to resonate in their respective fields.

Hyesoo Christina Valentine
Associate Director, ArtCenter Galleries
Curator, Exhibitions

Installation Views

Seeing the Unseeable: Data, Design, Art at the Alyce de Roulet Williamson Gallery, ArtCenter College of Design, Pasadena, California, 2024–25

Map of the installation

→

Peggy Weil, *77 Cores*, 2024

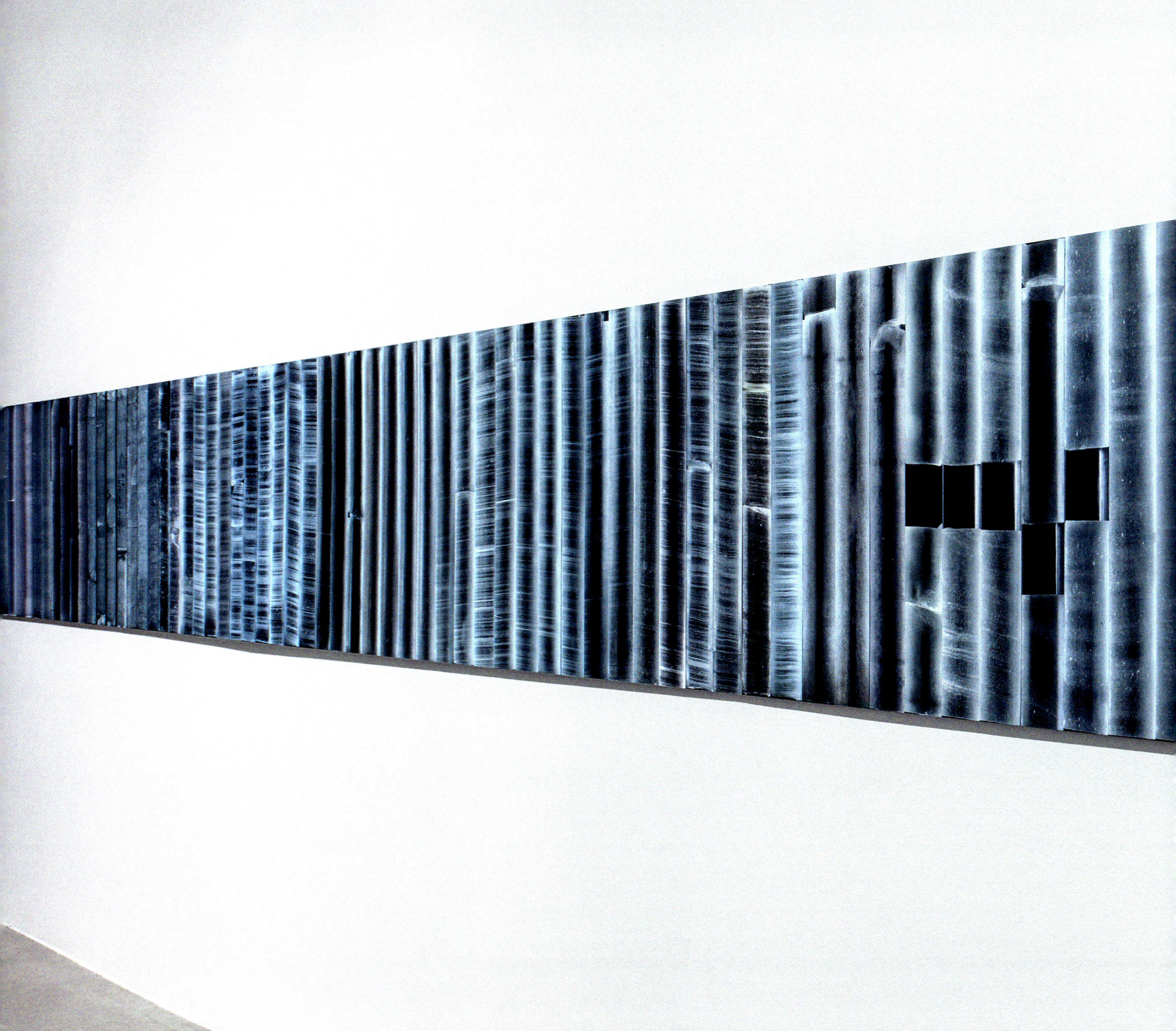

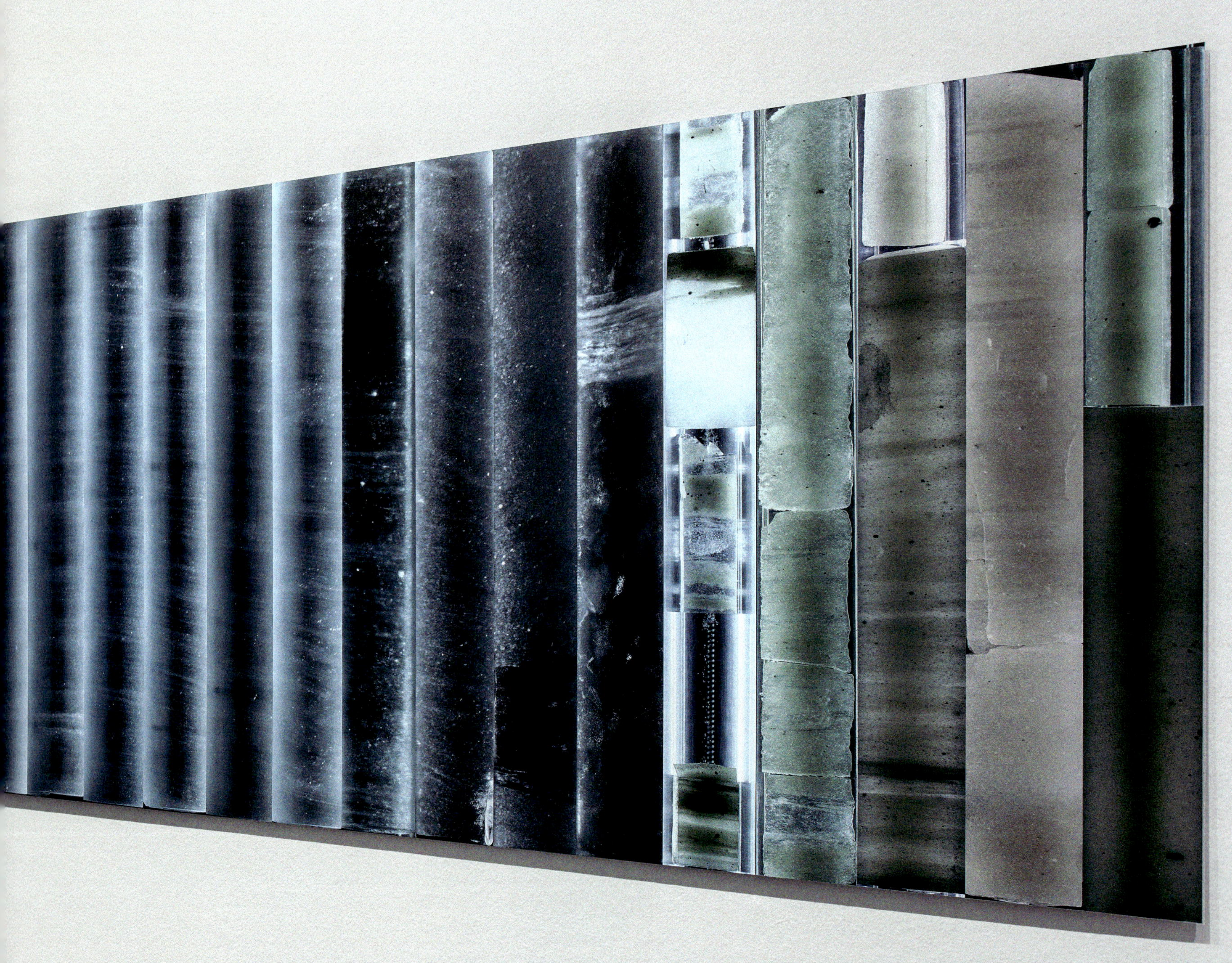

←
Peggy Weil, *77 Cores*, 2024

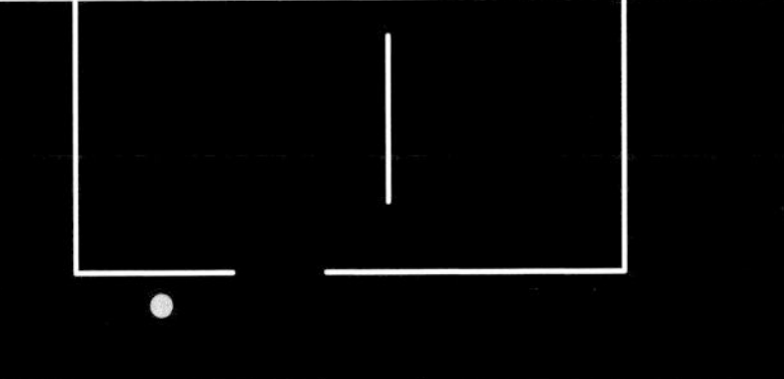

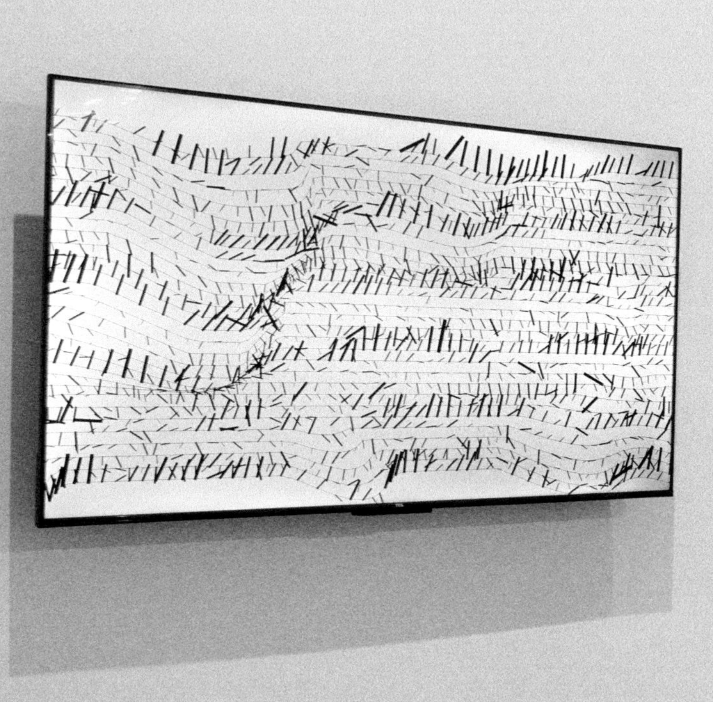

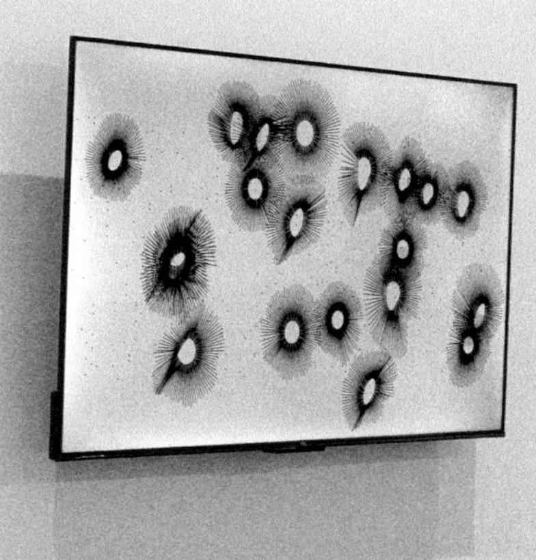

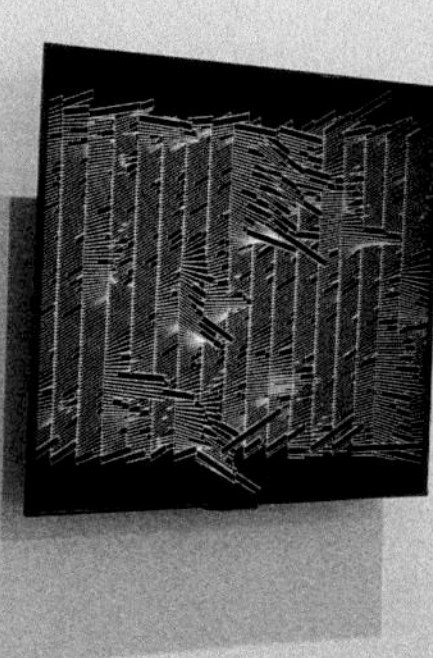

↑
Hyojung Seo

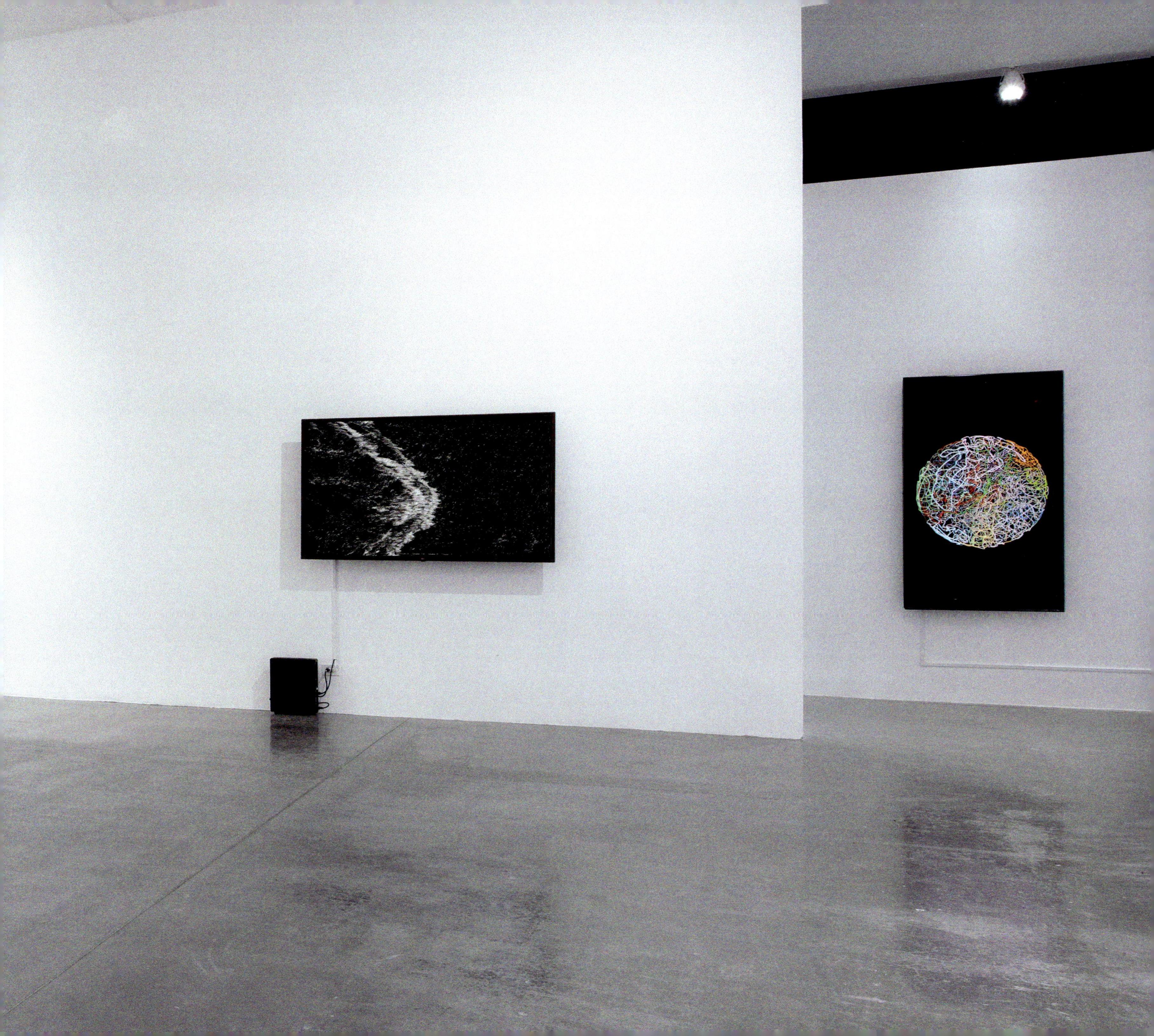

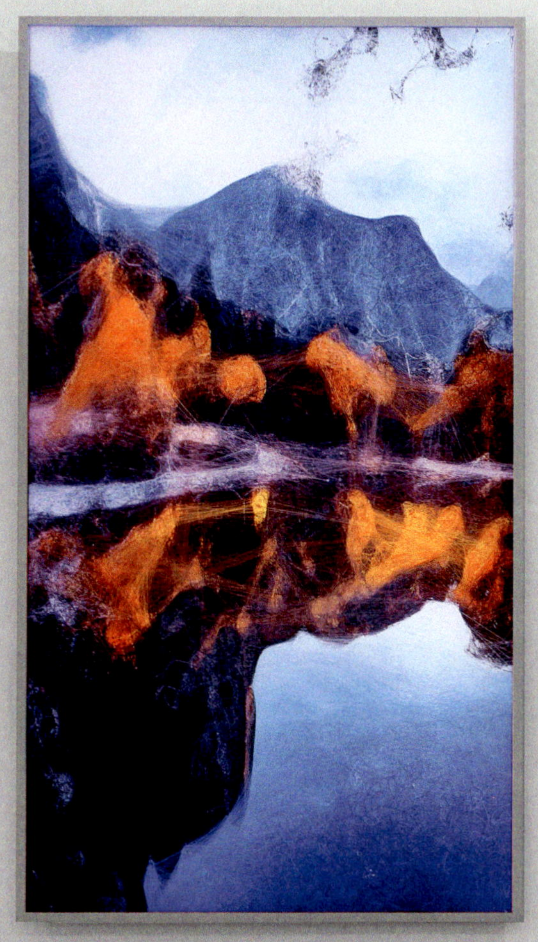

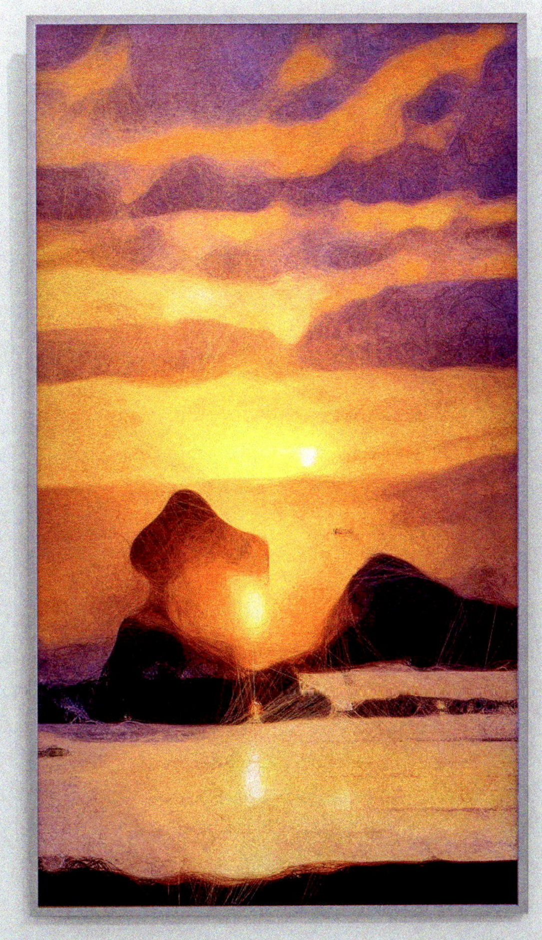

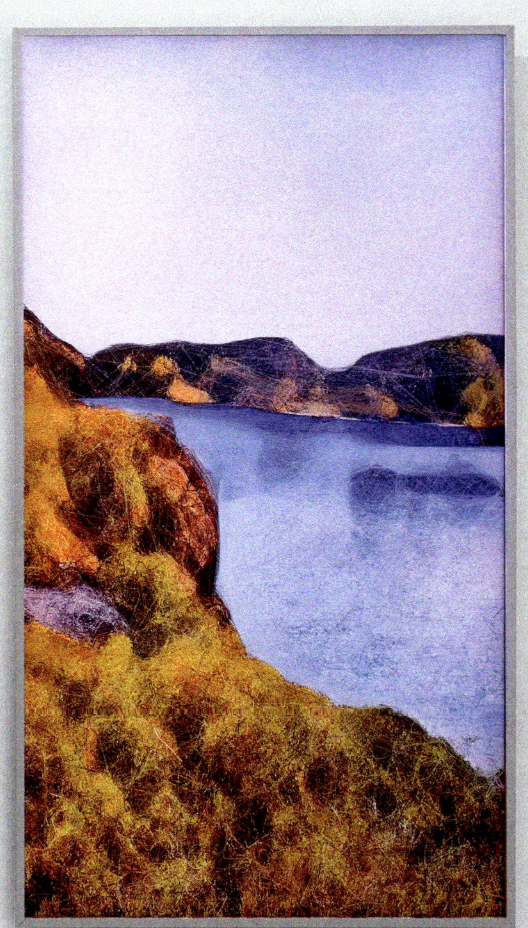

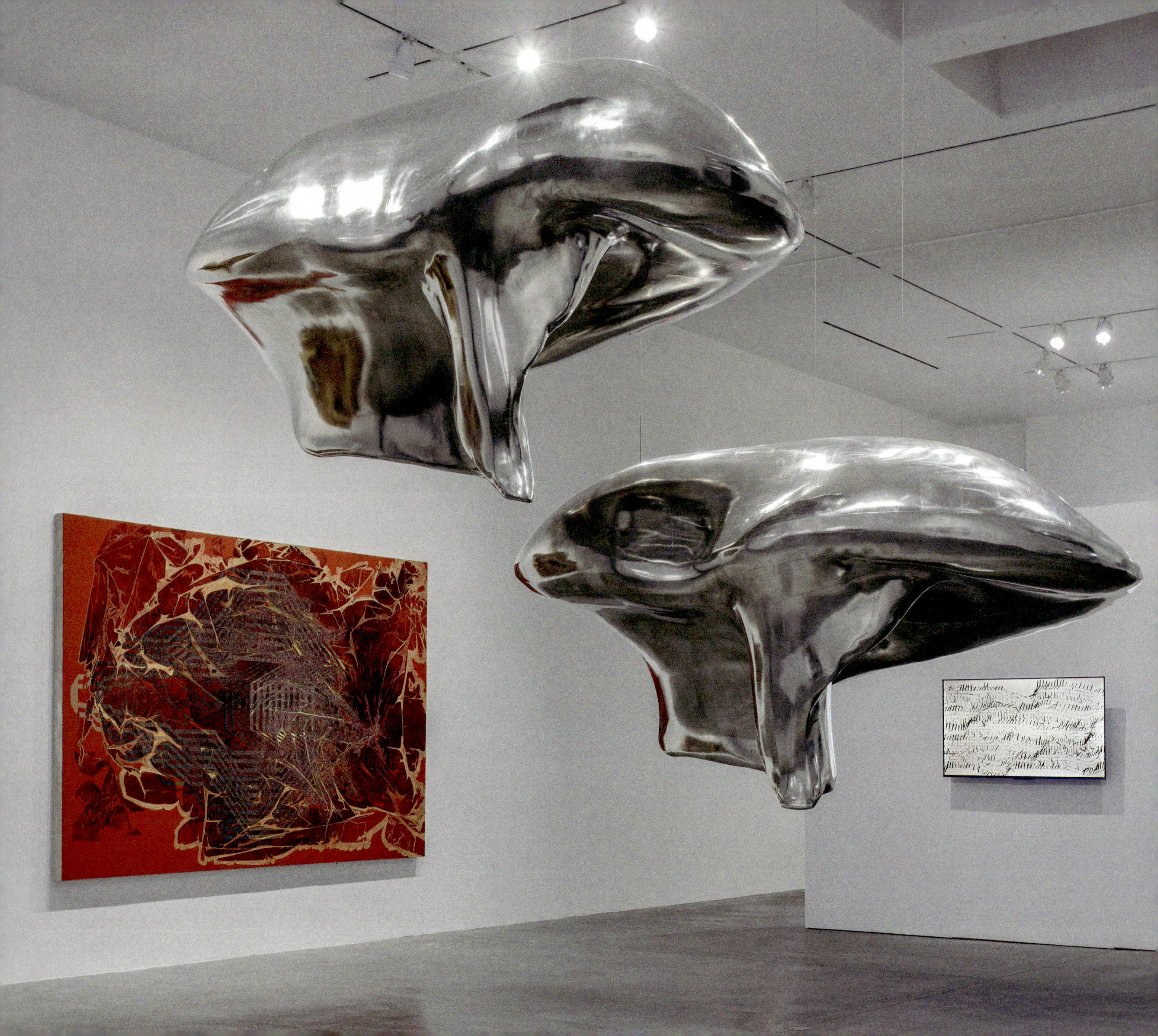

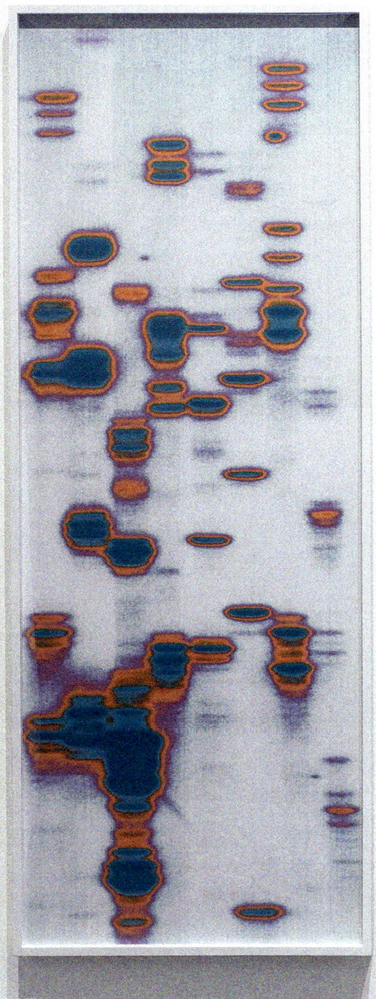
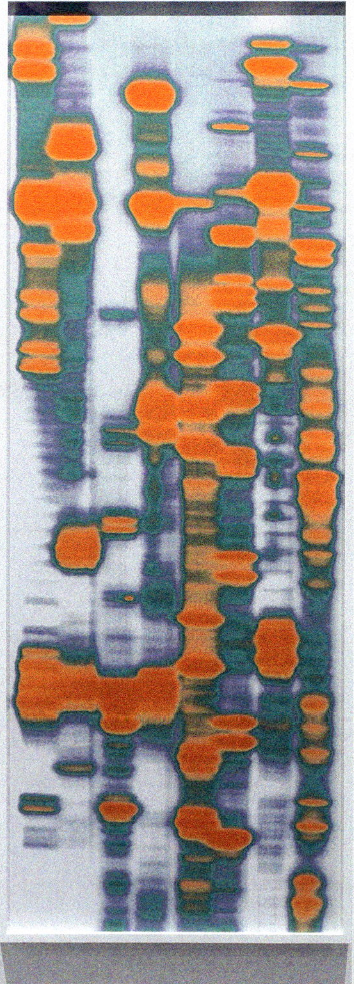
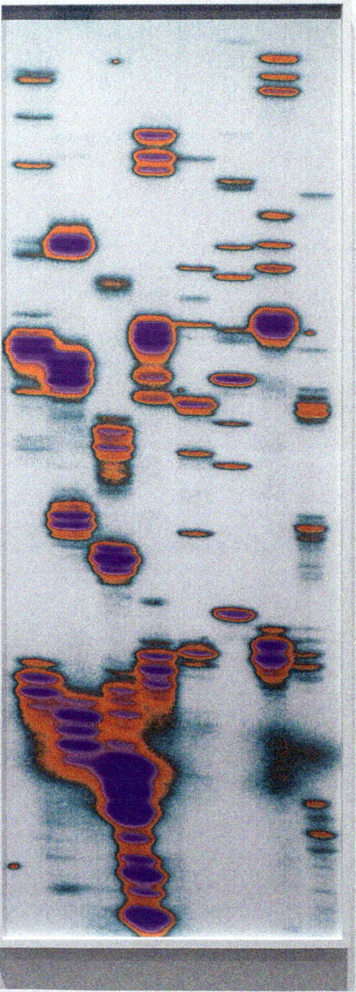

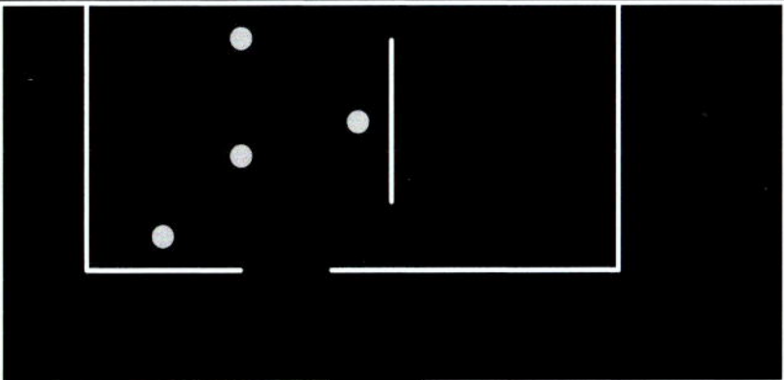

↑
Iñigo Manglano-Ovalle, *Lu, Jack and Carrie* (from *The Garden of Delights*), 1998

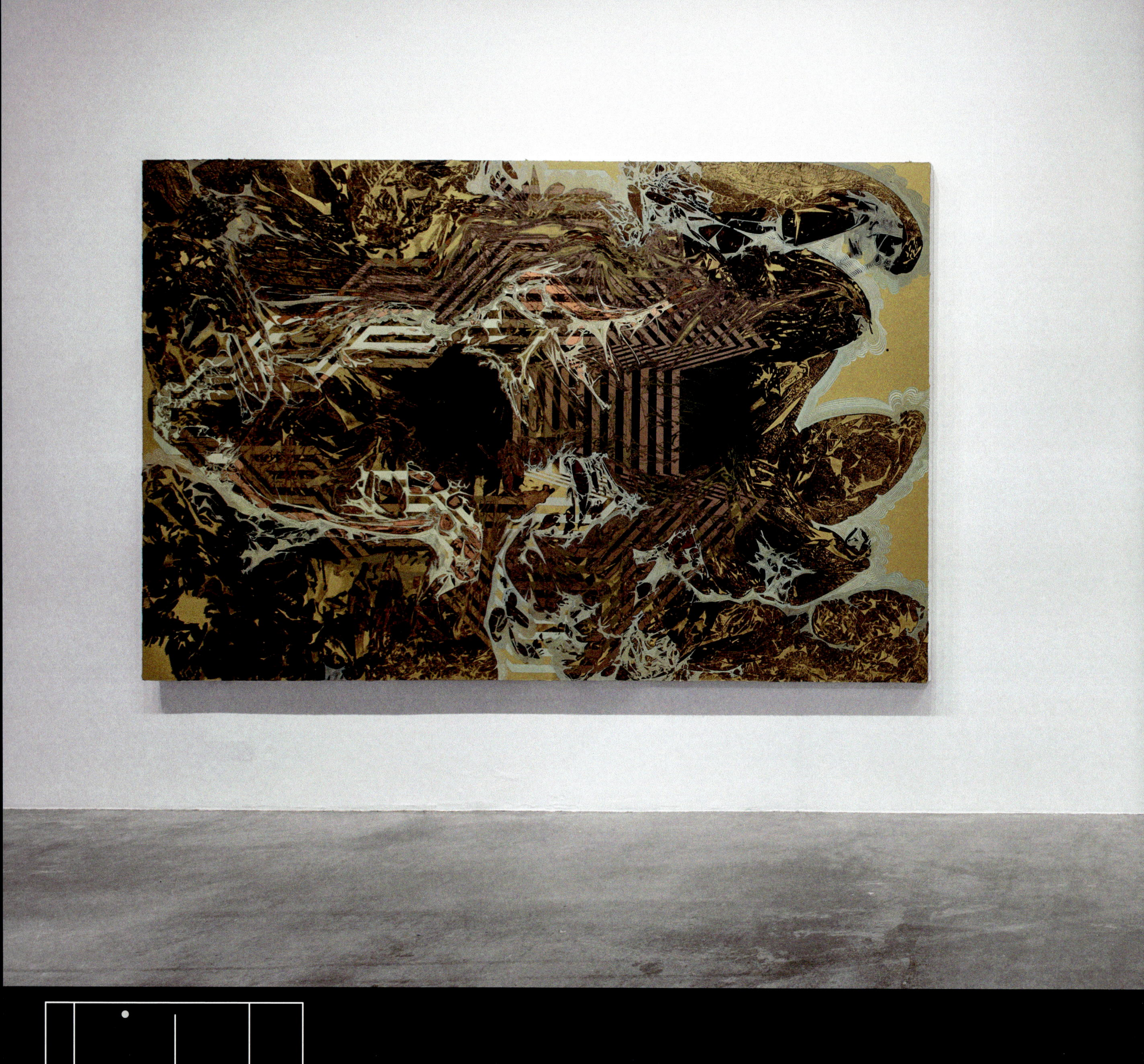

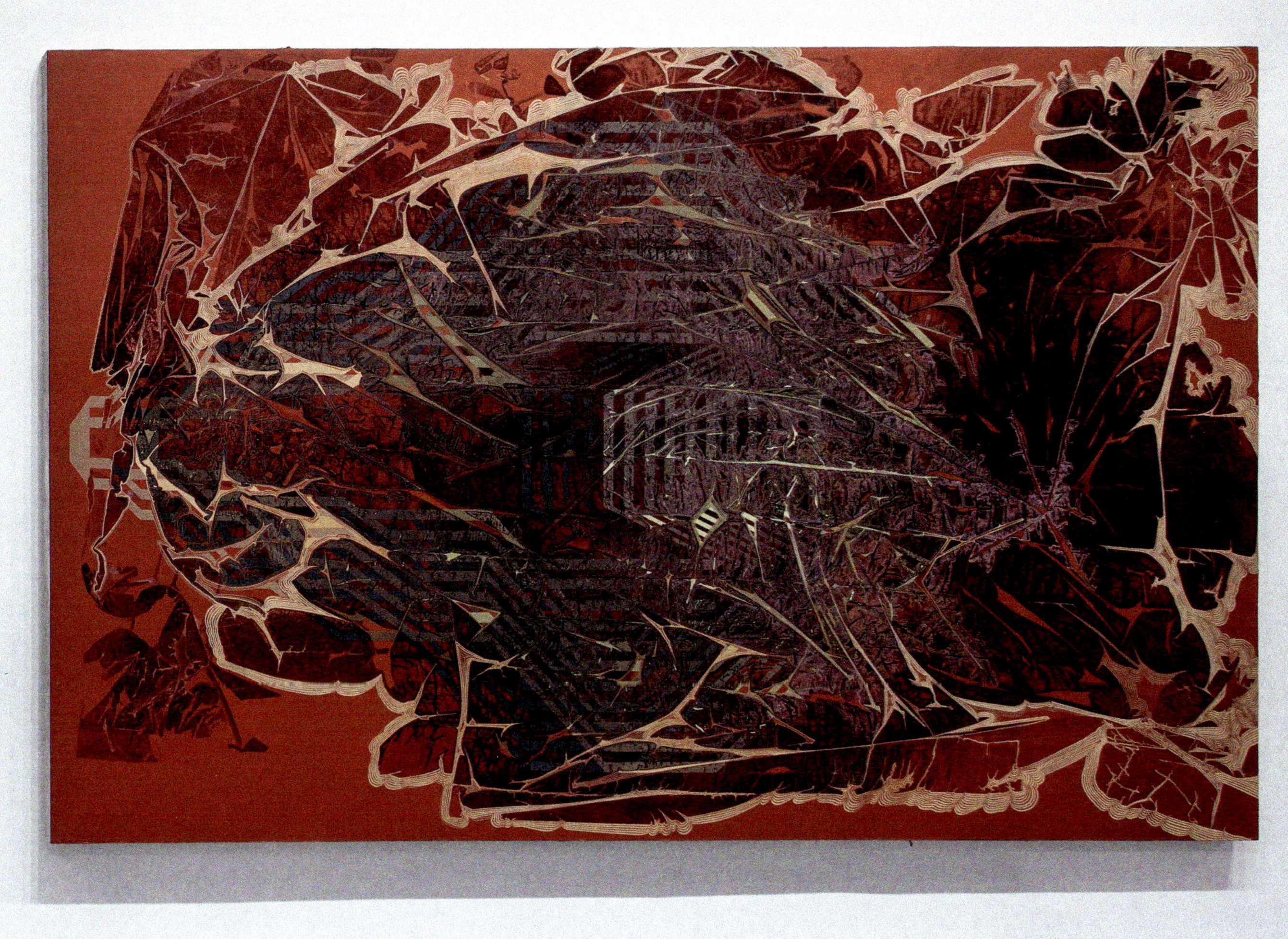

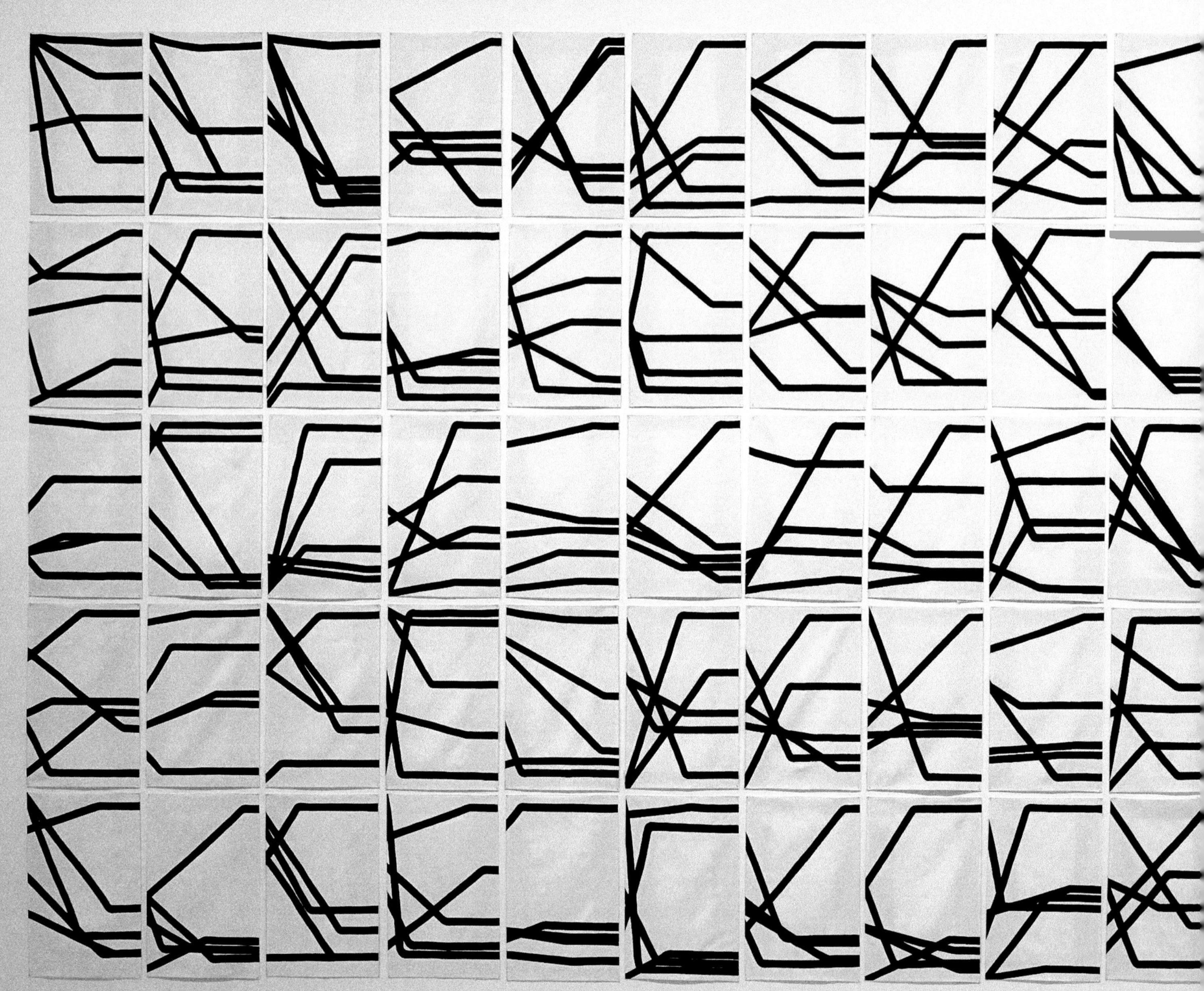

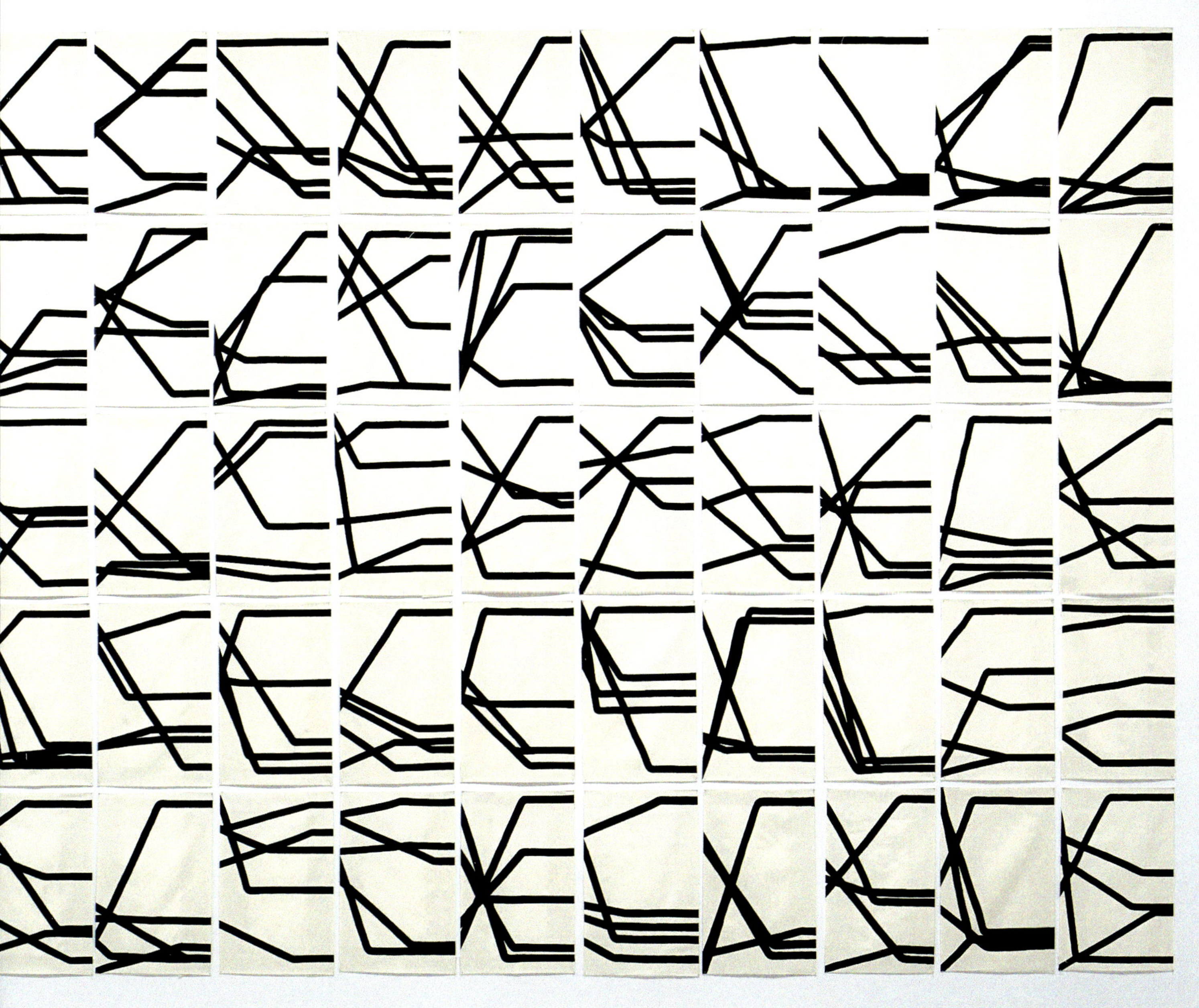

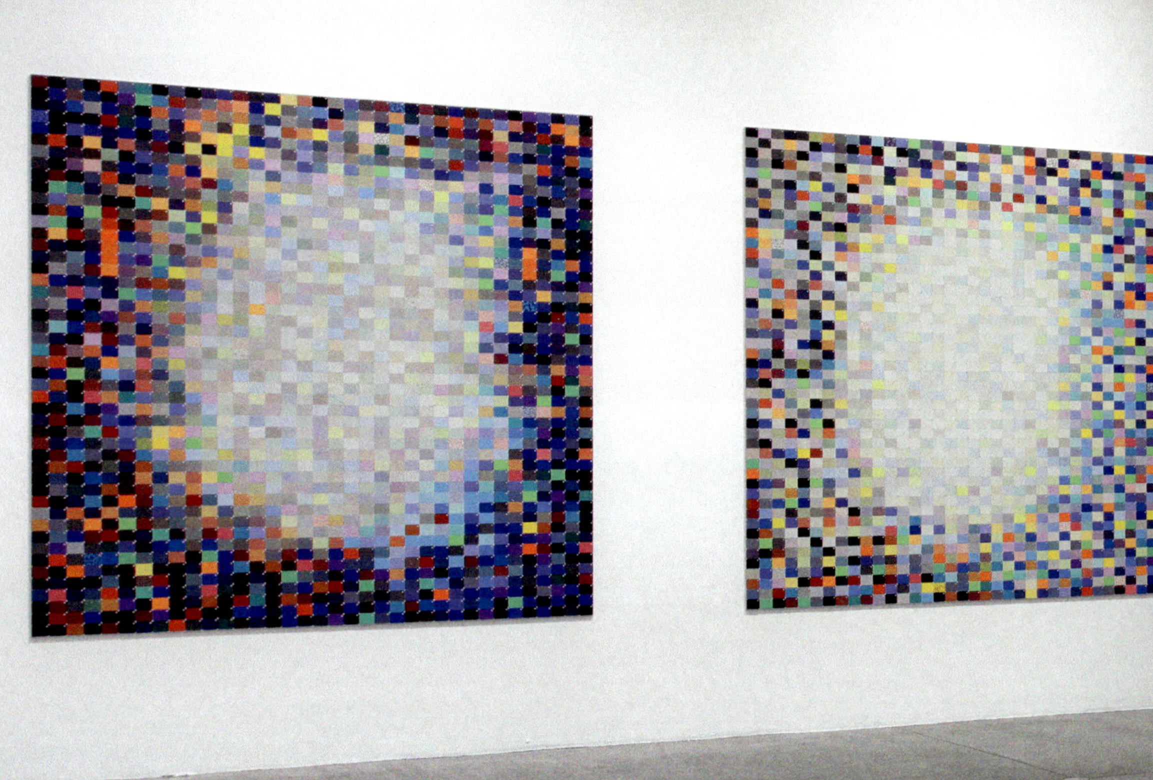

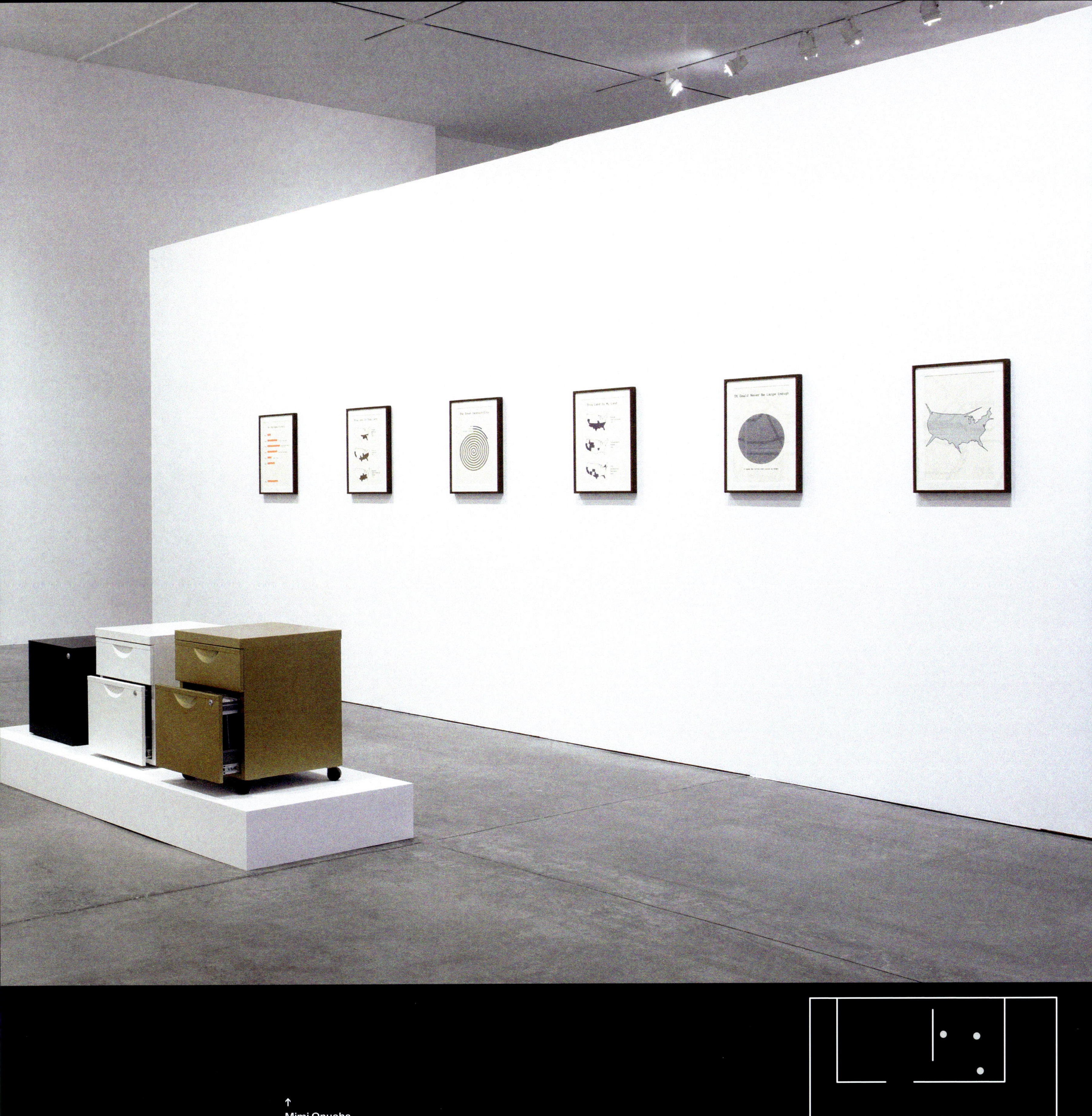

↑
Mimi Ọnụọha

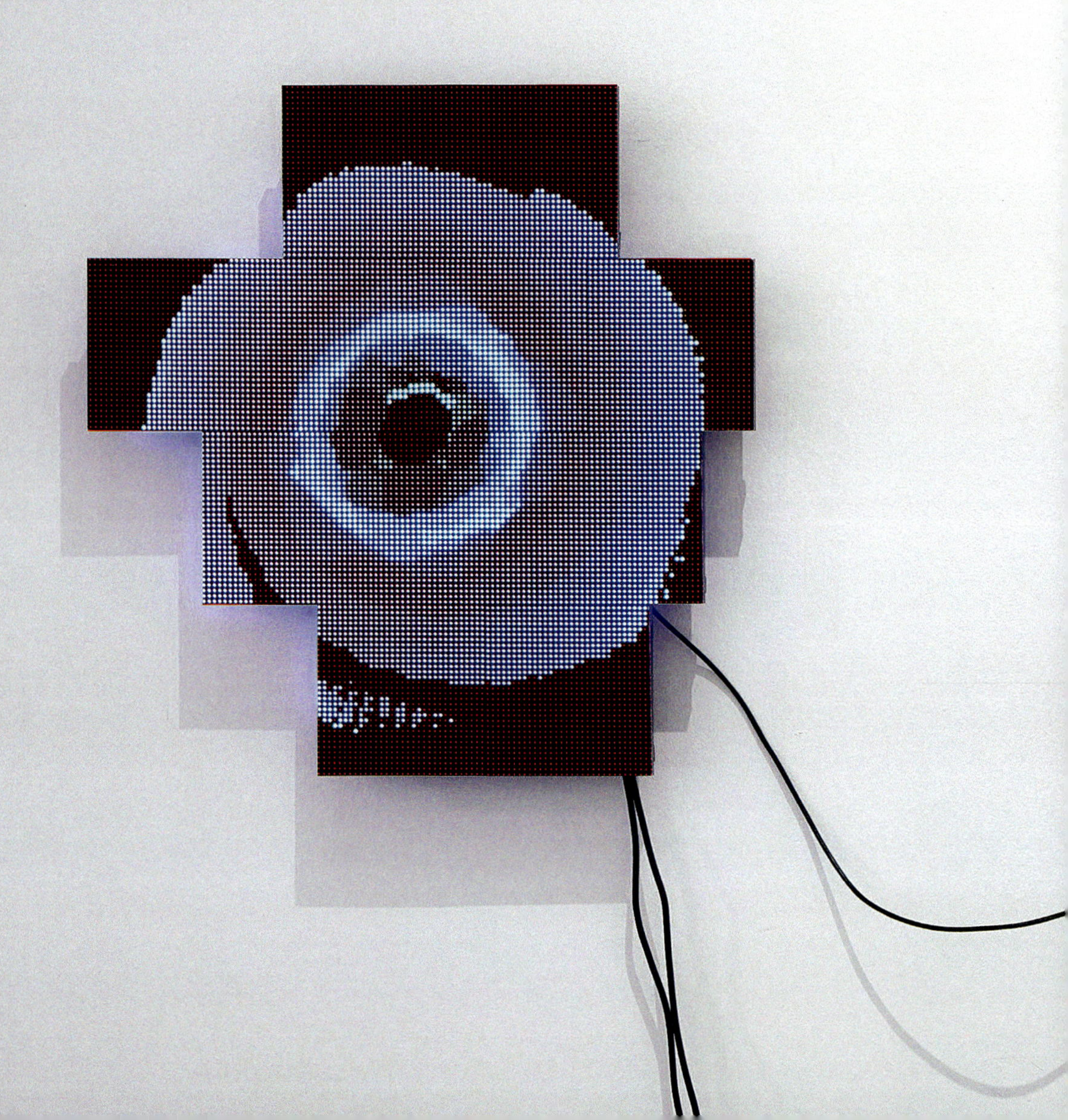

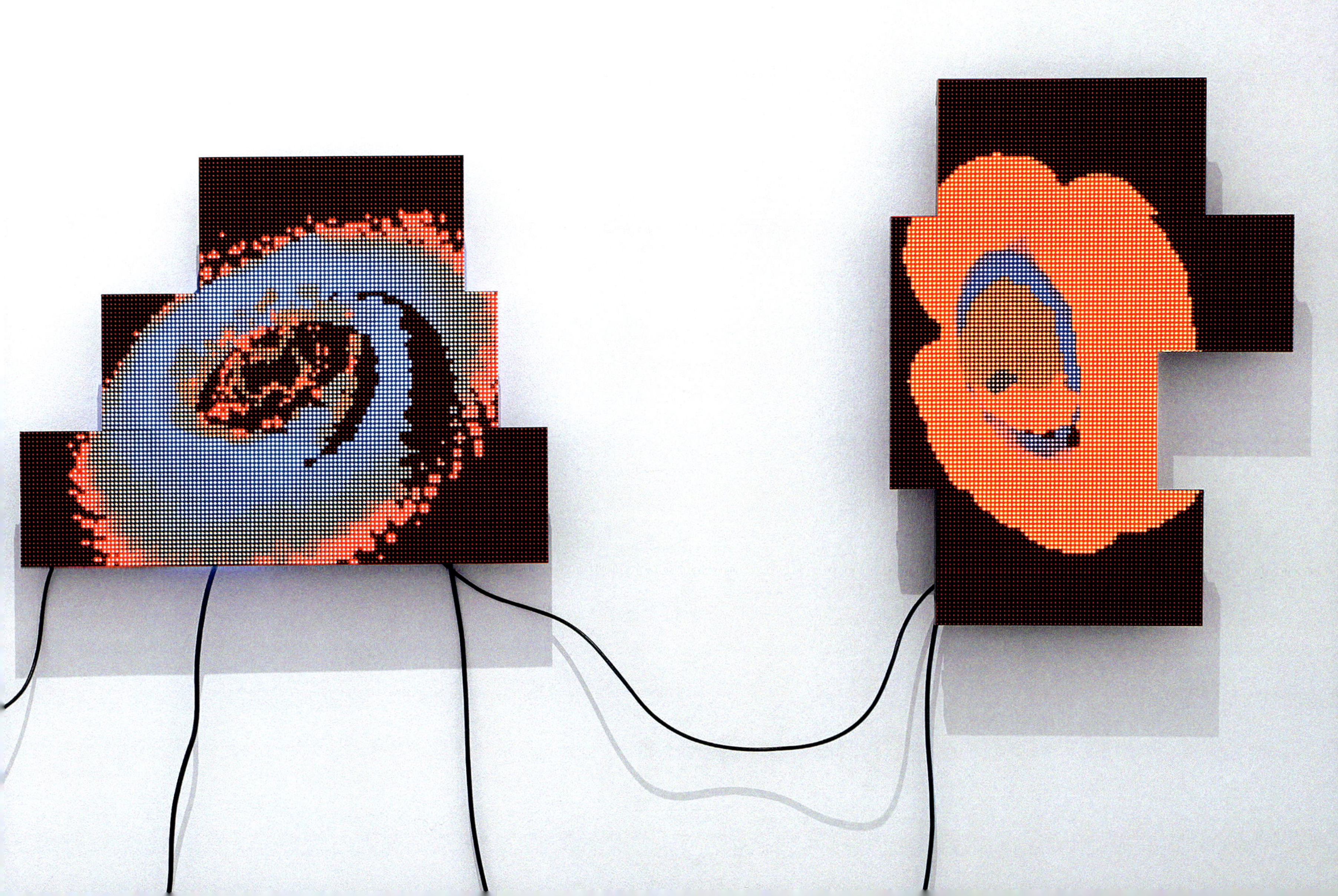

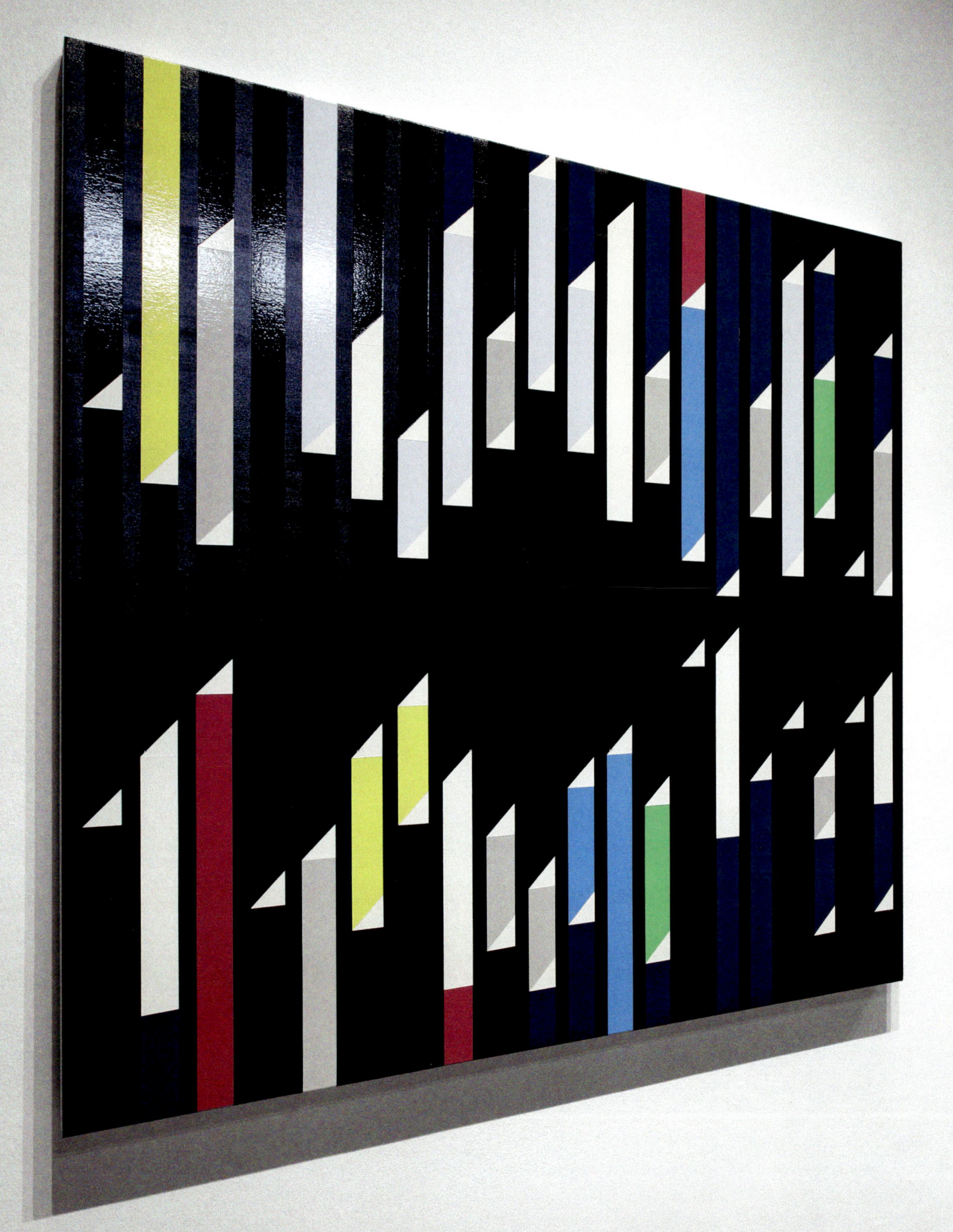

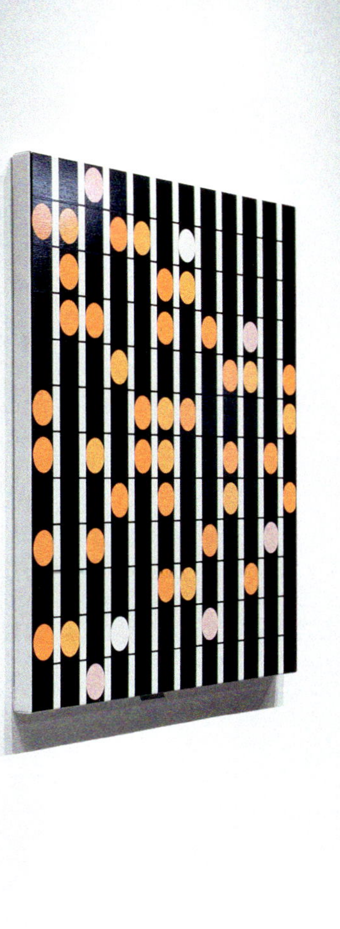

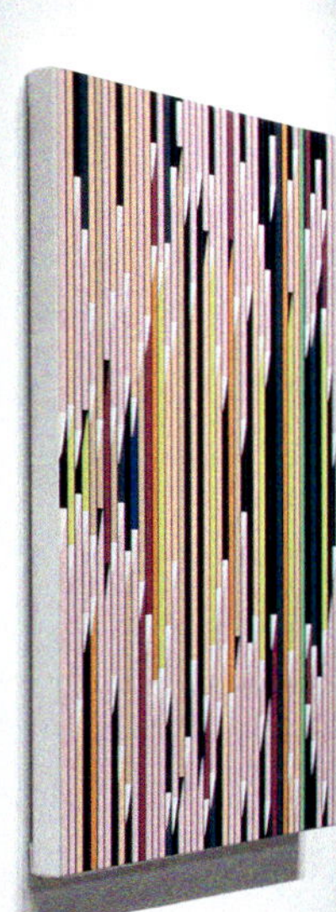

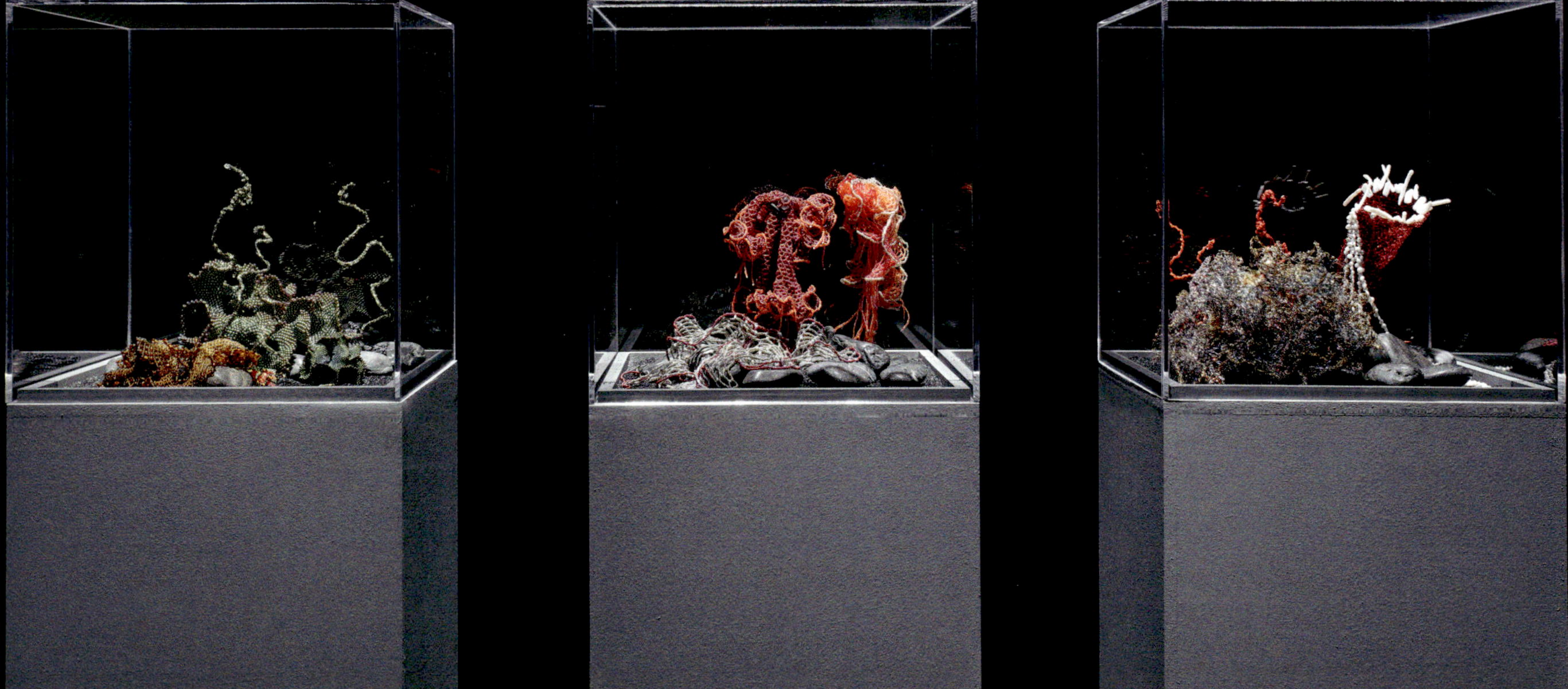

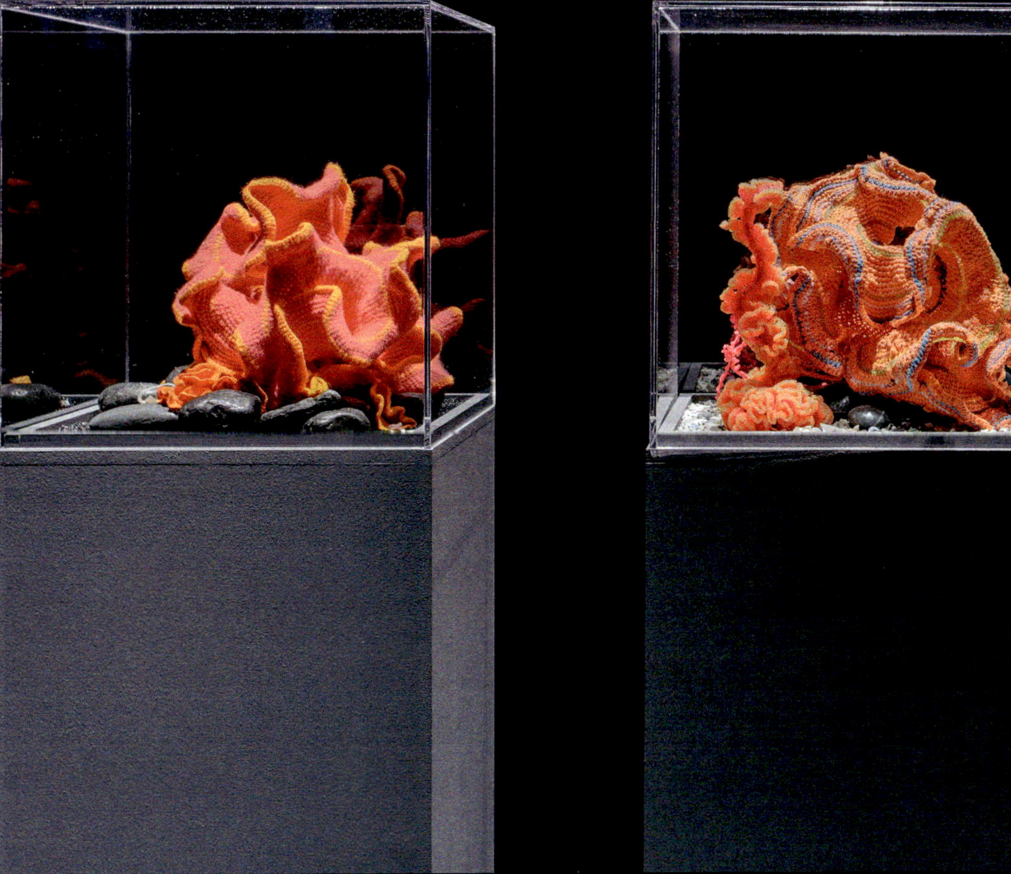

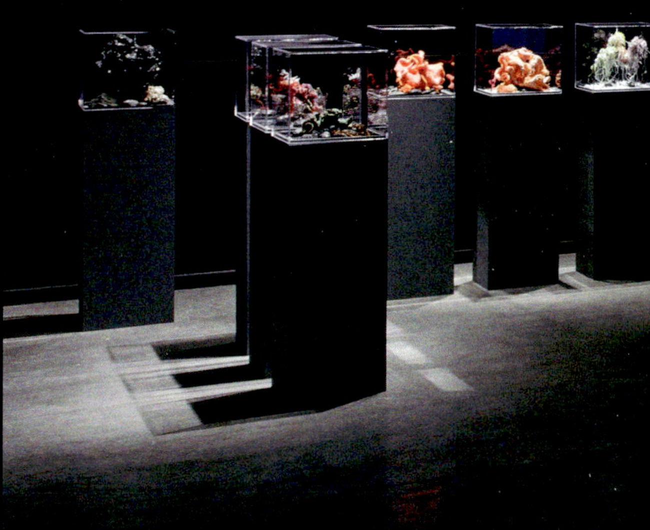

↑
Christine Wertheim, Margaret Wertheim, and the Institute For Figuring

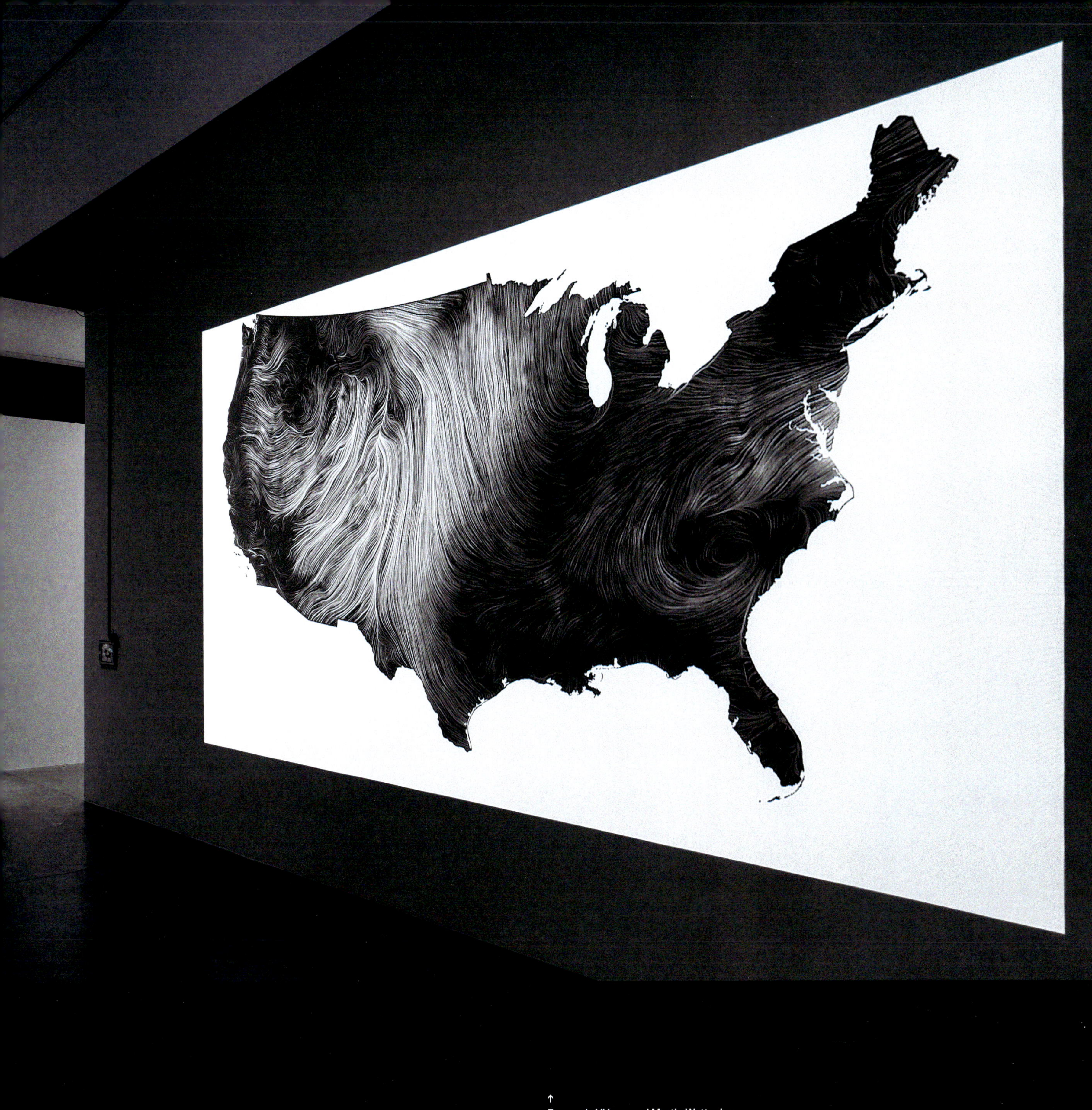

↑
Fernanda Viégas and Martin Wattenberg

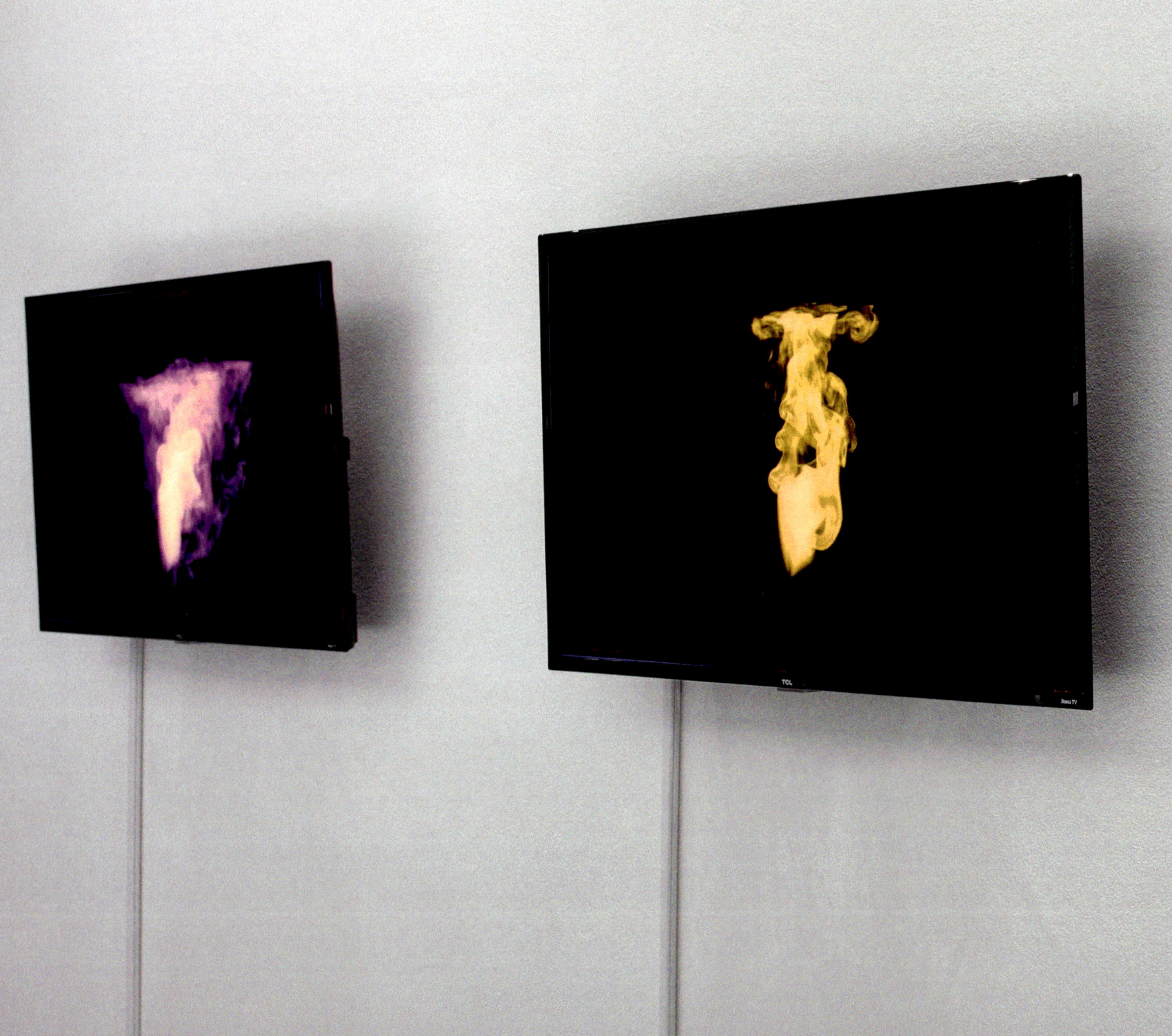
TCL
Roku TV

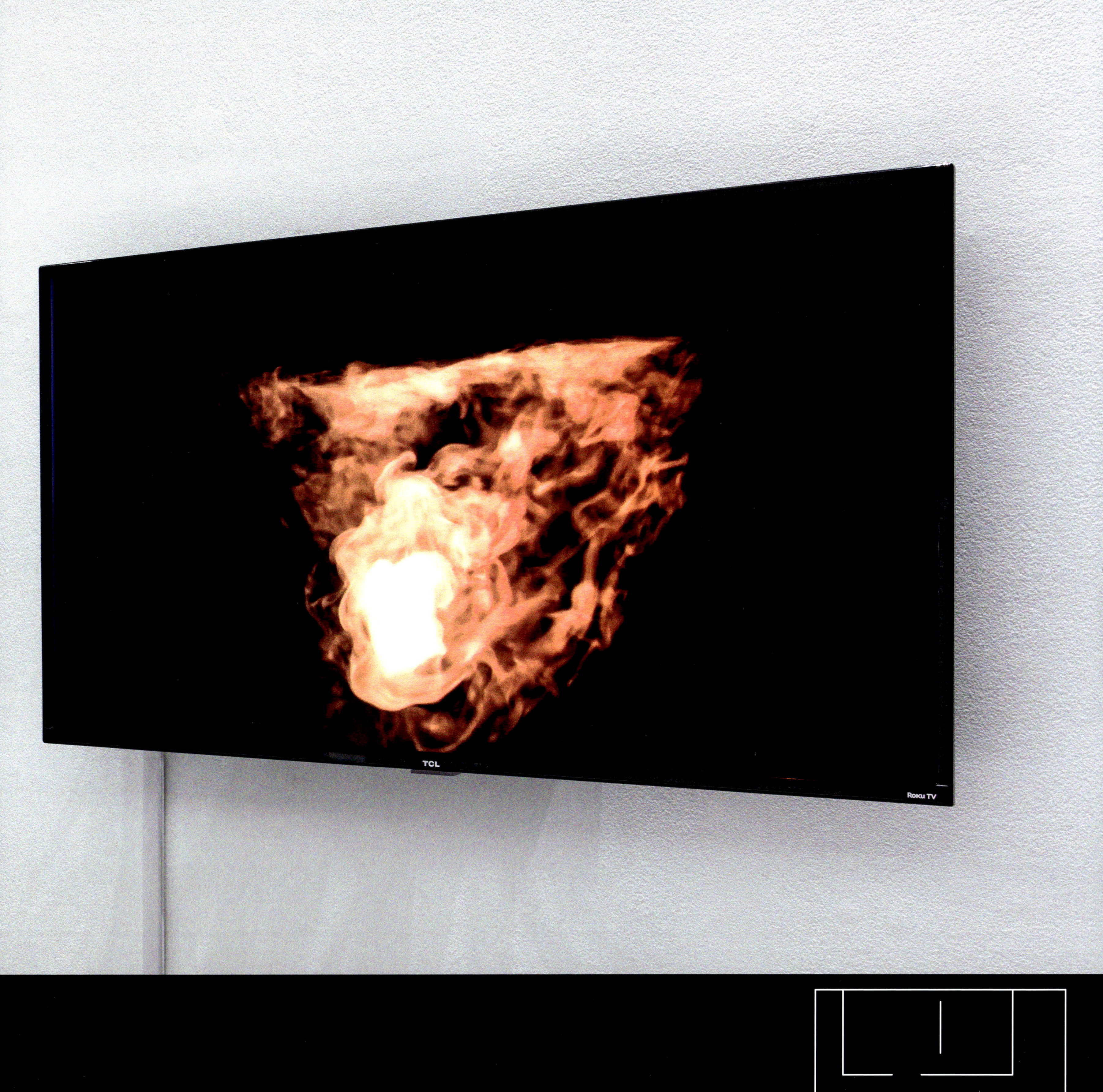
TCL
Roku TV

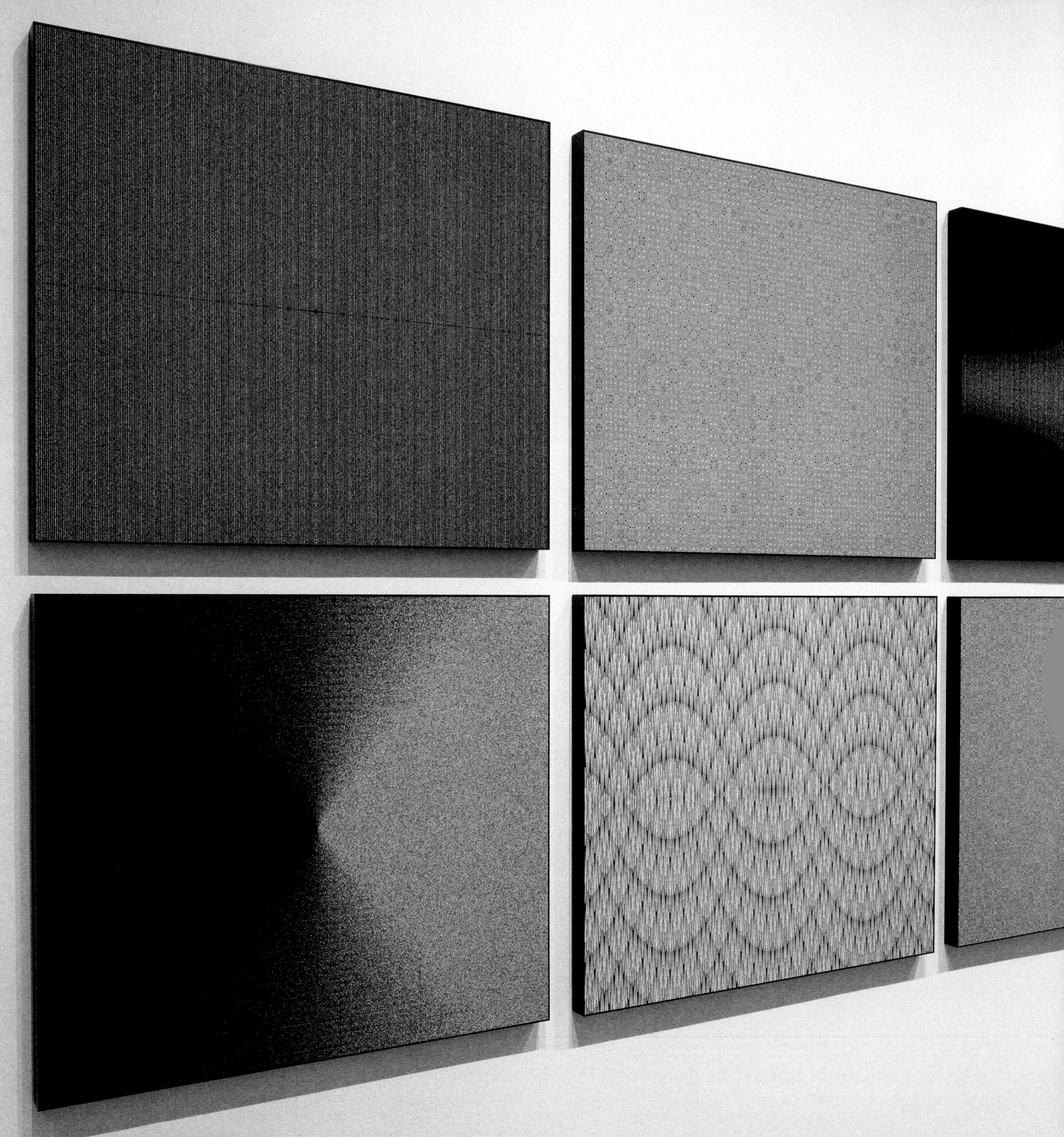

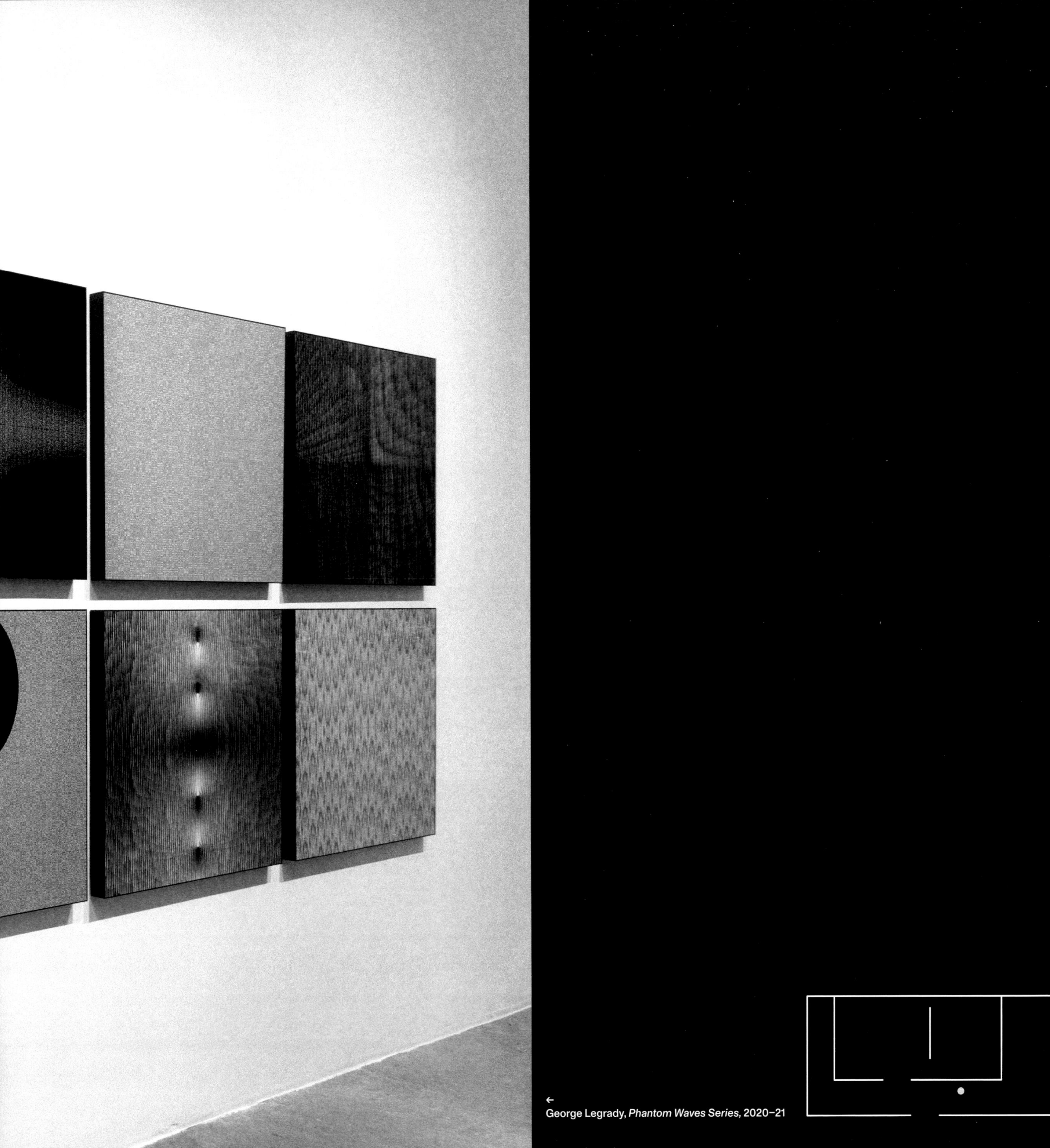

←
George Legrady, *Phantom Waves Series*, 2020–21

Essays

Jason Forrest
Stephen Nowlin
Margaret Wertheim

DATA

HAS BEC

FOR THE

HUM

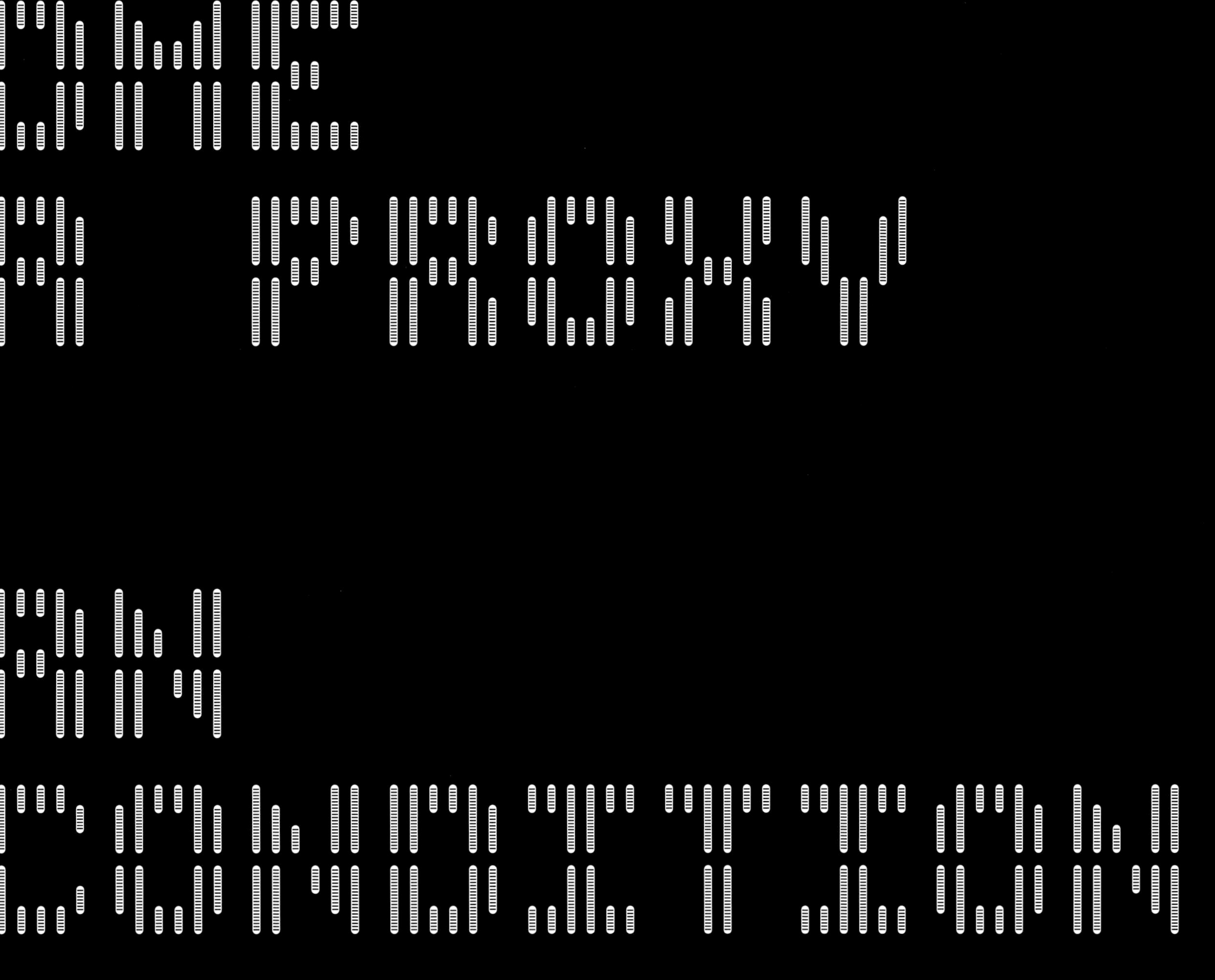

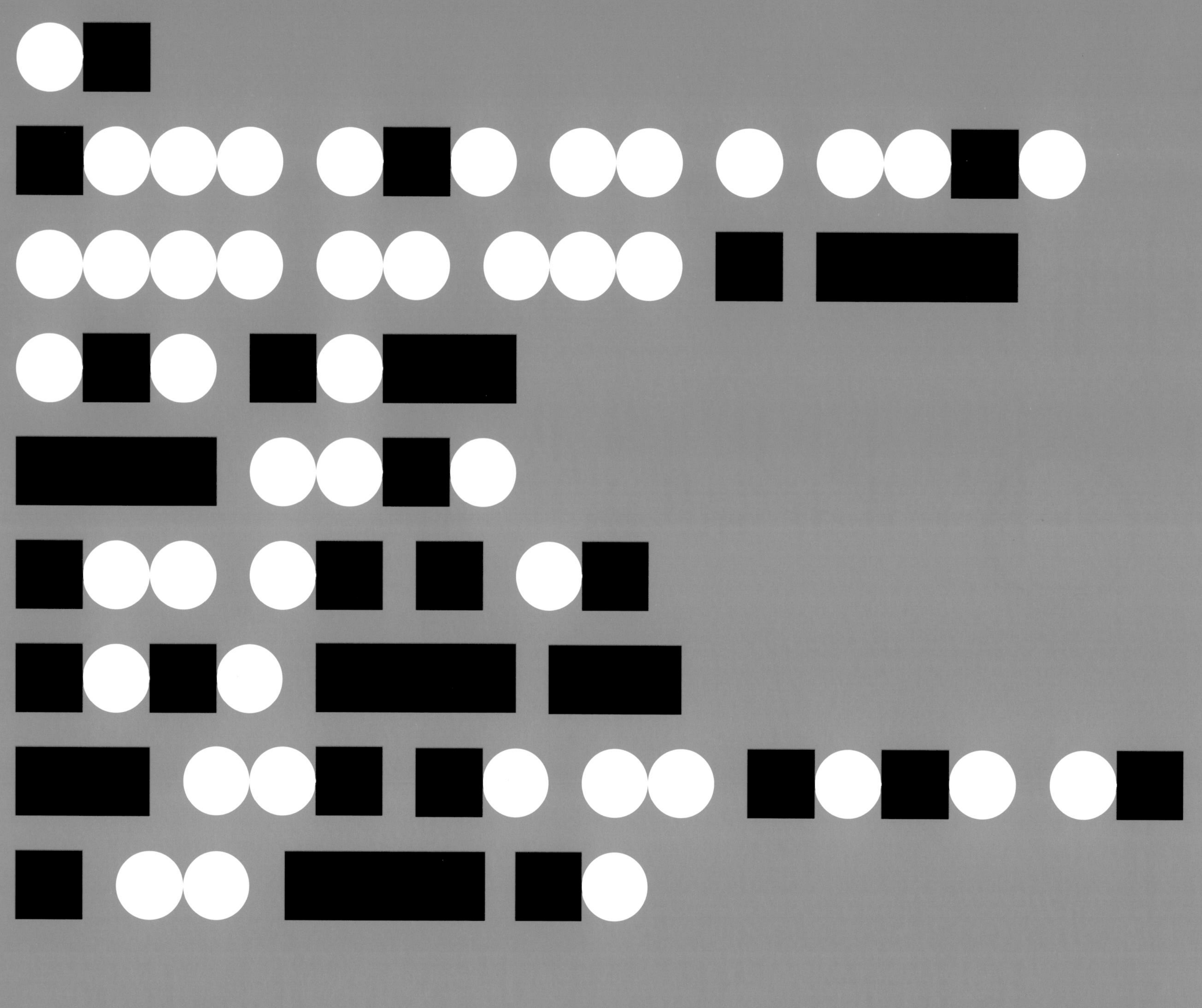

A Brief History of (Data) Communication

JASON FORREST

The history of communication is as intertwined as the sweeping movements of technology, marketing, and data that bind us together.[1] At every stage in human history, innovations in technology impacted approaches to sharing knowledge and shaped the design of our world. Exploring the history of data alongside the evolution of marketing and technology reveals how it became a powerful tool for communication. Understanding data is crucial to understanding communication in relation to the historic innovations that contextualize and define it.

While art and data may not commonly be associated, both are fundamental to the human experience: data fuels our contemporary world, but our ability to transform it into an artful response[2] reflects how we live in and interact with society. Since communication is an inherently human response to other people, we build on societal constructs shaped by generations of interactions. Therefore, to truly understand data, we need to start at the beginning of communication.

Prehistoric tallies, the marketplace, and the birth of the image

The first forms of recorded human communication are rock paintings and petroglyphs dating from about thirty thousand years ago. The earliest example of data may be the Ishango bone, a ten-centimeter-long piece of mammal bone covered in tally scratches from a piece of quartz (fig. 1).[3] Found in present-day Democratic Republic of the Congo, it was likely a mathematical tool used by a pre-sapiens species twenty thousand years ago at the end of the Paleolithic age—almost exactly at the same time as Venus figures would have been carved for fertility rituals across Europe.

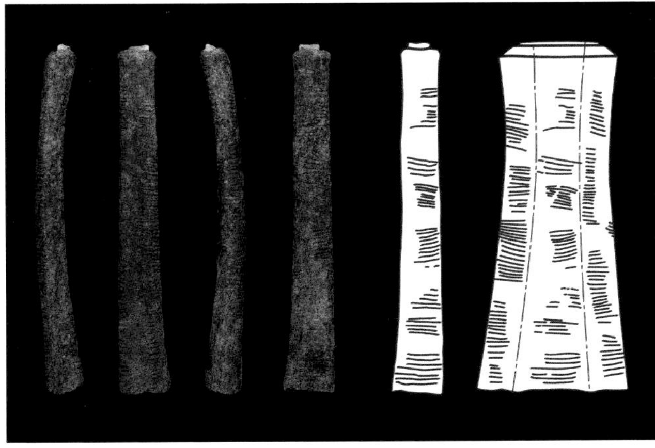

↑
Figure 1: Ishango bone, Upper Paleolithic era, with sketch by geologist Jean de Heinzelin de Braucourt, who discovered the bone in 1960

Petroglyphs evolved into symbols, which became written language in Mesopotamia, Egypt, and China. Although more complex mathematics might have started earlier, the first written examples are from the Sumerians, who wrote multiplication tables and division problems on clay tablets in Mesopotamia around 2500 BC.

Marketing is a social institution[4] created as a means to satisfy human needs through the exchange of goods and services. Ancient examples of what we might think of as the first advertisements can be found as early as 4000 BC, with inscribed rock paintings in India, and brickmaker stamps can be found in ancient Egypt as early as 2700 BC.

The first examples of design were also the earliest forms of money: that's according to Ruben Pater, a research theorist who builds a compelling case that design is inexorably connected to capitalism.[5] One of his examples—the first silver and brass coins, the Mesopotamian shekel circa 650 BC, were designed to identify a fixed value by a government—literally joins the concept of design to money.

As communities moved beyond meeting their own needs[6] they created exchange-based economies, and skilled professions were identified through signboards representing trades, such as a boot for cobbler, needle for tailor, tongs for blacksmith, etc.[7] These trademarks demarcated the marketplace while town criers were hired to shout messages in public places to advertise skilled laborers.

Communication was direct and symbology was simple, but as wealth began to accumulate, the social status of the wealthy became increasingly important. Art critic and provocateur John Berger[8] considers the beginning of the image not with prehistoric art, but with oil painting.

> Gradually it became evident that an image could outlast what it represented; it then showed how something or somebody had once looked—and thus by implication how the subject had once been seen by other people. Later still the specific vision of the image-maker was also recognized as part of the record. An image became a record of how X had seen Y. This was the result of an increasing consciousness of individuality, accompanying an increasing awareness of history.[9]

The age of mechanical information

As civilization evolved, so did the bond between design and business. This led to the next big innovation: the printing press, a technical evolution centuries in the making. The history of printing starts with highly crafted manual activities, ancient Chinese and Japanese wood prints among them, but the Gutenberg printing press in 1440 began the age of mechanical reproduction. This changes everything. Canadian media theorist Marshall McLuhan elaborates in his 1967 treatise, *The Medium Is the Massage:*

> Printing ... provided the first uniformly repeatable "commodity," the first assembly line—mass production. It created the portable book, which men could read in privacy and in isolation from others. Man could now inspire—and conspire. Like easel painting, the printed book added much to the new cult of individualism.[10]

Each new technology enabled a new sense of scale in disseminating knowledge. Before the nineteenth century, written language itself was a secure channel of information, as literacy was relatively low.[11] Because personal and public libraries could now afford mass-produced books, the sciences[12] became traded within expert communities and knowledge began to spread.

With the invention of the printing press, the speed of information becomes increasingly important. Printed words and pictures were still relatively slow, and important news needed to spread faster than a person could travel. A novel invention was the Chappe telegraph in 1790: a series of physical structures placed every five to fifteen kilometers across France. At the top of each tower, hinged planks formed semaphores that were transmitted tower by tower by operators using specially designed telescopes (fig. 2). A coded message sent from Paris could reach Marseille in roughly two hours—by horse it took a week.

By spreading information by sight, the speed of information became optical. The study of optics had been a field of study since the ancient world, with documentation of the first magnification lenses in 1 AD by Roman emperors. Exploration continued into the sixteenth century when optical magnification evolved into the microscope and optical correction became the camera obscura, used as a drawing tool. Photography was invented in the 1830s as a result of advances in optics (plus the ability to fix a photographic image on paper).

William Playfair, a Scottish engineer and economist living in France, published *The Commercial and Political Atlas* in 1801. This book featured a radical new concept that explained statistics on England's trade balance through a series of graphic abstractions that we now call data visualization. While met with mixed success initially, his graphic innovations—the line chart, the area chart, and the pie chart—spread quickly through scientific communities.

Innovation becomes the speed of information

Everything set the stage for the nineteenth century, an era of innovation that redefined human possibility—economically, artistically, and spiritually. By 1800, design and illustration in the form of advertisements in newspapers were common, and innovations in printing expanded the design possibilities of handbills and posters to feature luxurious illustrations. Lithography was introduced in 1796 by Aloys Senefelder as an inexpensive method of reproducing artwork; and color lithography was introduced in France in 1837. The use of statistics in books became common by the end of the nineteenth century, predominantly in the format of printed tables of data, shared under the auspice of expert knowledge.

Across the nineteenth century, print production becomes faster, cheaper, and more common. In 1844, the cylinder printing press was patented, enabling rapid newspaper production in the following years (fig. 3). In 1840, Volney B.

↓
Figure 2: A Chappe telegraph displaying the symbol for Q, 1850

→
Figure 3: Illustration of Richard March Hoe's cylinder printing press, 1860s

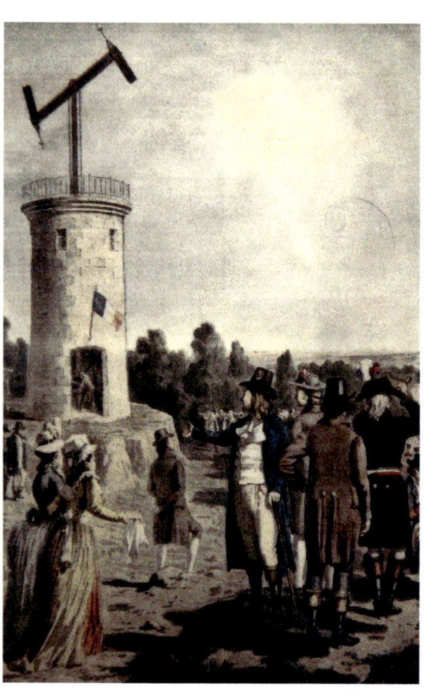

The history of printing starts with highly crafted manual activities, ancient Chinese and Japanese wood prints among them, but the Gutenberg printing press in 1440 begins the age of mechanical reproduction. This changes everything.

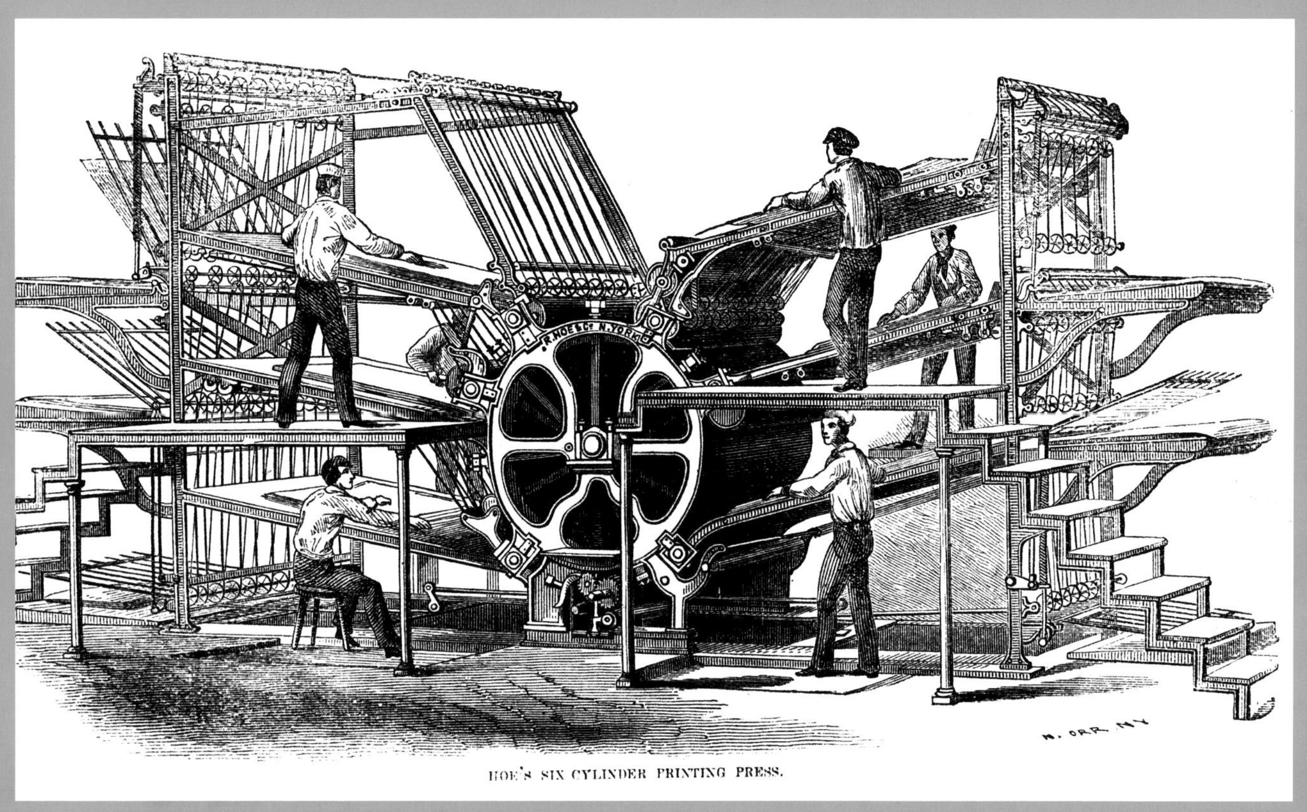

HOE'S SIX CYLINDER PRINTING PRESS.

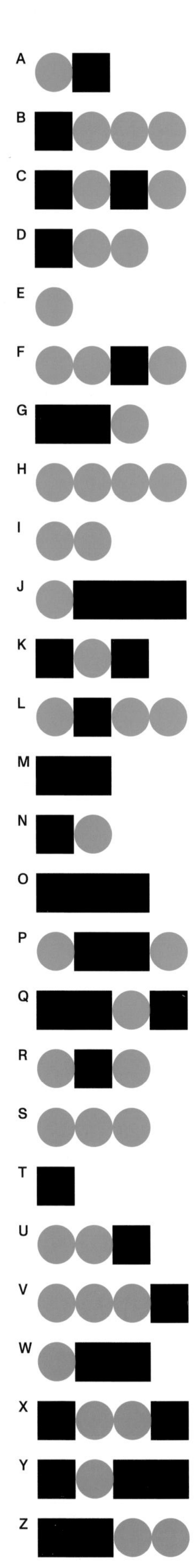

Palmer established the first advertising agency in Philadelphia as a side hustle for his real estate businesses. He found immediate success by showing his business clients how "to advertise judiciously, effectively, and safely."[13]

In 1858, healthcare pioneer Florence Nightingale used elaborate data visualizations to lobby Queen Victoria for support in changing sanitation standards in healthcare. Nightingale became an international hero in the field of public health largely due to her success in convincing governments by presenting statistical data in the form of detailed, hand-colored data visualizations. Frenchman Charles Joseph Minard achieved a similar prominence for his innovations by visualizing civil engineering and trade statistics a few years later in 1869.

The Industrial Revolution, now fully underway, proved the importance of speed via mechanical engineering into all aspects of society. Because information was able to move faster, scientific and engineering communities were able to push ideas from concept to practice faster, and this was certainly the case with electromagnetism, which became the foundation of many twentieth-century innovations. One of them was the electric telegraph, which helped information move faster and more freely across the world.

It was also the birth of electrical engineering. As information became electronic, the format of information became more important. To create a faster, more reliable way to transmit information over further distances with the electric telegraph, Samuel Morse created a code in 1837 to translate natural language into a series of electrical pulses and the silences between them (fig. 4). This reduced language to a binary format of transmission, allowing for nearly instantaneous communication across vast distances.

The modes of communication continued to diversify as the telephone was invented in 1876. That same year, the first advertising agency was acquired by N. W. Ayer & Son, establishing the industry's first art and copy departments. A few years later, the American Charles Sanders Peirce formulated the tenets of modern statlstlcs In "Illustratlons of the Loglc of Sclence" In 1877; hls "A Theory of Probable Inference" (1883) established the notion of probability in scientific correlation.

In photography, George Eastman invented the film negative in 1884, replacing cumbersome glass plates and allowing for more images to be captured quickly. By 1888, the first Kodak camera allowed amateurs to take photographs for the first time; Eastman marketed the product with the slogan "You press the button, we do the rest," selling 2,500 cameras that year.

The race to capture and record sound was split between Thomas Edison's low-quality cylinders in 1877 and Emile Berliner's high-quality gramophone, patented in 1887. Two years later, Edison assigned an assistant, William Kennedy Dickson, the task of making a device that produced visuals to accompany the sounds of the gramophone. This became the kinetoscope, the first moving-picture device to use celluloid film. Illuminating a continuous loop of film with a small lamp, images were viewed through a peephole window of a cabinet housing the components (fig. 5). A few years later, in 1895, the French brothers Auguste and Louis Lumière created the first commercial film screening by editing together a series of ten short films and projecting them at the Salon Indien du Grand Café in Paris.

The rapid development of machines to record data happened in much the same way as it did in cinema. Although Edison first patented an electric vote recorder in 1869, he had a hard time monetizing his invention and moved toward recorded sound instead. In 1889, German American statistician Herman Hollerith was awarded a patent for the first punch-card system of collecting data (called the Electric Tabulating System). He immediately went to work for the 1890 US Census, and his system reduced the time to collect and tabulate the data by two years.

Illuminating a continuous loop of film with a small lamp, images were viewed through a peephole window of a cabinet housing the components.

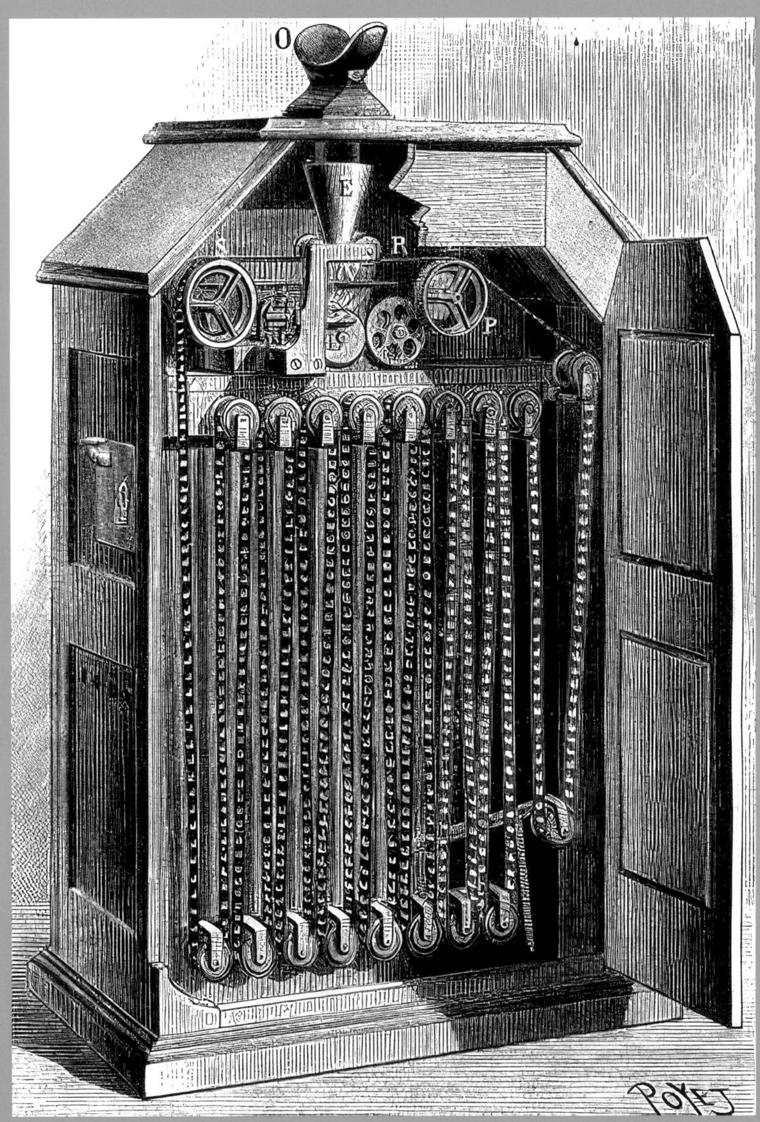

←
Figure 4: International Morse Code chart of the twenty-six letters of the alphabet

↗
Figure 5: View of kinetoscope with cabinet door open to reveal components, illustration in *La Nature*, 1894

The romanticism of decades previous gave way to the influence of the machine as a representation of a world beyond the visible.

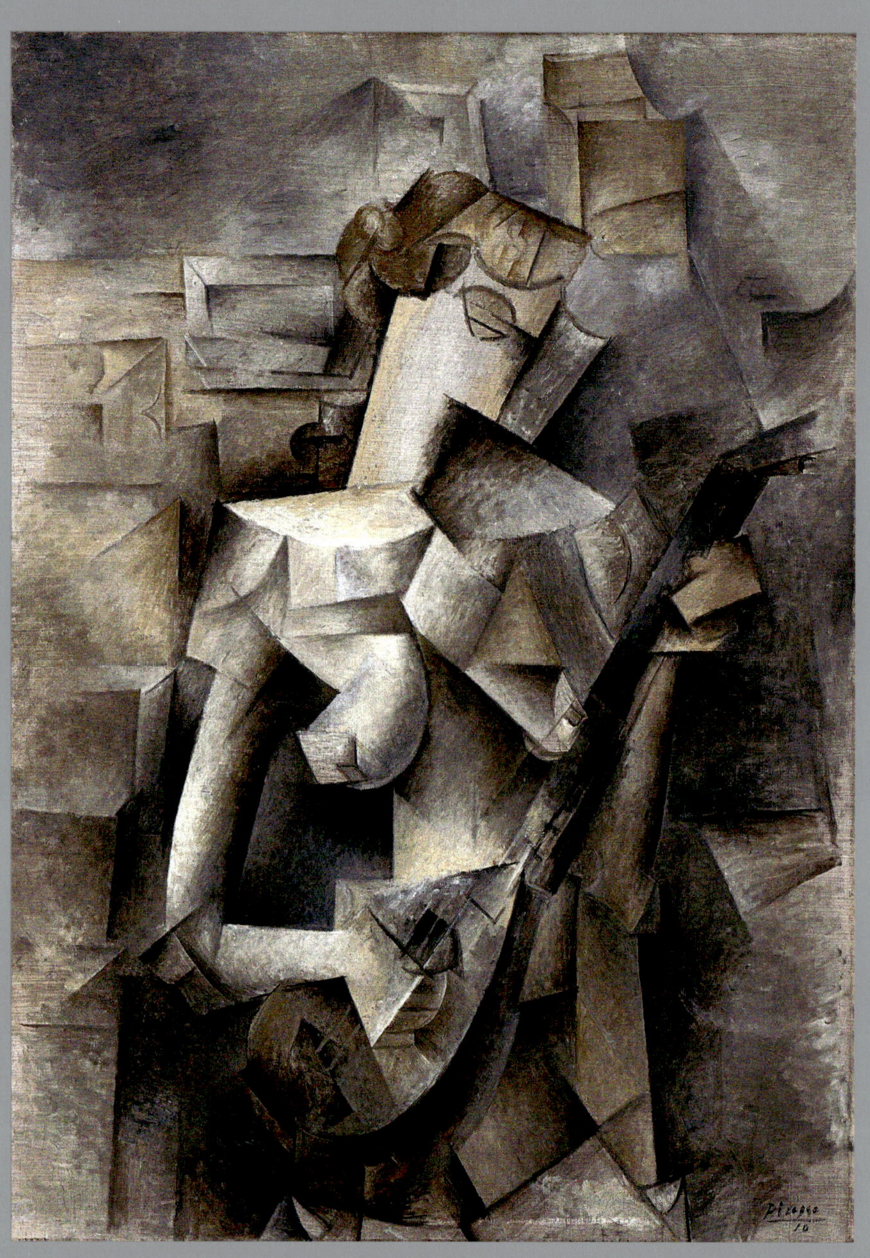

While methods to collect sound, light, and motion through technology were developing, so did the exploration of electromagnetic radiation. German physicist Heinrich Hertz transmitted electromagnetic waves (better known as radio waves) through the air in 1888. While many scientists explored Hertz's research, it was a young Italian inventor, Guglielmo Marconi, who perfected the idea of long-distance wireless transmission; by 1895, he was broadcasting radio waves over two miles.

As advertising grew with each new type of media, it became more scientific in its approach to its efficacy. In 1897, Elias St. Elmo Lewis began developing a useful structure for how to write good advertisements:

> The mission of an advertisement is to attract a reader, so that he will look at the advertisement and start to read it; then to interest him, so that he will continue to read it; then to convince him, so that when he has read it he will believe it. If an advertisement contains these three qualities of success, it is a successful advertisement.[14]

This develops into the AIDA (Attention, Interest, Desire, Action) framework, which is still widely used across the advertising industry today.

1900–40: Abstraction, science, and speed

The first decade of the twentieth century fundamentally changed how we think about the world. First, Sigmund Freud's *The Interpretation of Dreams* (1900) is published and becomes one of the most important books of the century by introducing the concept of the unconscious, inspiring artists and audiences for generations. The Kodak Brownie is mass-marketed a year later for a fraction of the price of any commercial camera, and the millions sold creates a generation of amateur photographers. Meanwhile, Frenchman Charles Pathé begins producing films that same year and founds Pathé Frères, which quickly becomes the biggest film company in the world and produces films on a variety of dramatic subjects and current events.

From 1910 on, filmed newsreels became a popular way of discovering the news. In 1911, Hollywood's first studio opened,[15] and soon after twenty companies were producing films in the area. By 1912 there are four thousand newspapers globally, printing about six billion copies a year. As film and newspapers boomed, the business of advertising became more visual. Vibrant graphic advertising becomes central to the profitability of the newspapers, and the mass media elevates commercial art and design to the dominant visual culture. With the continued technical, scientific, and metaphysical innovations, the fine arts reject the traditional, creating a modernist movement that embraces the technological and the urban and rapidly redefines the aesthetics of the era in art, architecture, fashion, and design. Modernism advances new realms of expression and social experimentation like never before. Everything was affected—cities expanded, buildings grew taller, transportation accelerated, and communication was faster, cheaper, and global—and it was all connected: the idea, the look, and the technologies that made them possible.

As art and design began to imagine a modern world represented by speed, it simultaneously explored abstraction, dreams, and the unconscious. The romanticism of decades previous gave way to the influence of the machine as a representation of a world beyond the visible. Inspired by the invention of the X-ray, Pablo Picasso (et al.) created "Cubist" paintings showing the transitory states of an object more as a concept than a descriptive representation (fig. 6).

In 1914, the field of market research was pioneered by Daniel Starch through his book *Advertising: Its Principles, Practice, and Technique*. In what became a primer for the business world, Starch set out to create a strategic methodology

←
Figure 6: Pablo Picasso, *Girl with a Mandolin (Fanny Tellier)*, 1910. Oil on canvas; 39 1/2 × 29 inches. The Museum of Modern Art, New York; Nelson A. Rockefeller Bequest, 966.1979

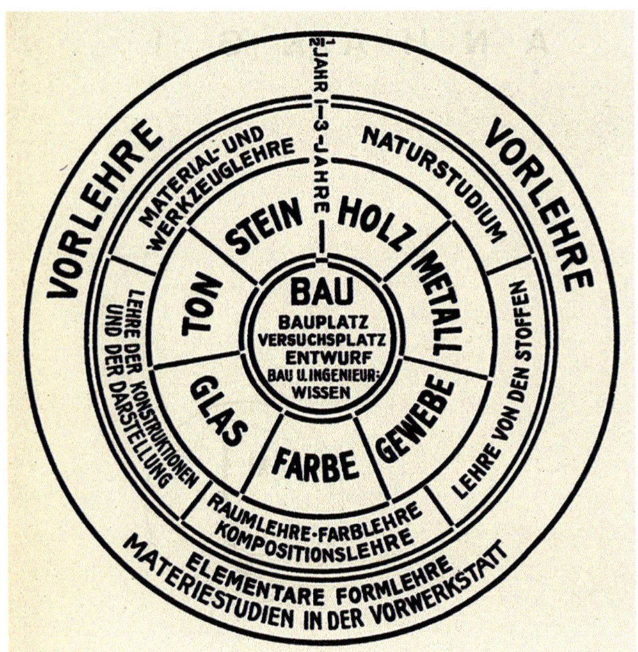

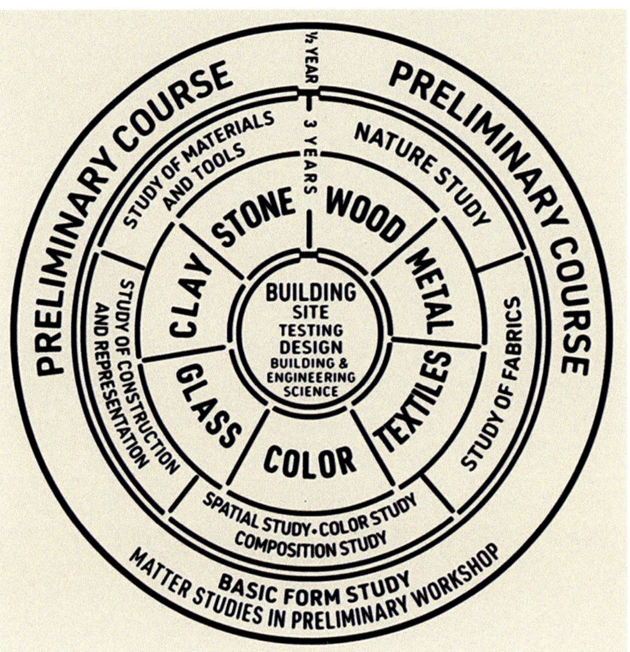

for understanding the effectiveness of advertising psychologically as applied to business needs in an increasingly saturated media landscape. As World War I began, the connection between agenda-oriented communication (such as advertising) and scientific evaluation became crucial, with the US and European governments heavily investing in mass-media propaganda to justify their efforts and shape public opinion from each side. Color posters, newspapers, and handbills were used extensively in combination with radio and newsreels for news and political dissemination.

As Germany rebuilt itself after World War I, a group of artists led by architect Walter Gropius established a school for the industrial arts known as the Bauhaus. It was initially founded in 1919 in alignment with William Morris's Arts and Crafts movement "to create a new guild of craftsmen, without the class distinctions which raise an arrogant barrier between craftsman and artist." By 1922, with the collaboration of such avant-garde artists as Oskar Schlemmer, Paul Klee, Wassily Kandinsky, and László Moholy-Nagy, the arts are taught as a radical functionalist response to problems in industry (fig. 7). While architecture is seen in the penultimate art form at the Bauhaus, all mediums of visual art are taught as an attempt to design a new, efficient, and systematic blueprint for society. Gropius captures the forward thrust of modernism: "We want an architecture adapted to our world of machines, radios, and fast cars."[16]

In 1925, electric recording made it possible to use sensitive microphones that greatly improved audio quality in phonographs and radio broadcasting. A year later, in 1926, the National Broadcasting Corporation (NBC) was founded by the Radio Corporation of America (RCA), and radio became the standard for hundreds of millions of Americans, enabling them to whistle the same jingle, hear the same story, and laugh at the same joke.

In 1926, Otto Neurath, a political economist and philosopher, created a museum dedicated to educating people in Vienna through a system of visual

↖
Figure 7: Walter Gropius, *Diagram of the Bauhaus Curriculum* (with translated version on the right), 1922. Bauhaus Typography Collection, 1919–1937, Getty Research Institute, Los Angeles (850513)

charts and diagrammatic approaches to visualize statistics. Neurath was highly aware of how visual media could be used for visual education:

> Modern man is conditioned by the cinema and a wealth of illustrations. He gets much of his knowledge during leisure hours in the most pleasing way through his eyes. If one wants to spread social knowledge, one should use means similar to modern advertisements.[17]

The charts were easy to understand, yet their details contained nuance and context. Over the years these pictorial statistics became known by the acronym ISOTYPE,[18] and the design process they used was deeply iterative, applying a scientific approach to their communication by testing their designs with school children for content clarity.

In 1927, Philo T. Farnsworth invented television by transmitting images without wires for the first time, using a dollar sign as a test pattern. That same year, Edward Bernays, nephew of Sigmund Freud, promoted the concept of sublimation (where socially unacceptable behavior can be converted to acceptable behavior) and, in doing so, becomes a pioneer of modern cigarette advertising. In 1928 he wrote in a book on propaganda:

> Those who manipulate this unseen mechanism of society constitute an invisible government which is the true ruling power of our country. We are governed, our minds are molded, our tastes formed, our ideas suggested, largely by men we have never heard of.[19]

As cinema matured and followed modernist trends, the appeal of the mechanical was maybe best expressed by Dziga Vertov,[20] director of the Russian tour de force *Man with a Movie Camera* from 1929, whose dizzying montages of the modern city made the camera the hero of the story:

> I'm an eye. A mechanical eye. I, the machine, show you a world the way only I can see it. I free myself for today and forever from human immobility.... Freed from the boundaries of time and space, I coordinate any and all points of the universe, wherever I want them to be. My way leads toward the creation of a fresh perception of the world. Thus I explain in a new way the world unknown to you.[21]

The 1930 US Census shows 40% of Americans have a radio. In 1931, George Gallup began using polls to understand local politics but quickly pivoted to applying his techniques to advertising, founding the American Institute of Public Opinion. After the popularity of radio, and the successful transmission of wireless images by Farnsworth a few years earlier, the promise of television as a mass medium became captivating for inventors around the world. The first commercial television program was broadcast in the UK in 1939, but much of the medium's development was halted by the outbreak of World War II. By 1940 90% of Americans were tuning in to their radios every night.

1945–2005: The digital age

For the field of communication, World War II may have been the most important period in human history. The technical, social, and psychological impact of the advances in this relatively short period of time still reverberate today. Vast resources were poured into the war effort, among them the field of cryptography to break secret codes. Advances in telecommunications expanded into devices that stored and transmitted data. In 1945, British mathematician Alan Turing built on earlier concepts to create, in secret, the first electromagnetic computer.

The impact of propaganda during World War II was significant across all media. Bernays compiles his writing in the book *Public Relations* (1945), which outlines the science of "advantageously releasing information to the public."[22] The war ends with the invention, and deployment, of two nuclear bombs in Japan, ushering in the atomic age. The mushroom cloud itself becomes a symbol of a new era of technical promise and terror.

In the decades after the war, technology develops so quickly that the way we communicate is rapidly shaped and reshaped, forcing mindsets to become cross-functional, flexible, and richly symbolic. The transistor was invented and the sound barrier was broken in 1947. A year later, Norbert Weiner published *Cybernetics: Or Control and Communication in the Animal and the Machine* in response to the need to engineer complex mechanical systems that respond to their environments (such as radar and servomechanisms). What began as an exploration of systematic inputs and outputs became the study of messages to control purposeful behavior in machines. This becomes the foundation for what would become the modern computer.

1948 was a pivotal year as Claude Shannon's book, *A Mathematical Theory of Communication*, established information theory,[23] setting a new mathematical threshold for the smallest quantity of information: the binary "bit." Between the two great thinkers, Shannon and Weiner, and their interconnected fields of study, the groundwork is laid for the evolution of digital systems and the world of data that followed. By the dawn of the internet forty years later, the *cyber-* prefix of Weiner's new science will be used to name a system for information so vast we call cyberspace.

As the concept of digital information was just forming, a new generation of British and American artists in the mid-1950s challenged many of the previously held notions of what could be considered art. Pop art[24] appropriated advertising imagery as a response to the pervasive mass media using such tools as photography, mechanical printing, and sculptural assemblage. By internalizing culture through its media, the influence of art, advertising, and entertainment increasingly became interchangeable on artists—it was all just information.

Sputnik launched in 1957, the first database management system was created in 1961, and the microprocessor was invented ten years later, in 1971, packing thousands of transistors into a single, tiny chip and dramatically improving the speed of calculating data.[25] That same year journalist Ben Bagdikian published his book *The Information Machines: Their Impact on Men and the Media*:

> Today we are on the threshold of a change in human communications which is more powerful and perhaps more significant than all past changes in the technology of information. The way [people] deal with each other and with the distant world is about to be transformed by a combination of the computer, innovations in the transmission of signals, and new ways to feed images into this system and to take them out. All informational systems, including the news media, will be more intertwined with each other than they are today.[26]

As we move into the 1970s, communication becomes indivisible from technology: 95.5% of all American homes have a television, while only 16% have air conditioning and 40% have indoor plumbing.

In the 1970s artists continued to explore personal worldviews instead of larger art movements. The resulting diversity of styles include both highly skilled painting and conceptual art, which moved away from traditional mediums and techniques to focus primarily on ideas; sometimes artists presented just a few written statements as the artwork to plant an idea that lives in the mind of the audience.

In 1970 the Museum of Modern Art in New York (MoMA) held a landmark exhibition simply called *Information*. The show was highly conceptual, with one hundred artists' takes on the theme through video, photography, performance, and site-specific installation. Mail art was requested and solicited while several artists created projects based on computation. A trio of artists from Yugoslavia's OHO Group visualized elements of chance as well as the flow of information through circuits. Dan Graham computed the miles to the edge of the known galaxy as well as the distance between the cornea and retinal wall within the human eye.[27] Artist Mel Bochner created an installation of a giant circle with a detailed formula for its drawing (fig. 8), while Sol LeWitt submitted instructions for four workers paid $4 an hour to draw lines for four hours. Conceptual artist Lawrence Weiner presented three statements on the creation of an artwork, including the option not to create it at all. Perhaps the most important work in the show was Hans Haacke's interactive sculpture *Poll of MoMA Visitors*, which allowed gallery viewers to vote on the politics of then–New York governor and MoMA board member Nelson Rockefeller (fig. 9). Haacke's sculpture showcased public sentiment literally by collecting color-coded ballots by museum visitors in plexiglass boxes. This mix of data and politics became a charged representation of a turbulent era's intergenerational conflict and communication.

After the 1970s, the speed of change becomes a blur. In 1976 Apple Computers was founded, the first "personal computers" showed up in stores a year later, and the Voyager spacecraft was set on its way as an ambassador of humanity to unknown planets. A year later, the Atari 2600 home video game system launched, ARPANET established the internet in 1983, DNA fingerprinting was introduced in 1985, and Powerpoint was released in 1987 a few years before the first digital cameras were for sale. By 1996, there were approximately forty-five million people using the internet; enough content was online by 1998 that Google was founded to improve the search for information. Only two years later, in 2000, there were 407 million users worldwide, an 800% increase. As people flocked to the internet, digital content became the next horizon. Wikipedia began crowdsourcing a new digital encyclopedia in 2001 and social media quickly spread with Facebook starting in 2004, then Twitter and YouTube in 2005.

2005–today: Data business and social apps

Just as the nineteenth century led to the innovations of the twentieth century, the successive revolutions in digitization keep redefining human possibility—economically, artistically, and spiritually. As communication moves from analog to digital, it all becomes data. The mechanism of the computer loses its importance in comparison to the significance of the communication and media it enables. With the popularization of the internet, business is also digitized, and data went from being measured in kilobits to zettabytes.[28] In 2006, internet advertising revenues increased 35% in a single year to reach $16.9 billion.

The launch of the iPhone by Steve Jobs in 2007 ushered a cultural revolution and a design inflection point. Through innovative new technology matched with an intuitive new user interface, the computer was suddenly free to roam untethered, changing how—*and where*—we collect data, impacting nearly every form of human communication.

2012 was declared "The Year of Big Data"[29] by *The New York Times*, and the *Harvard Business Review* published the article "Data Scientist: The Sexiest Job of the 21st Century,"[30] although there were only around six thousand data scientists in the world at the time. Ten years later, in 2022, five billion people are using the internet,[31] and there are 11.5 million posted data science jobs.[32] In 2020, the Covid-19 pandemic closed down the entire world, and the majority of human interaction is now online.[33] In 2023, social-media advertising revenues were $225 billion. In 2024, 70% of the world's data is now user generated.

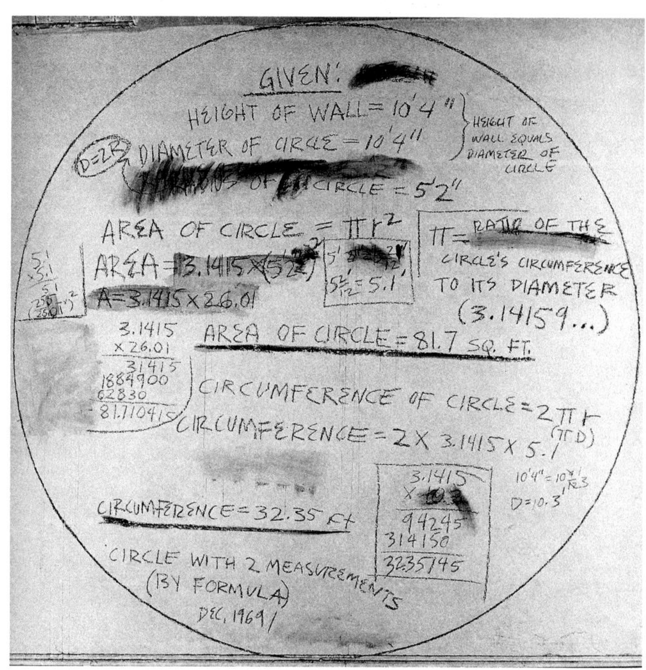

↑

Figure 8: Mel Bochner, *Circle with 2 Measurements (By Formula)*, 1969/2022. Charcoal and wall paint on wall; size determined by height of wall

→

Figure 9: Hans Haacke, installation view of *Poll of MoMA Visitors* (1970), in *Hans Haacke: All Connected*, New Museum, New York, 2019–20

Haacke's sculpture showcased public sentiment literally by collecting color-coded ballots by museum visitors in plexiglass boxes. This mix of data and politics became a charged representation of a turbulent era's intergenerational conflict and communication.

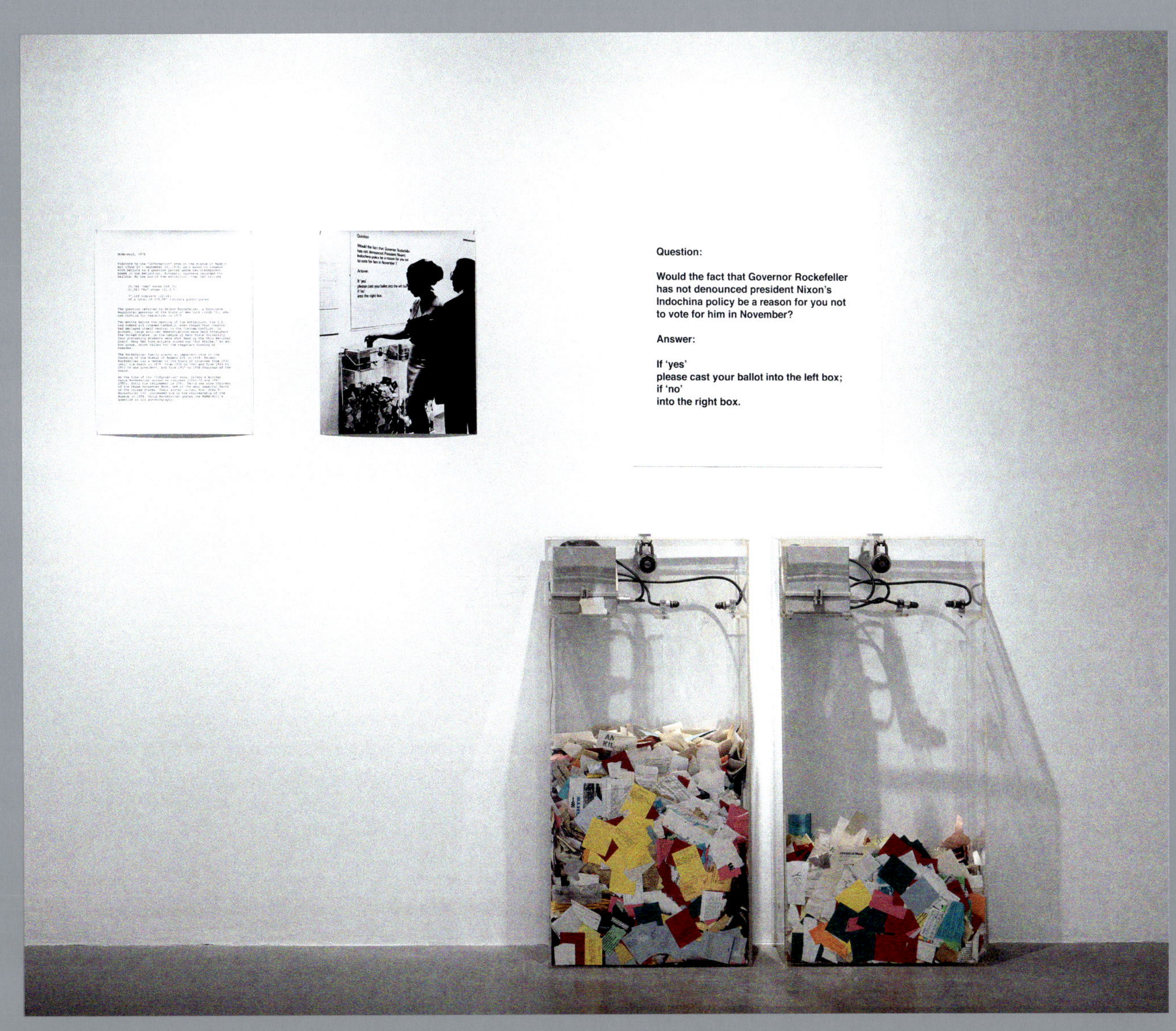

Starting from the earliest forms of human communication and building a narrative spanning thirty thousand years, this essay aims to establish data as a cultural construct intertwined with advertising and media as much as technology. We developed technologies to learn and communicate more efficiently and established systems to collect and transmit information as data, but in the end, the data represents far more than knowledge or communication; it became the raw material of our lives[34] and for expression. In the same way as the camera became the roving eye to capture the experience of the artist, or the pen inscribed paper as an expression of the will of the individual, data has become a proxy for the human condition.

Information designer and proponent of "data humanism" Giorgia Lupi elaborates:

> Data represents real life. It is a snapshot of the world in the same way that a picture catches a small moment in time. Numbers are always placeholders for something else, a way to capture a point of view—but sometimes this can get lost. Failing to represent these limitations and nuances and blindly putting numbers in a chart is like reviewing a movie by analyzing the chemical properties of the cellulose on which the images were recorded.[35]

Along with the digitization of nearly all communication, and the pervasive collection of data in general, it comes as no surprise that data has also become power. Back in 1997 Michael H. Goldhaber revived the concept of the "attention economy" first at a conference called "Economics of Digital Information" and shortly after in the pages of *Wired* magazine:

> If you get attention, that means you have some control over both the thoughts and actions of those paying it to you.... The very act of paying attention may seem voluntary, but often it is not completely so.[36]

Our conscious awareness of data in communication and in practice only amplifies its importance. That is why data is too important for us not to reinterpret its power through art.

NOTES

1 This exercise is anything but complete. Your complaints and suggestions are welcome and likely be added to subsequent versions.

2 By this, I mean that any response to data is inherently an act of choosing what data to react to, how it is charted, labeled, designed, engineered, etc. I think any data visualization is a response to the data and subject matter regardless of the format or domain (whether business intelligence, journalistic, or contemporary art).

3 Jean de Heinzelin, "Ishango," *Scientific American* 206, no. 6 (June 1962): 105–16.

4 *In The History of Marketing Thought* from 1962, Robert Bartels has this handy framing of how marketing accomplishes social objectives: "Reciprocity is a social system wherein material needs are met through exchange carried on between individuals and groups in the form of gift-giving. Redistribution is a social system involving the assembling of goods at a point from which they are redistributed by a duly constituted authority. Householding, or oecomomia, is a social system accomplishing what marketing does in our society. It involves production for use, not for exchange; Self-sufficiency of trade. Trade is a form of exchange which may be carried on in the absence of markets. It involved prices, in the form of equivalencies, determined by treaty or administrative decision and not by behavior in a marketplace. The market is the fifth type of social system supplying society's material needs. Originally, the market was a local institution. It was entirely separate from the trade carried on outside the country. The market supplied the common people with daily provisions."

5 Ruben Pater, *CAPS LOCK: How Capitalism Took Hold of Design, and How to Escape From It* (Amsterdam: Valiz, 2021).

6 Early marketplaces evolved naturally across the world, but documented marketplace signs date to the ancient Greeks in 550–350 BC. A few hundred years later, the Roman-built Trajan's Market was the equivalent of the shopping mall, with vendors set up in multi-level buildings.

7 Interestingly, the sign for a tavern in Roman times featured a bush, derived from the proverb "A good wine needs no bush."

8 John Berger was an art critic, philosopher, and provocateur whose 1972 four-part BBC TV series and book of the same name, *Ways of Seeing*, was an introduction to art history as a progressive study of images. The first episode begins with the author taking a box cutter to a fifteenth-century painting in a museum, cutting out the face of a woman.

9 John Berger, *Ways of Seeing* (London: Penguin Books, 1972).

10 Marshall McLuhan, *The Medium Is the Massage* (New York: Bantam Books, 1967). McLuhan's book was not actually written by McLuhan but was an image-laden, pop-digest version of his previous essays as designed and edited by Quentin Fiore. While McLuhan is widely cited for his brilliant insights, he was made a household name by the efforts of Fiore, the less-remembered designer. Let that be just one more example of the power of image and text in communication!

11 From a historical perspective, literacy levels for the world population have risen drastically in the last couple of centuries. While only 12% of the people in the world could read and write in 1820, today the share has reversed: only 14% of the world population, in 2016, remained illiterate. Max Roser and Esteban Ortiz-Ospina, "Literacy," Our World in Data, 2013, https://ourworldindata.org/literacy.

12 The Wikipedia entry for the word "science" feels relevant: "Science is a rigorous, systematic endeavor that builds and organizes knowledge in the form of testable explanations and predictions about the world." https://en.wikipedia.org/wiki/Science, accessed June 2024.

13 Megan Corinn Crouse, "Business Revolution: The Ad Agency," article for Pennsylvania Center for the Book website, Penn State University Libraries, 2010, https://pabook.libraries.psu.edu/literary-cultural-heritage-map-pa/feature-articles/business-revolution-ad-agency.

14 "Catch-Line and Argument," *The Book-Keeper* 15 (February 1903): 124.

15 While D. W. Griffith was the first person to make a film in Hollywood, in 1910, it was the Nestor Film Company that first opened on the northwest corner of Sunset Boulevard and Gower Street on October 27, 1911.

16 Herbert Bayer, Walter Gropius, and Ise Gropius, eds., *Bauhaus, 1919–1928* (New York: The Museum of Modern Art, 1938).

17 Otto Neurath, "The Social and Economic Museum in Vienna'" (1925), collected in Neurath, *Empiricism and Sociology*, ed. R. S. Cohen and M. Neurath (Dordrecht, The Netherlands: Reidel, 1973), 214.

18 ISOTYPE, or International System of Typographic Picture Education, was named by its chief practitioner and co-inventor, Marie (Reidemeister) Neurath. The team that developed ISOTYPE featured a subject-matter expert, Otto, a designer named Gerd Arntz, and a design/data science hybrid role called "the Transformer," Marie Neurath.

19 Edward Bernays, *Propaganda* (New York: Horace Liveright, 1928).

20 Dziga Vertov was born David Abelevich Kaufman in Białystok, Poland, which was part of Russia at the time. After studying psychology, he took the pseudonym Vertov around 1918 as a futurist neologism derived from the Russian verb *vertit'sia* (to spin or turn), and Dziga from the Ukrainian word for a "(spinning) top." Vertov experimented with concrete poetry and sound recording before moving into film, ultimately becoming one of the most celebrated Russian avantgarde film makers with *Man with a Movie Camera*. It is regarded as one of the most important films of the twentieth century despite being forgotten for over thirty years after its release and widely dismissed by his peers until its reevaluation in the 1990s/2000s.

21 Vertov, "Kino-Eye Manifesto" (1923), reprinted in *Kino-Eye: The Writings of Dziga Vertov*, ed. Annette Michelson, trans. Kevin O'Brien (Los Angeles: University of California Press, 1984), 82–83.

22 Edward Bernays, *Public Relations*, Vocational and Professional Monographs, no. 58 (Boston: Bellman, 1945).

23 Wikipedia defines information theory as the mathematical study of the quantification, storage, and communication of information.

24 Pop art being a hallmark for art about media in a long lineage beginning at least with Surrealist collage, Marcel Duchamp's "readymades," and Robert Rauschenberg's "combines."

25 The size of the microprocessor was equal to the importance of its speed. The Intel 4004 microprocessor was equal in computational power to earlier computers weighing thirty tons. James L. Pelkey, "2.25: The Microprocessor—1971," in *The History of Computer Communications*, 2021, https://historyofcomputercommunications.info/section/2.25/The-Microprocessor-1971/.

26 Ben Bagdikian, *The Information Machines: Their Impact on Men and the Media* (New York: Harper & Row, 1971).

27 It's worth noting that Ray and Charles Eames created two versions of a similar project, *Powers of Ten*, in 1968 and then a higher quality version in 1977. In the Eames film, a trip to the edge of the known universe and then back to the smallest known particle, then a quark, is made by adding or subtracting from the exponent of ten each second as the image zooms out or in.

28 Initial magnetic-core memory in the 1950s contained 32 kilobits per cubic foot of physical memory. A zettabyte is equivalent to 1,000,000,000,000,000,000,000 (10^{21}) bytes. Storage for the entire world's internet passed a zettabyte in 2012, but data creation and transfer has exploded largely due to video-streaming services.

29 Steve Lohr, "How Big Data Became So Big," *The New York Times*, August 11, 2012.

30 Thomas H. Davenport and DJ Patil, "Data Scientist: The Sexiest Job of the 21st Century," *Harvard Business Review* (October 2012), https://hbr.org/2012/10/data-scientist-the-sexiest-job-of-the-21st-century.

31 That's 66% of the entire global population.

32 Maha Taqi, "2023 and Beyond: The Future of Data Science Told by 79,306 People," *Jetbrains* (blog), https://blog.jetbrains.com/pycharm/2023/10/future-of-data-science/. It turns out that determining the number of data scientists in the world is fairly difficult, mainly because the skills of a data scientist are more widely used than the term data scientist.

33 "As of March 2021, 65% of people communicated more digitally than in person on a daily basis, with the number even higher in English-speaking countries. For example, 73.7% of Americans and 74.4% of UK residents communicate more digitally than in person." Alicea Lieberman and Juliana Schroeder, "Two social lives: How differences between online and offline interaction influence social outcomes," *Current Opinion in Psychology* 31 (February 2020): 16–21.

34 From our movements, and health, to our thoughts, relationships, and emotions. It's hard to imagine just how much data each person has, representing all aspects of our recordable lives, for every moment that is tracked. While our memories and internal lives are not stored, there are certainly ways of capturing data that may represent our inner selves.

35 Giorgia Lupi, "Data Humanism: The Revolutionary Future of Data Visualization," *Print* 70 (2016): 76.

36 Michael H. Goldhaber, "Attention Shoppers!" *Wired*, December 1, 1997, https://www.wired.com/1997/12/es-attention/.

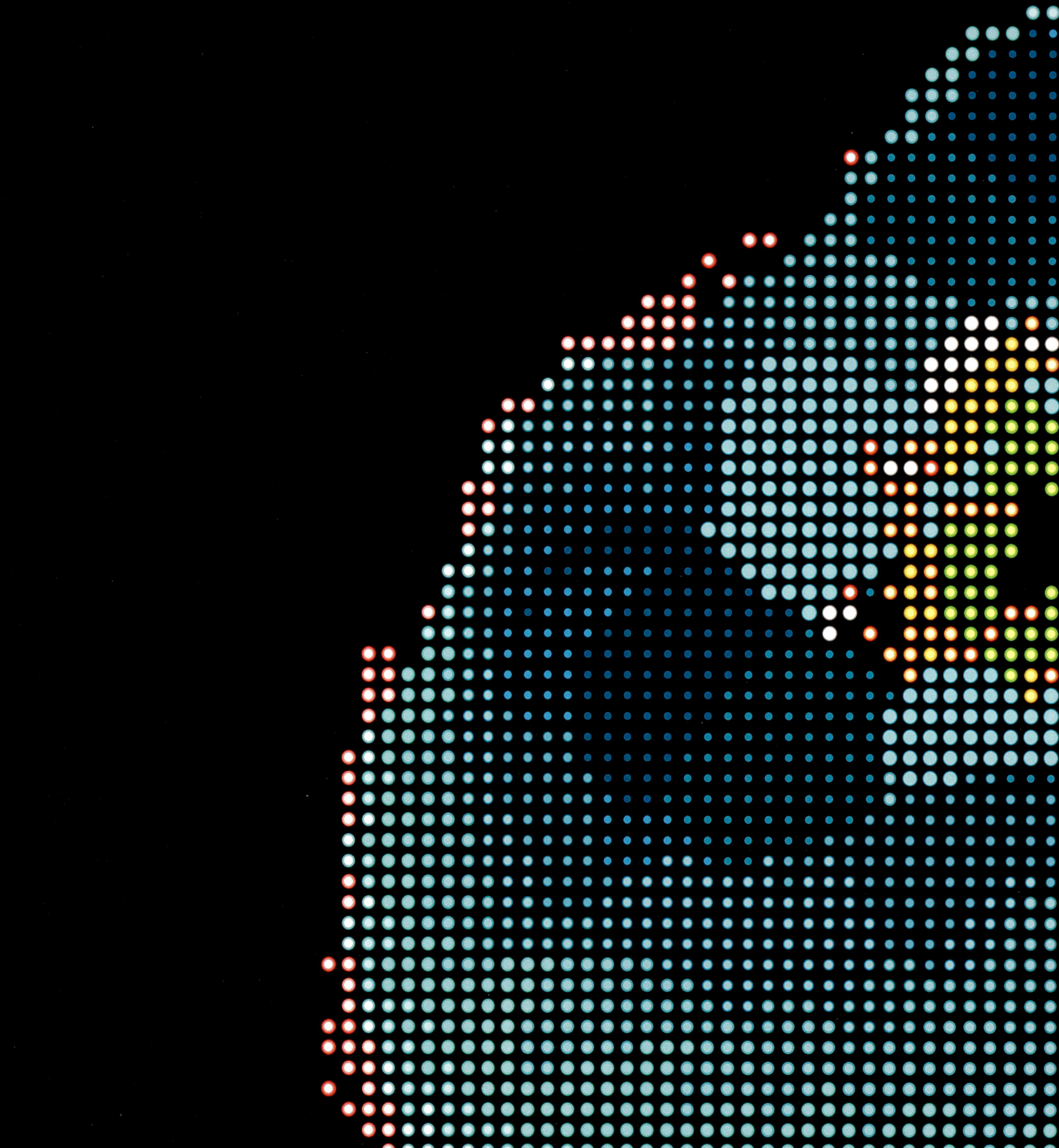

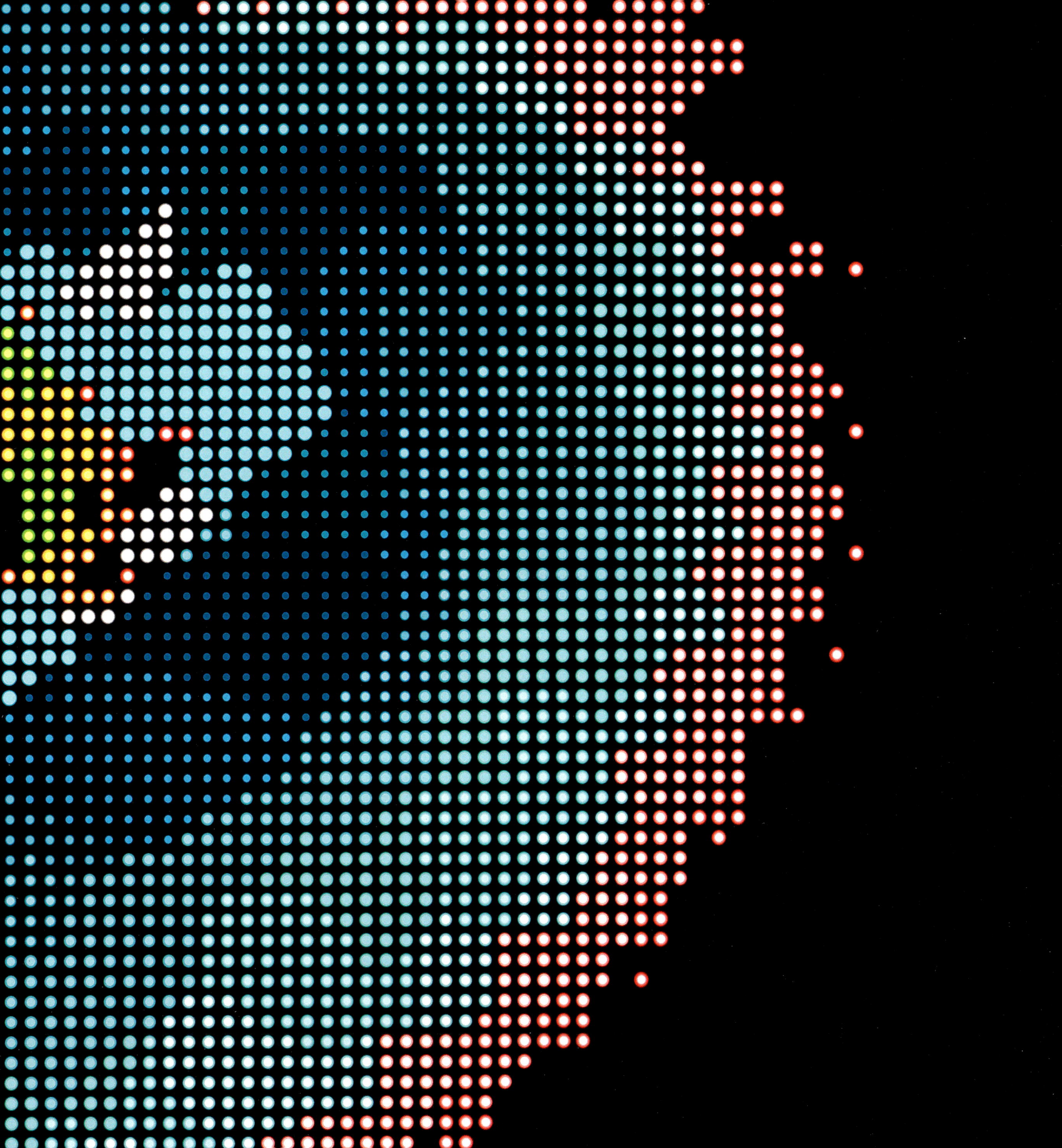

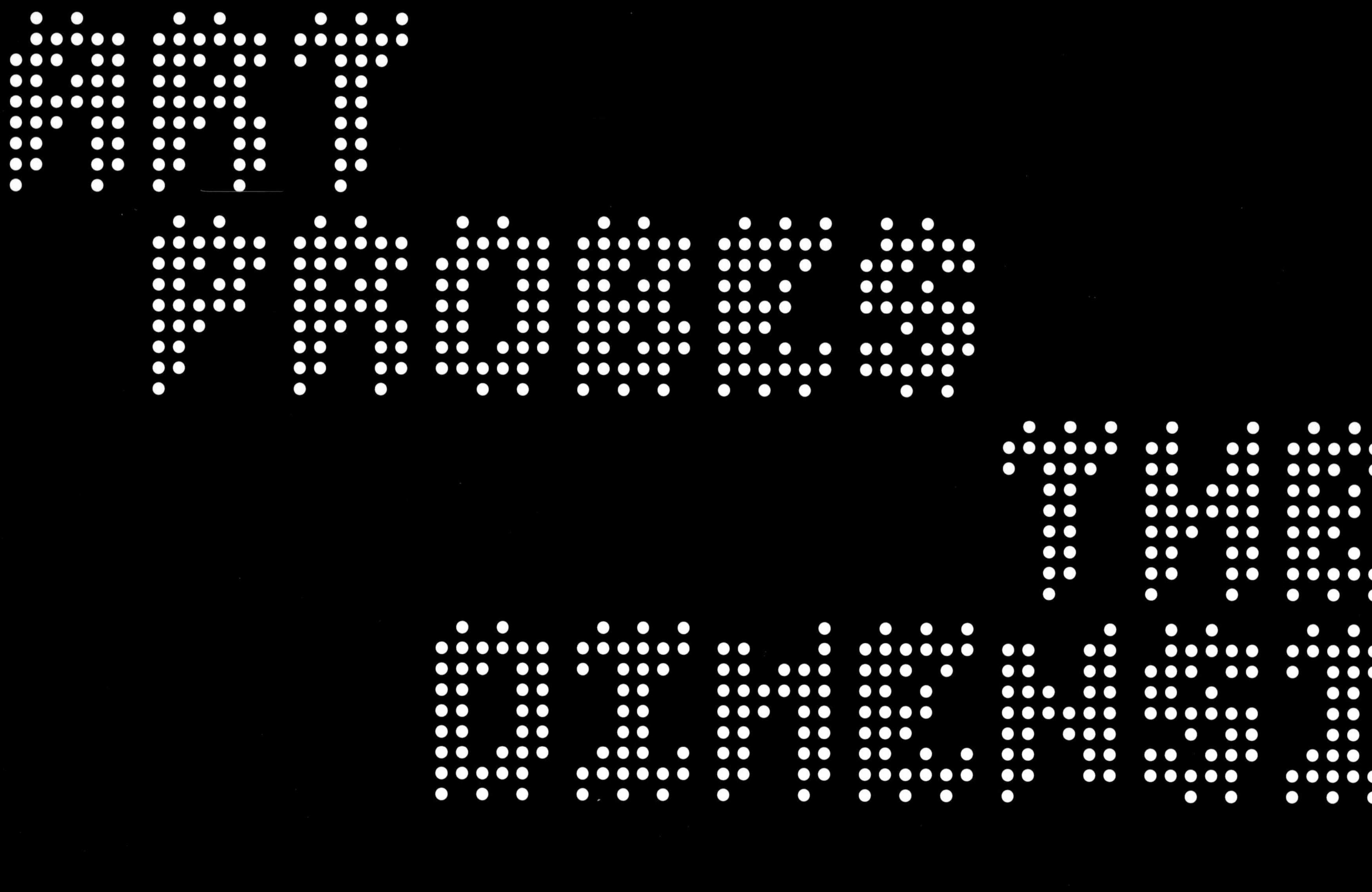
ART
PROBES

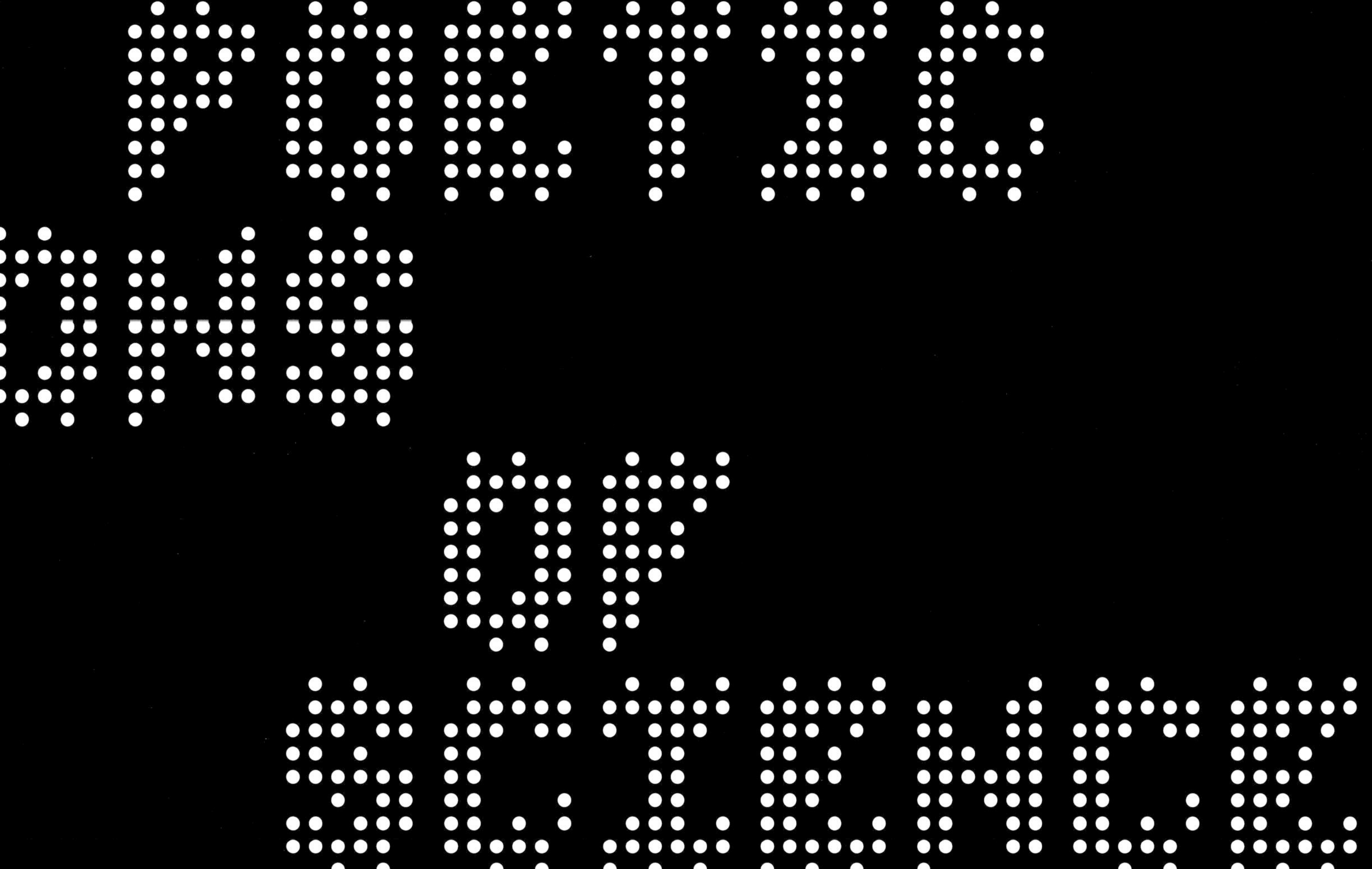

STEPHEN NOWLIN

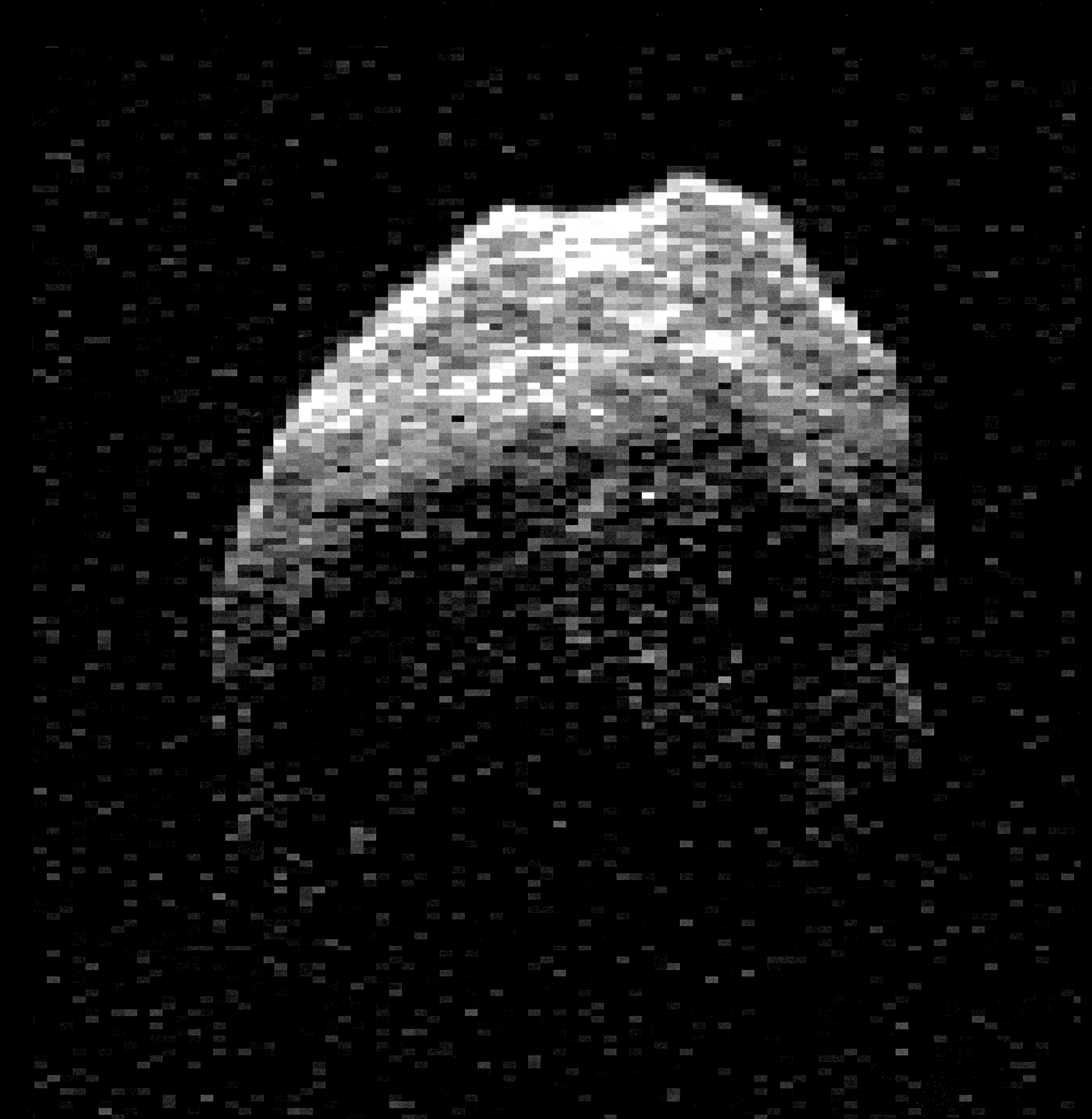

Beauty Found (Where It Wasn't Meant to Be)

STEPHEN NOWLIN

↖
Asteroid 2015 TB145

A 2015 radar image of an asteroid achieves aesthetic effect without artistic intention.

On its trek running circles around the sun, an asteroid skirts past silent Earth. Perhaps the remains of a primordial comet, the solitary assemblage of space rubble known as Asteroid 2015 TB145 is about to have its picture taken. More precisely, it's about to be microwaved.

Deep within California's high Mojave Desert, near the barren ghost town of Goldstone, sits one of three facilities comprising NASA's Deep Space Network. On an early Halloween morning in 2015, the largest of the site's five giant radio telescopes tilted toward a patch of sky surrounding TB145's journey—and began hurling microwaves at it. Three hundred thousand miles away, those pulses bounced off their target and were sensed by another massive antennae, at Green Bank Observatory in West Virginia. The outcome of this scientific operation was a set of images: rough first-ever portraits of the hitherto unknown face of TB145 set against its backdrop of eternal deep space.

Radar images appear as a field of pixels in which their target's shape is approximated by a backscatter of microwaves. Comprised of tiny rectangles in a complex array of shades from black to white, the sparkling grayscale that demystified TB145's craggy profile provided a valuable yield of scientific data. The asteroid thus joined with nature's other previously hidden phenomena upon which humans have, for the first time, cast an analytical eye.

In addition to its scientific harvest, the portrait of TB145 is much like a work of art. Its raw beauty is an alloy of truth and the ineffable that, significantly, was an artistic outcome without artistic intent. In science, art makes itself.

Today, artists using data and other objective sources are in search of outcomes that tap into the same beauty–truth alliance. Theirs is a type of generative art: the byproduct of structured procedures employed in lieu of more traditional and subjective artful choices. Such methodologies involve self-imposed limits circumscribed by rules, systems and patterns, data, code, algorithms, chance, and physical elements such as gravity or other natural forces that comprise an artwork's conceptual and procedural framework.

Generative art can be likened to tossing random factors into complex physics equations and following through to see what sort of world might emerge—it's art that could serve as a metaphor for how our real world came into existence. The operational elements of generative art systems create visual outcomes that, like scientific knowledge of things, are not "meant to be" in the sense of having been consciously manipulated to satisfy subjective intentions, but rather are discovered indiscriminately by adherence to the integrity of a discrete process. Generative art is the relishing of form as a consequence.

Nature itself is the model. In his 1917 book *On Growth and Form*, Scottish biologist D'Arcy Wentworth Thompson describes appearances throughout the natural world with the observation that "form is a diagram of forces."[1] The form of an object in nature is related to nothing other than its causal processes as an outcome, or byproduct, of interactions subject to the laws of physics. Forms like a tree are understood as a diagram of how physical forces acted upon and interacted within an organism and ended up as arching and twisted branches. The shape of the branch diagrams the history of its making. It is, in essence, a type of memory, like how a weather chart's zigzagging lines are a record of climate data. Natural form in all its wonder and beauty is not a creation of godly or artistic willfulness but is instead the unintended outcome of nature's complex algorithmic forces interacting.

Science works in the same way, when it follows evidentiary methods to generate knowledge outcomes. As an action toward knowing, science is more a verb than a noun. It's what an infant is doing when it attempts to rise up on all fours, gathers evidence of gravity's effects, and experiments with successes and failures—then crawls. We're not all scientists, but we all do science.

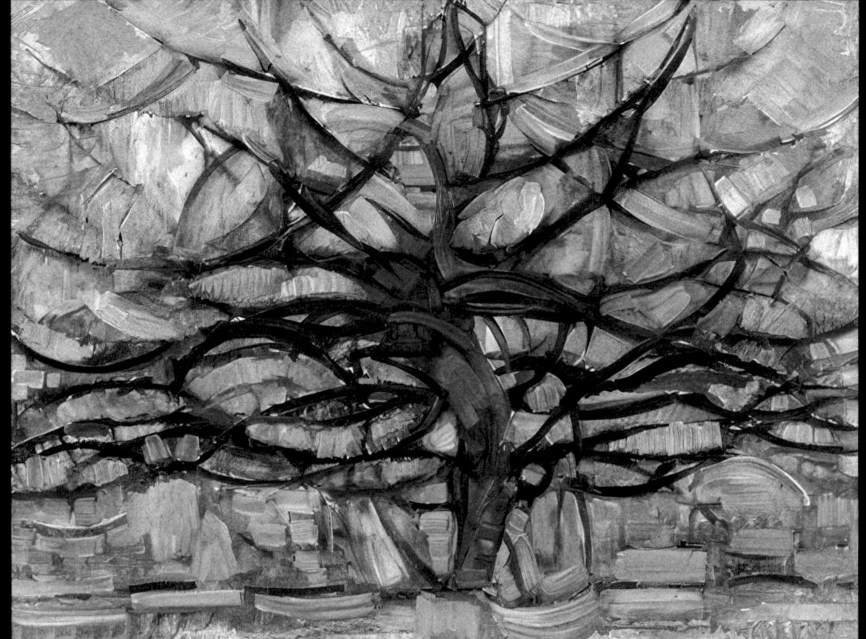

Like art, science arouses sensations of the poetic, of having queried the depths of mystery in search of new truths and sensations of beauty. In generative art, the conceptual decision to employ an externally determined order as the substitute for personal choice infuses visual expression with organizing principles echoing those of science and nature. The devotion to such procedure by an artist can itself be viewed as symbolic of how science seeks to understand the world.

In the present, a wave of generative and other science-informed artmaking has appeared, in part as a response to advanced digital technology's flood of big data inundating social and intellectual corridors, offering opportunities for artistic analysis of critical subjects at an increasingly granular level. For an era struggling with debates about multiple versions of the truth, the presence of objective criteria, facts, and data are increasingly relied upon for wayfinding. Artists are drawn to this nexus and its social provocations.

More than a century ago, antecedents in the mutual influences of science and the arts stirred radical changes in artists' strategies for reflecting reality, prompting a shift away from the primacy of figurative representation and acute craftsmanship. Piet Mondrian was prominent among a string of luminaries in forging a new sense of artistic beauty and truth that he declared as equal with that of nature, rather than simply imitative of it. He sought a "purely pictorial form that appeared eminently 'real' and 'concrete.' It existed in its own right, a fully fledged artistic reality."[2]

> All the arts strive to attain an aesthetic plastic of the relationship existing between the individual and the universal, the subjective and the objective, nature and spirit.... The essential characteristic of the New Plastic in painting is a composition of rectangular color planes that expresses the most profound reality.[3]

Limiting himself to forms bounded by a Cartesian grid, Mondrian surrendered much of what had been left to personal choice in artmaking up to that point. His vertical and horizontal black lines functioned like a simple dataset. He'd narrowed his options to permutations generated by adherence to this set, limiting his own personal subjectivity and achieving in works of art a metaphorical reference to how objects in nature had come to exist. For Mondrian, art *was* an act of nature.

Science around the time of Mondrian accounted significantly, perhaps exclusively, for such evolving artistic practices. By the nineteenth century's final years and the beginning of the twentieth's, assaults on the status quo had included Charles Darwin's theory of evolution, Gregor Mendel's genetics, James Clerk Maxwell's science of electromagnetism, Dmitri Mendeleev's creation of the periodic table, Louis Pasteur's germ theory of disease, the rise of knowledge in thermodynamics, the confirmation of atoms, the discoveries of x-rays and electrons, the inventions of the telegraph and telephone, Max Planck's development of quantum theory, and Albert Einstein's special theory of relativity. It was an era of acceleration in radical new views of how nature works, the tenor of which implied an earlier history where truth may have been riddled with errors and fictions.

In paintings of the same era, the changing position of linear perspective's vanishing point diagrammed for modern art a journey parallel to that of science, whereby the pictorial space in which art had previously notarized orthodox views of nature began to accommodate a new aesthetic based upon emerging science. Perspective's vanishing point began its sojourn deep in the illusionistic pictorial space of Neoclassicism, ricocheted through the shallower pictorial spaces of Impressionism and Cubism, and ultimately disappeared on the flat material surfaces of Suprematist and Constructivist paintings. The

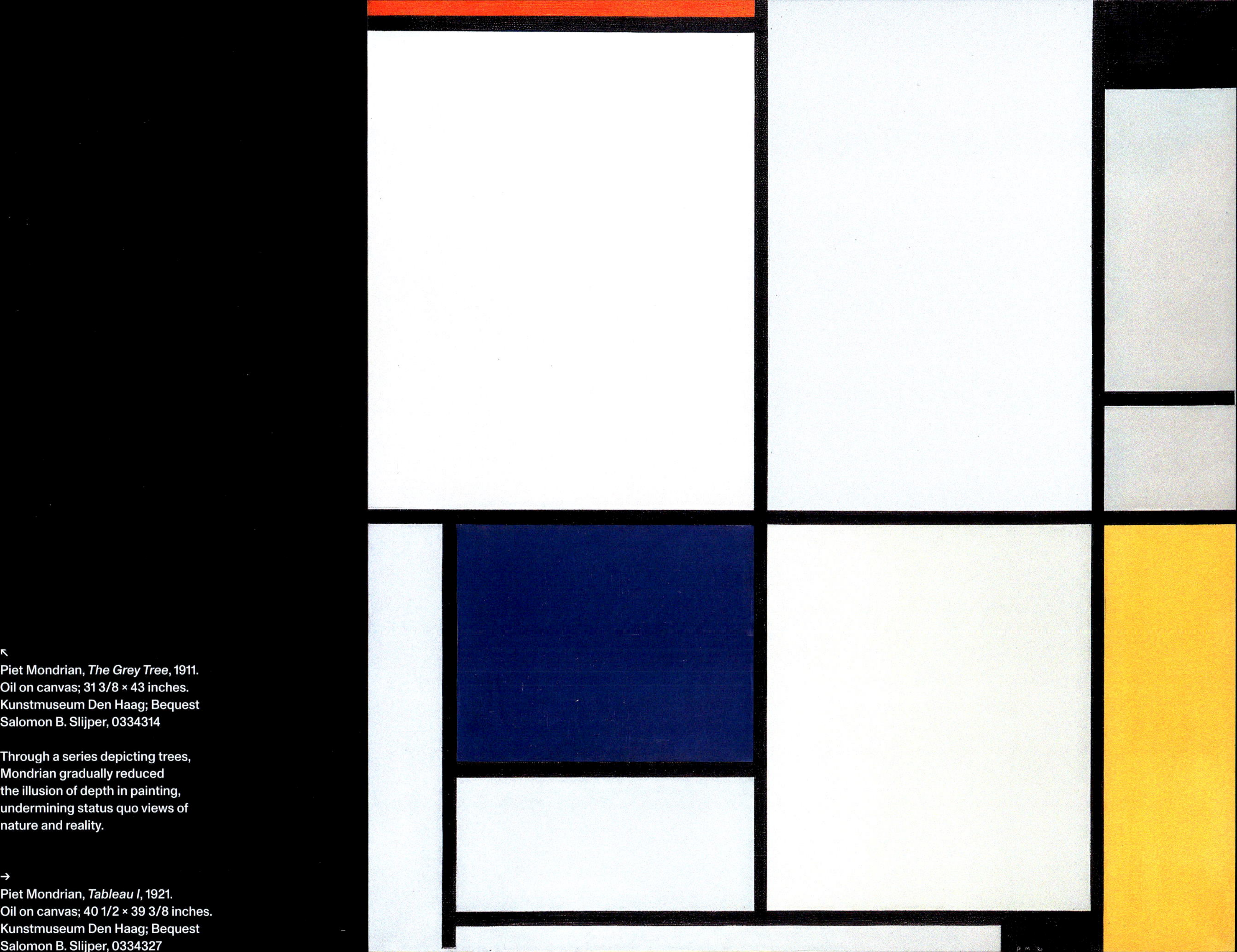

↖
Piet Mondrian, *The Grey Tree*, 1911.
Oil on canvas; 31 3/8 × 43 inches.
Kunstmuseum Den Haag; Bequest
Salomon B. Slijper, 0334314

Through a series depicting trees, Mondrian gradually reduced the illusion of depth in painting, undermining status quo views of nature and reality.

→
Piet Mondrian, *Tableau I*, 1921.
Oil on canvas; 40 1/2 × 39 3/8 inches.
Kunstmuseum Den Haag; Bequest
Salomon B. Slijper, 0334327

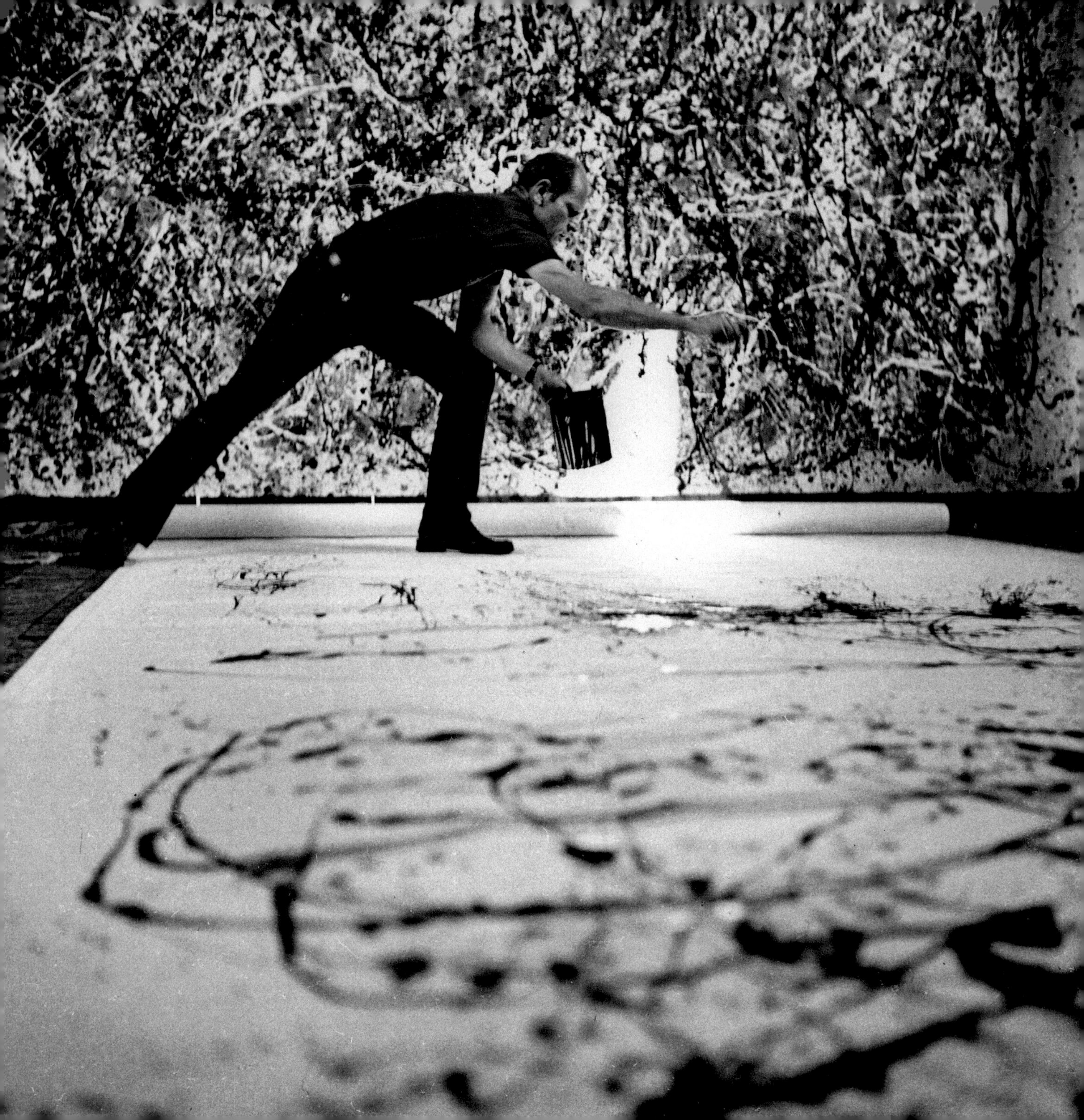

Generative art can be likened to tossing random factors into complex physics equations and following through to see what sort of world might emerge—it's art that could serve as a metaphor for how our real world came into existence.

↖
Hans Namuth, *Untitled (Jackson Pollock)*, 1950. Photograph. Center for Creative Photography, University of Arizona

Jackson Pollock harnessed and foregrounded the natural interactions of gravity, velocity, and liquidity to aesthetic effect.

force of rapid scientific advancement elevated principles of an evidence-based search for truth, disrupting longstanding beliefs about reality and sparking the inevitable agitations of new knowledge contradicting old. Its tensions were manifest in art's exchange of the pictorial for the real, analogizing science's exchange of fictional for factual.

The beginnings of a generative impulse simmered beneath the science of the time, emerging from the endeavor to make sense out of accelerated change. While Impressionism, Cubism, Constructivism, Suprematism, Dada, and beyond were being mischaracterized as "anti-art" by their critics, science raced ahead. Attempting to keep up, artists had in common their refusal to participate in orthodoxies that had served the past with an art that no longer adequately represented changing views of reality.

As a result, a science-laced generative impulse gestated throughout the ensuing twentieth century's art, trailing the implication that an inclusion of made-by-itself elements in a work of art will imbue it with qualities of beauty found in a nature that was being redefined by science. Scattered variations on the theme appear throughout the century's medley of radical stylistic forays: repurposed forms and "readymades" whose origins lay not in artistic intent but in functional usage; experiments in randomness and chance; candid foregrounding of process; gravity-directed drips and splashes; raw canvas into which paint aimlessly spilled, soaked, and stained according to the dictates of its chemistry; and unplanned flourishes, smears, erasures, and apparently unauthorized marks. All can be seen as referencing, whether consciously or not, an allegiance with the beauty model provided by nature: form without deliberate intent.

Further discourse underlying generative art gathered momentum in the early 1960s with the advent of Experiments in Art and Technology (EAT).[4]

In generative art, the conceptual decision to employ an externally determined order as the substitute for personal choice infuses visual expression with organizing principles echoing those of science and nature.

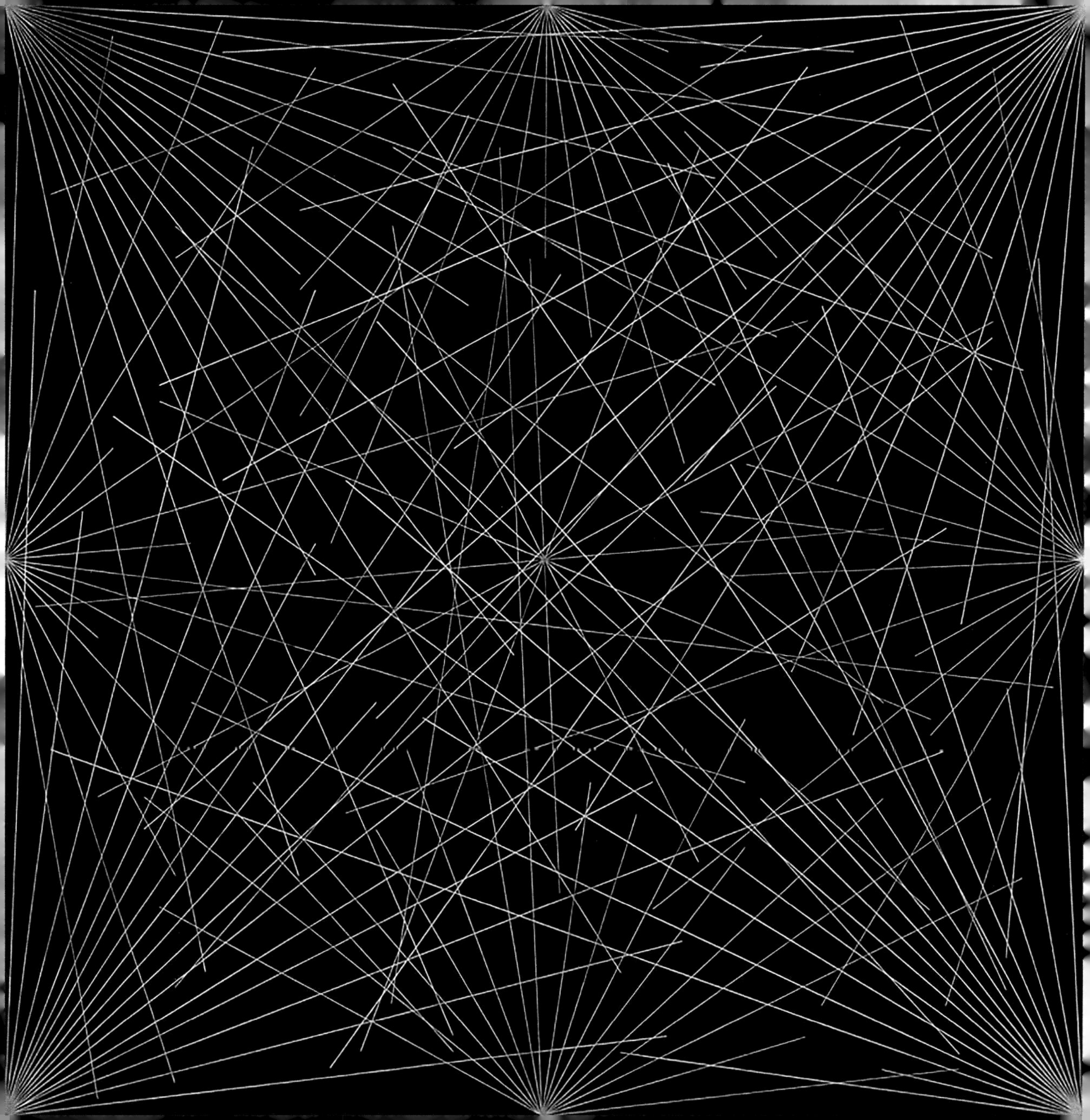

Established by artist Robert Rauschenberg and Bell Laboratories engineer Billy Klüver to support collaborations between artists and engineers, the project prompted an expansion of artists' palettes and visual vocabularies into alluring new arenas of electronic media and industrial materials. More significantly, it spawned appropriations of the language and models of science itself for use in artistic expression.

EAT was accompanied by the birth of the ecology movement and its awakening to nature as a delicate balancing act of the laws of physics, the consequences of global industrialization, and the poetics of a nature–human symbiosis. Concerns over the ultimate fate of Earth's natural environment converged in an increased collaboration between the science and art worlds, thawing their icy Two Cultures[5] relationship and opening doors to further modes of collaboration.

Additional appropriations of mathematics, patterns, algorithms, and eventually computation and coding served to fashion generative modes independent of subjectively biased choices and more involved in an art made by its own internal machinery, shifting the role of the artist from omniscient creator to that, like the scientist, of an instigator or proctor of experimentation and its outcomes. Throughout, such artmaking strategies implied a Mondrianesque investigation of the universal and the real, and queried evolving ideals of beauty.

Traditional artistic purpose, and the conventional notion that a creation is meant to be the way it is only by the conscious will and artistic dexterity of a creator, were thus repeatedly called to account. The use of impersonal criteria to generate an artistic outcome provokes the realization that beauty and its inveterate companion truth do not have to result from the personal esoteric designs of a creator. As a linkage to science and the ways and outcomes of nature, the symbolic character of generative art is that beauty and truth are already there to experience, where intent is absent. In that, art begins to probe the poetic dimensions of science.

Historically, a perception of the beauty–truth alliance permeates the poetic, philosophical, and spiritual discourse around the human relationship to nature and the universal. As poet John Keats wrote in 1819,

> Beauty is truth, truth beauty,—that is all
> Ye know on earth, and all ye need to know.[6]

Among others, generative art continues history's quest to wrestle with Keats's edict. As science changes the playing field upon which reality is understood, stubborn mythologies and misunderstandings crocheted into the fabric of social institutions and knowledge conventions begin to unravel. Truth along the way can become tortured in a maelstrom of disputed anxieties over the old and the new. Beauty can become hostage to the insistence that there must be a creator for it to embody truth.

A perennial subject of contemplation, disputes over the beauty–truth duality include deep questions of what is known and needed to be known of existence. Like the enigmas of space-time, explorations of beauty or truth lead inevitably from one to the other and back again. From its perspective as a metaphor for the workings of science and its outcomes, generative art is implicated in such a contemporary discourse and its considerations of existence, transcendence, and meaning.

Today the past, as if only yesterday, is echoed in iterations of art made by using methodologies not unlike those inherited from an art restricted to permutations of horizontal and vertical lines plus primary colors, or as well from the self-generated appearance of an encounter between archaic asteroids and a

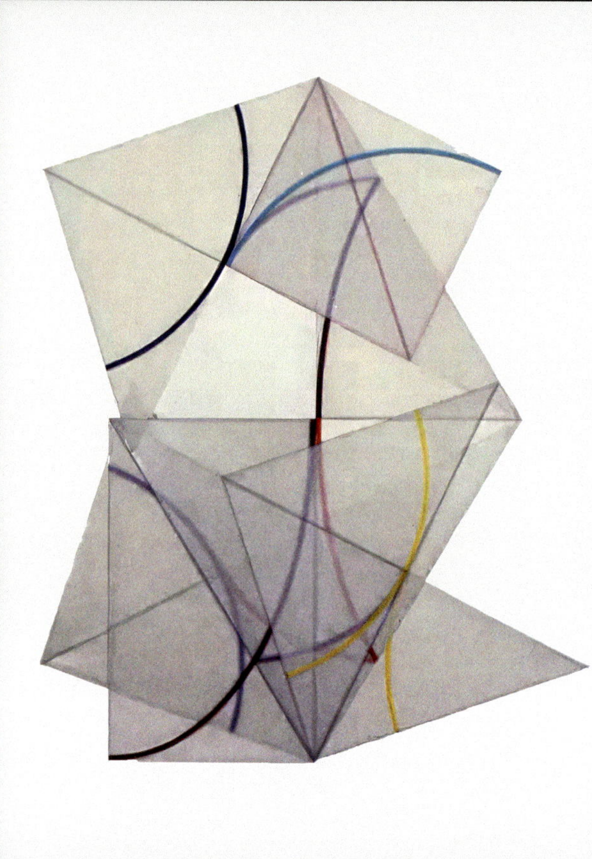

↑
Dorothea Rockburne, *Arena III (from the Arena Series)*, 1978. Vellum paper, colored pencil, varnish, glue, and rag board; 54 1/2 × 47 inches. Cranbrook Art Museum; Gift of Rose M. Shuey, from the Collection of Dr. John and Rose M. Shuey, CAM2002.37

Rockburne depended upon mathematical equations and the Golden Ratio to create folds and overlaps in her series *Drawing Which Makes Itself.*

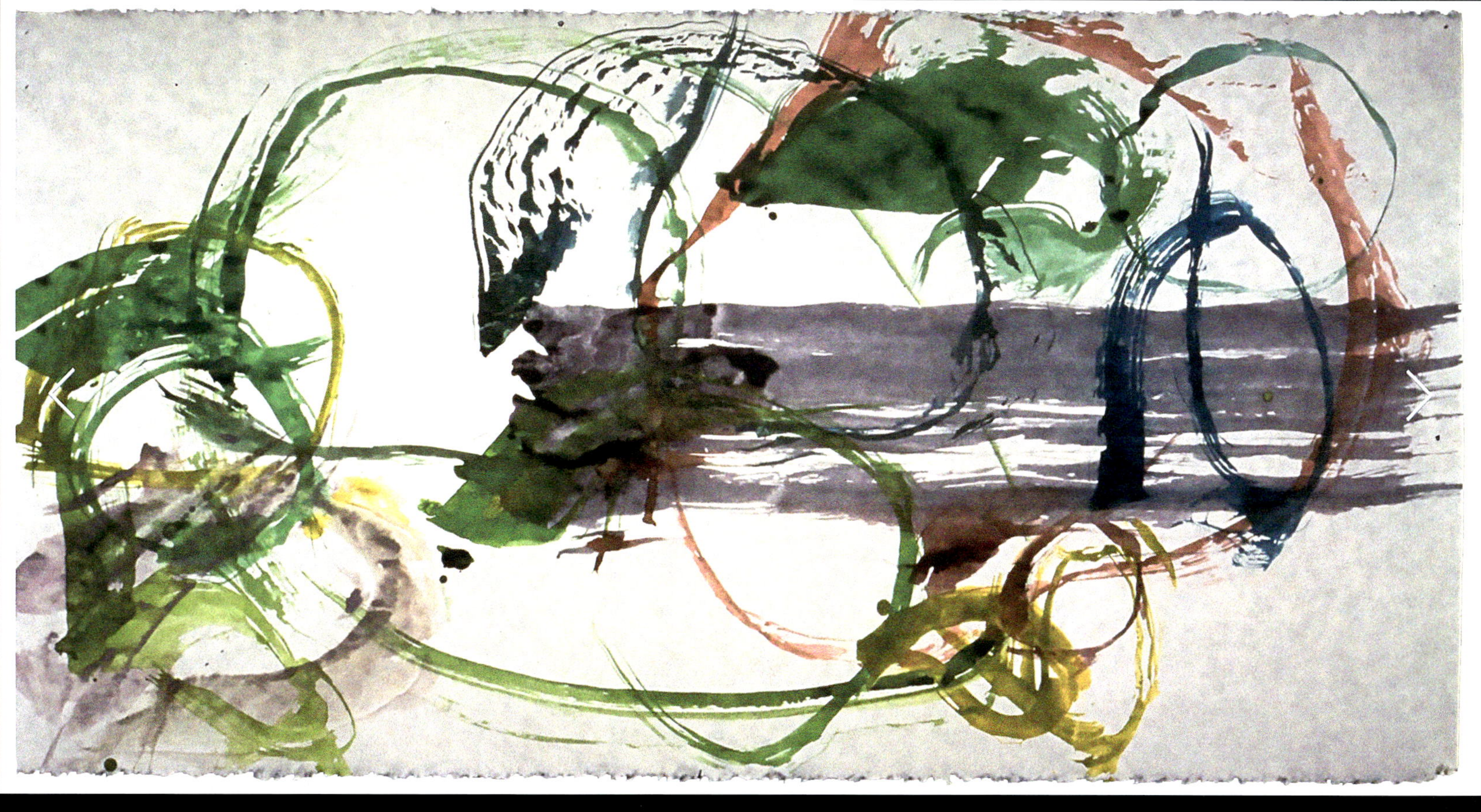

↑
John Cage, *New River Watercolors: Series 1 #4*, 1988. Watercolor on paper; 18 × 36 inches. Courtesy of Ray Kass, The Mountain Lake Workshop, Virginia

Starting with fifteen stones randomly selected from a river, Cage placed them on large sheets of watercolor paper to be brushed using computer instructions. Modeling his practice on nature's absence of artistic intention, Cage used chance interactions as means to create form.

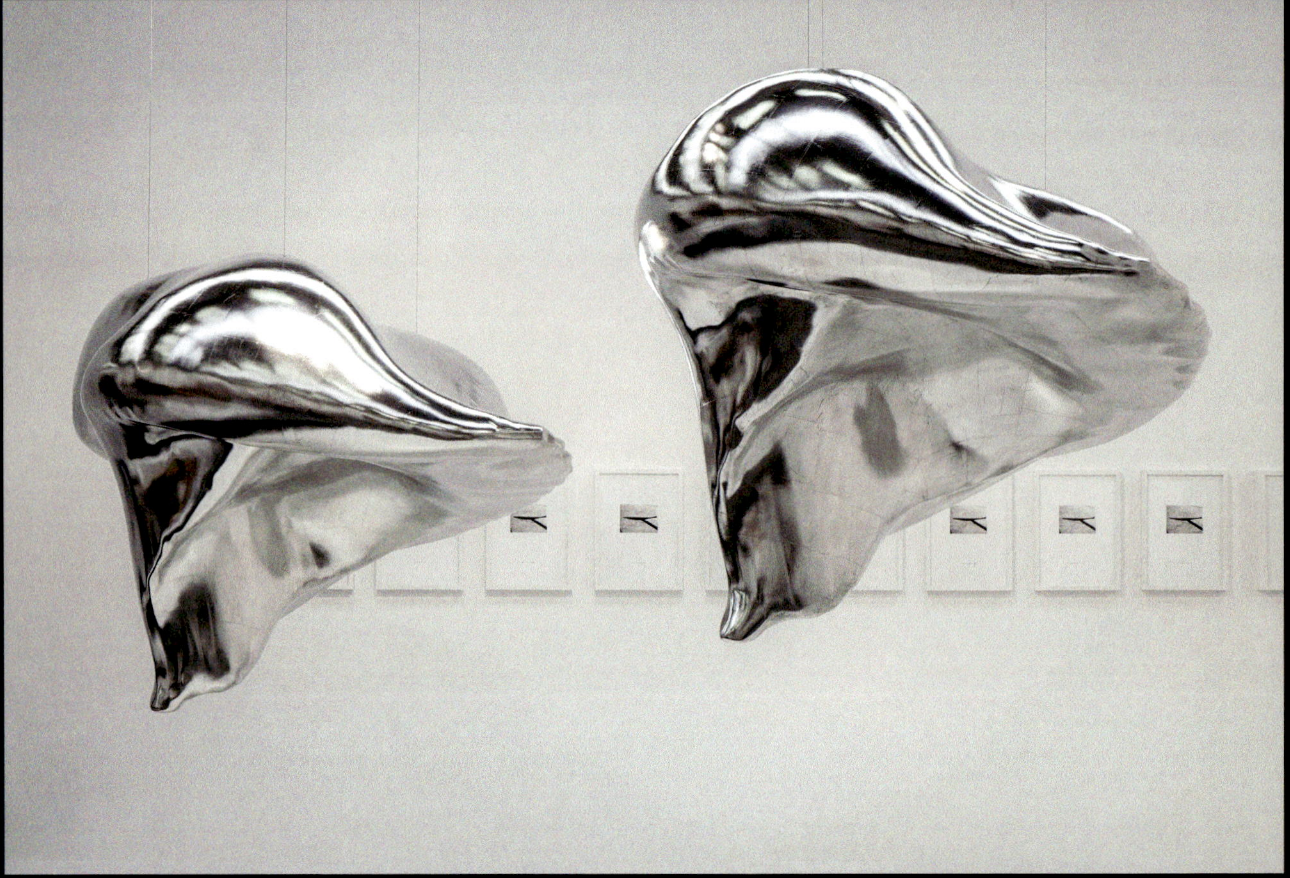

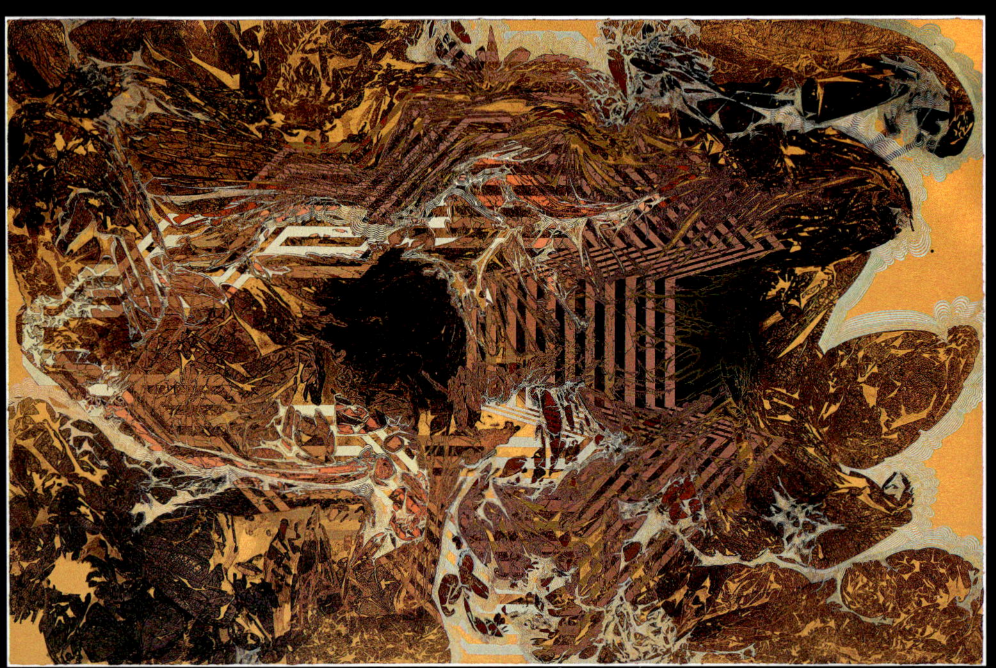

The impulse toward generative art harkens to the same thread of radical change begun by artists a century ago, when they gave expression to how science then, as it continues to do now, precipitated reconsiderations of how the universe works and our place in it. Beauty, truth, and eroding orthodoxies of fictional beliefs are interwoven into the shifting paradigm of a human relationship to nature. The arc of science compels that, along with all of nature's other forms, we ourselves are outcomes of generative processes. In nature, which is us, beauty does not glorify the conscious intentions of a creator but, rather, emanates from within us as an emergent sensation of something ephemeral, profound, and true.

A perk of human biology and a gift of having traversed long evolutionary pathways, we are the lucky finders of beauty where it wasn't meant to be.

↖

Iñigo Manglano-Ovalle, *Storm Prototype: Cloud Prototype No. 2* and *Cloud Prototype No. 4*, both 2006

Manglano-Ovalle's pair of thunderstorm clouds were an outcome of three-dimensional data supplied by the Department of Atmospheric Sciences, University of Illinois at Urbana-Champaign.

←

Linnéa Gabriella Spransy, *Prime Mover*, 2019

Spransy's abstract paintings and drawings are the result of a process of following predetermined rules and exploring the complexity of unanticipated visual outcomes.

NOTES

The phrase "We, the lucky finders of beauty where it wasn't meant to be" first appeared in my writing as part of an essay for the exhibition *ENERGY*, which took place at the Williamson Gallery, ArtCenter College of Design, in 2010.

1 D'Arcy Wentworth Thompson, *On Growth and Form* (Cambridge, UK: Cambridge University Press, 1917), 11. *On Growth and Form* was a seminal work in the field of biology, emphasizing the role of physical and mathematical principles in shaping the forms of living organisms.

2 Werner Haftmann, *Painting in the Twentieth Century*, vol. 1 (New York: Frederick A. Praeger, 1960), 202.

3 Piet Mondrian, *New Design: Neoplasticism* (Bauhausbücher 5, 1925) (reprint, Zürich: Lars Müller, 2019), 6, 10.

4 Experiments in Art and Technology's proactivity in promoting art–science relationships in the mid-1960s to early 1970s opened avenues of communication and interaction between the two domains that facilitated the eventual use by generative artists of quasi-scientific methodology.

5 "The Two Cultures" was a 1959 Rede lecture by British scientist and novelist C. P. Snow. It was widely understood as a despair over the notion that the arts and sciences existed hopelessly on polar ends of a cultural spectrum, and that their individual contributions to society were handicapped by this separation. The lecture was published as a book, *The Two Cultures and the Scientific Revolution*, that same year. Its premise permeated the discourse as various social forces began to bring the two cultures closer in the second half of the twentieth century.

6 In "Ode on a Grecian Urn" (1819), the message the English Romantic poet John Keats conveys to the urn is summarized in the ode's final lines:

> When old age shall this generation waste,
> Thou shalt remain, in midst of other woe
> Than ours, a friend to man, to whom thou say'st
> "Beauty is truth, truth beauty,—that is all
> Ye know on earth, and all ye need to know."

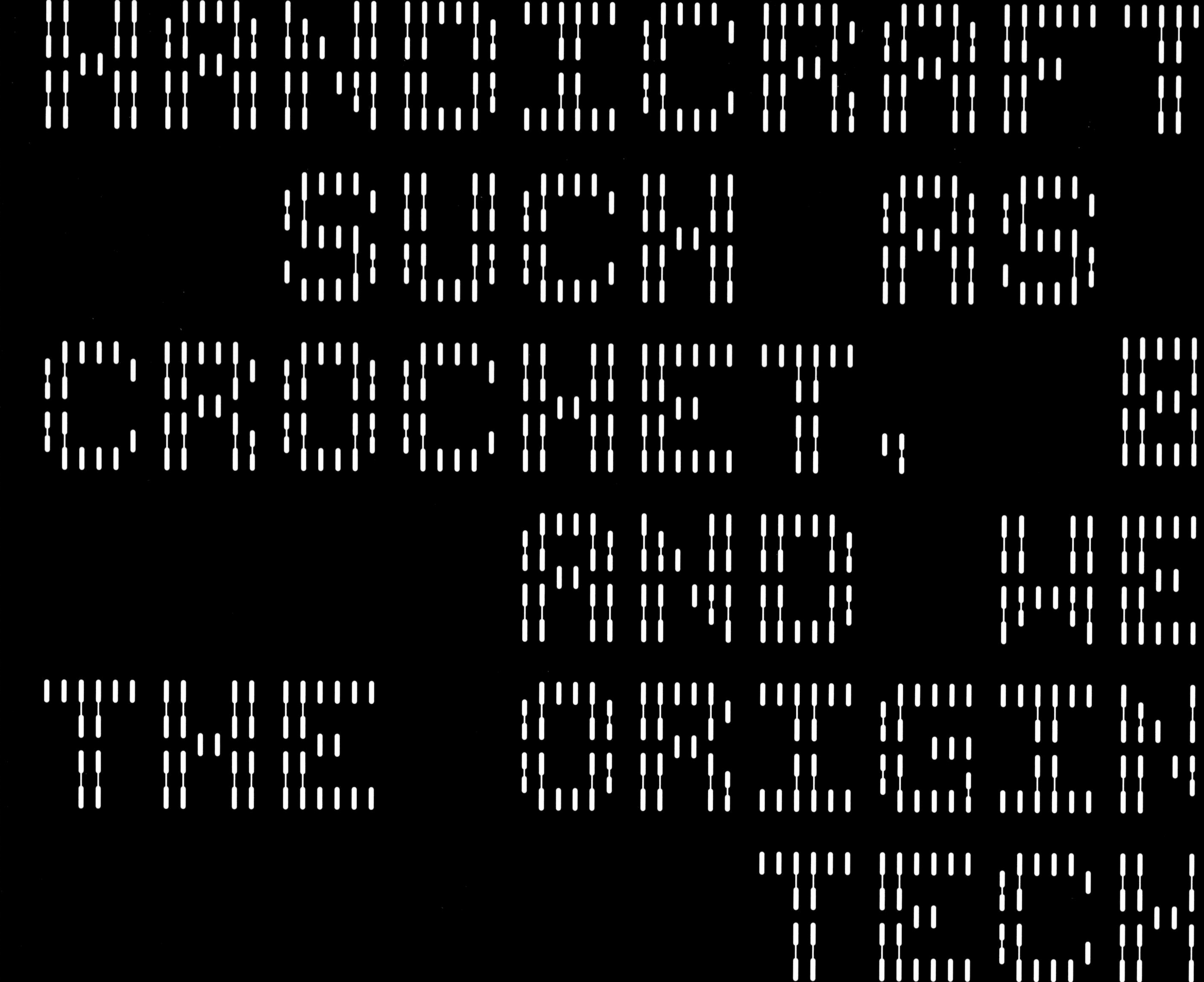
HANDICRAFT
SUCH AS
CROCHET, B
AND WE
THE ORIGIN
TECH

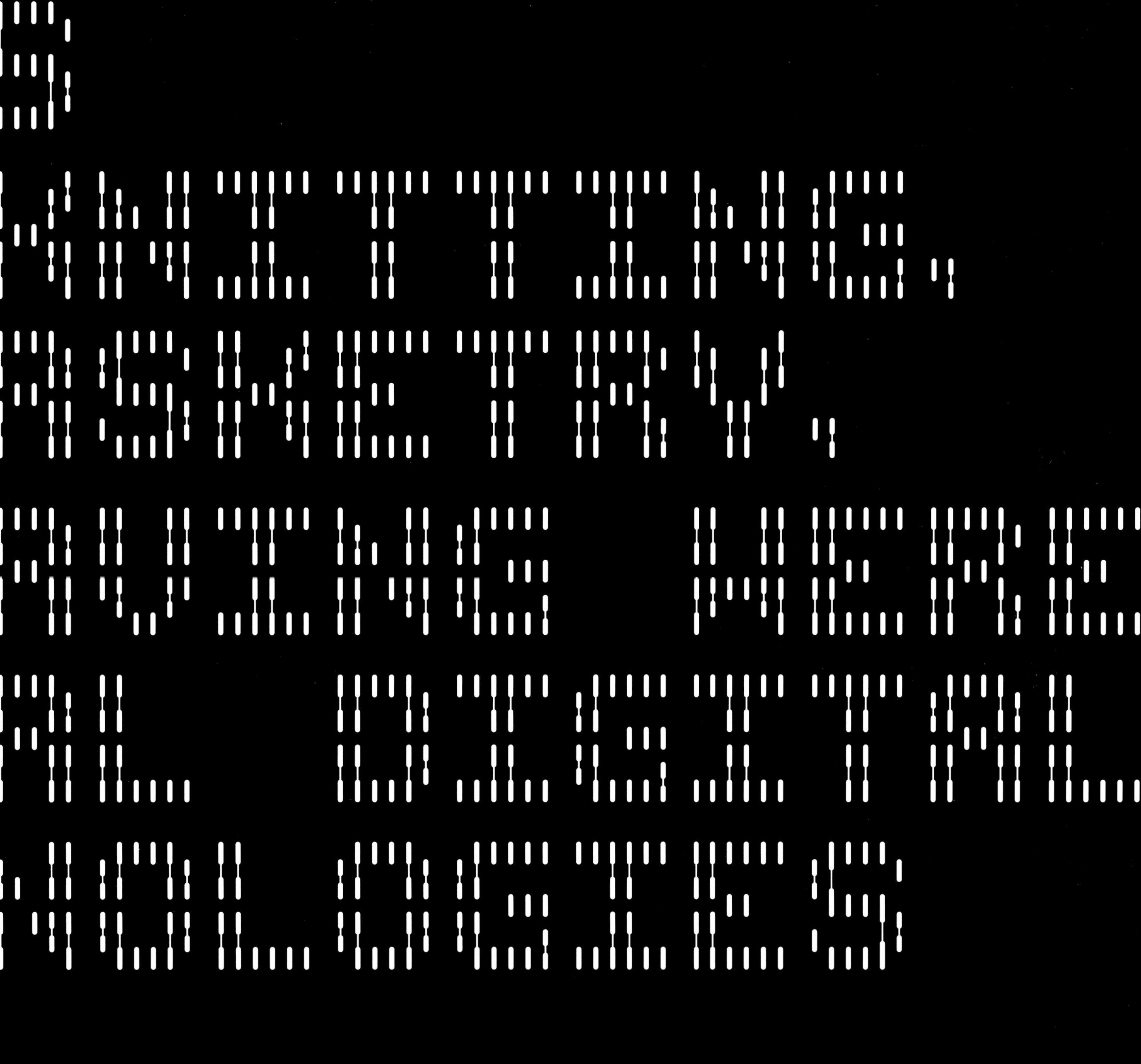

MARGARET WERTHEIM

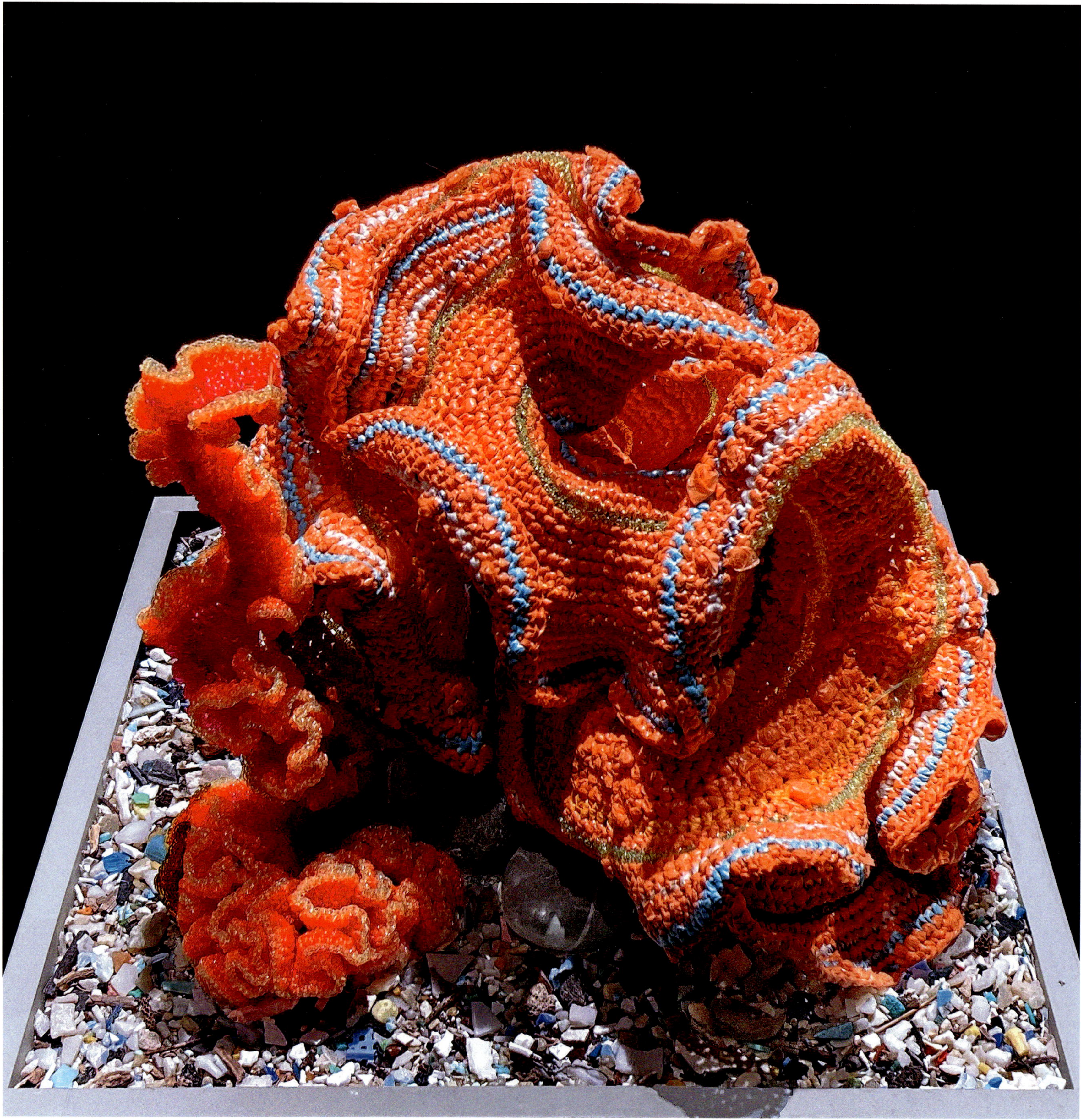

Making and Knowing: The Vernacular Science of the Crochet Coral Reef

MARGARET WERTHEIM

In the elegant anthology *Ways of Making and Knowing* (2014), science historian Pamela H. Smith proposes that "histories of science and art are not simply histories of styles, but histories of the making and using of objects to understand the world."[1] We come to knowledge of the world around us, Smith notes, "through material and human interaction with, and manipulation of, nature." *Interaction with* and *manipulation of* nature are processes we instinctively associate with science—what, under the banner of "science," are enfolded into the term "experimentation." But Smith and her fellow essayists want to alert us to the ways in which artists and artisans also manipulate materials and employ experimental practices in the service of knowledge production.

As a Renaissance expert, Smith's focus is the influence of artisanal culture on the emergence of science in the early modern period. For the purposes of this essay, my interest lies in her assertion that artists working today with material processes can also be said to be engaging in a kind of science.[2] Various artists in this exhibition, for example, use material substrates for cognitive explorations and ontological engagements. In *Ways of Making and Knowing*, Smith gives us a framework for thinking through such relationships. She writes: "an examination of material practices makes it clear that the methods of the artisan represent a process of knowledge making that involves extensive experimentation and observation that parallel similar processes in the sciences."[3] I agree wholeheartedly and present here a case study of a contemporary craft-based practice that constitutes an elaborate form of what I call "handmade science."

←
Christine Wertheim, Margaret Wertheim, and the Institute For Figuring, *Pod World: Plastic Fantastic Too*, 2015, corals by Christine Wertheim and Kathleen Greco for the *Crochet Coral Reef Project*, 2005–present

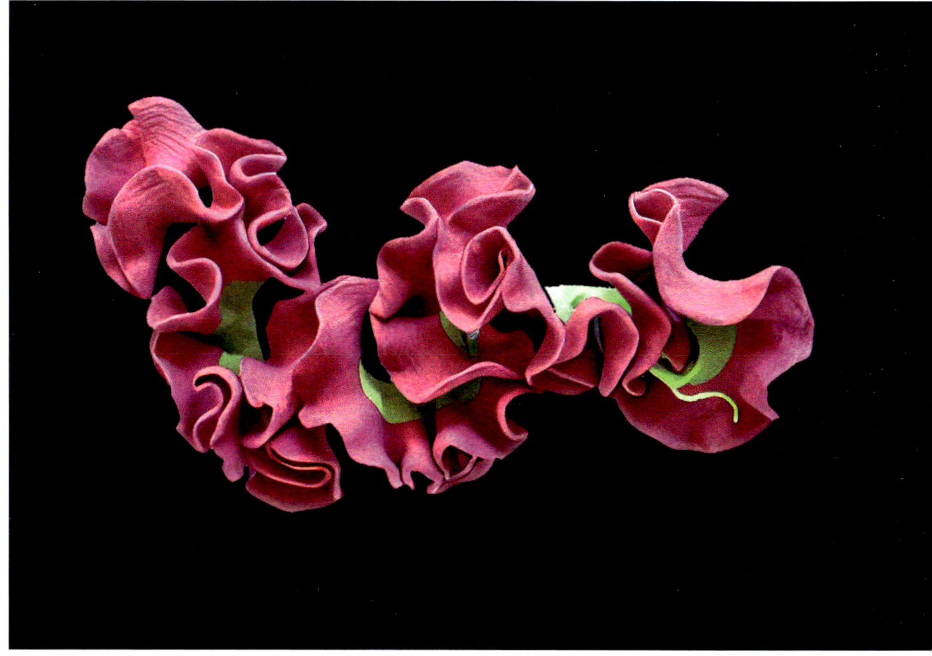

→
Figure 1: Geometrically precise hyperbolic crochet coral by Anitra Menning for the Institute For Figuring, 2006

Coral *contrefaict*

Smith speaks of "imitation as knowledge making," and her research zeroes in on artisanal techniques from the fifteenth through nineteenth centuries developed to represent and imitate nature: How were pigments created and applied to emulate distinct qualities of animals, flowers, and so on? What "lifecasting" techniques were invented to capture the soft bodies of lizards, snakes, beetles, and roses? And how did artisans then reproduce these forms in durable materials? What methods did they concoct to make imitations of precious stones or *coral contrefaict* (a faux version of branched red coral) to cater to a growing market for these exotics and as a means to understand how nature makes itself? Smith's work, however, extends far beyond the usual modes of academic scholarship, for at Columbia University (in 2014) she founded the Making and Knowing Project, where she set up laboratories to re-create processes described in centuries-old texts. Not content to have her students merely read such manuscripts, she challenges them to actually *make* faux jasper and coral, to cast lizard toes, to taxidermy rats.

Smith argues that early modern artisans who developed these techniques should be seen as partners in the evolution of science, for their explorations helped shed light on how nature works. Moreover, from around 1400 CE, artisans began to formalize the knowledge they were producing in "written documents such as handbooks, guides, treatises, tip sheets, graphs, and recipe books." In addition to passing along knowledge in their workshops, "literate artisans" started to publish their findings for a wider audience, thereby creating "an early kind of technical writing" which, Smith writes elsewhere, helped to "lay the groundwork for how we think about scientific knowledge today."[4] To recognize the contributions to science of these nonacademic *material thinkers*, Smith proposes the term "vernacular natural history" to be understood as a parallel practice to the usually told story of science as the progress of increasingly academic *conceptual ideas*.

In what follows, I describe a project of contemporary "vernacular natural history" that I and my sister Christine Wertheim created and spearhead—the *Crochet Coral Reef*—a worldwide endeavor now engaging tens of thousands of women across the globe who are emulating coral reefs using the craft of crochet. To draw on another term Smith deploys, the *Crochet Coral Reef* is "*a material imaginary*—a knowledge system that articulates relationships between materials and provides a framework for practice."[5]

Along with Smith's Renaissance artisans, our *Crochet Coral Reef* begins with a desire to model a natural phenomenon, in this case the Great Barrier Reef. We grew up in its home state, Queensland, where the Great One's fragile beauty looms large in public consciousness; during our lives, coral bleaching events have become ever more frequent and dire. As I write, in mid-2024, the Great Barrier Reef is experiencing the worst bleaching on record.[6] Average earthly temperatures are now more than 2° Fahrenheit (1.2° Centigrade) above preindustrial levels, far beyond the comfort zone of corals. Being delicate creatures, corals were among the first organisms to signal the here-and-now of climate change, and coral bleaching has become a kind of organismal meter for gauging water temperature, a living index as it were of the rapid transformation of our climate.

The aquatic equivalents to rainforests, reefs are home to perhaps a quarter of all marine species. They protect coastlines, provide sustenance, and fuel tourism. Yet reefs are tricky structures for humans to imitate because the frilly shapes we recognize as their hallmark don't conform to the kind of geometry we learn at school and to which modern Western aesthetics has often reverted. The straight-edged Euclidean geometry Renaissance painters strived to

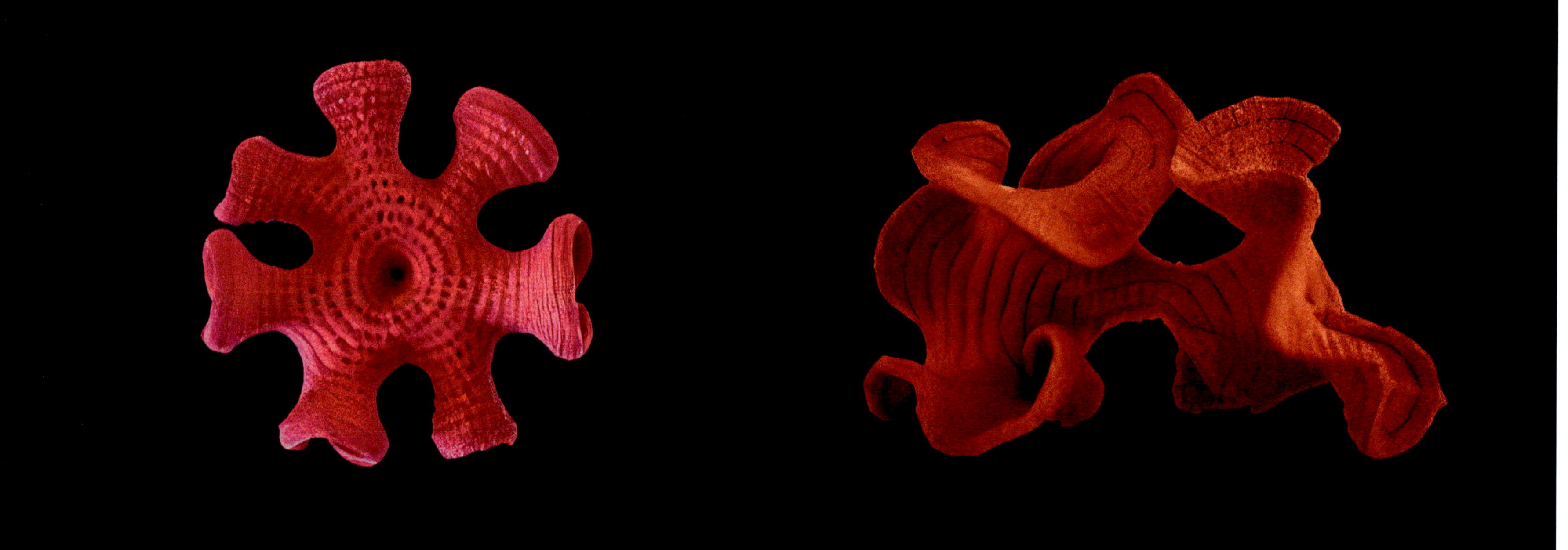

Using a female-coded craft, we can generate coraline frills and ruffles that follow the conformations of hyperbolic space, realizing in yarn an idea that shook mathematics to its core and helped lead Einstein to the general theory of relativity.

←
Figure 2: Geometrically precise hyperbolic crochet corals by Margaret Wertheim for the Institute For Figuring, 2006–7

represent doesn't apply to corals, kelps, and sea sponges. These ancient lineages are biological manifestations of an alternative geometry, known as *hyperbolic*, which distinguishes itself in swoops and curves. Although human mathematicians spent centuries trying to prove that anything like it was impossible, reef creatures have been *making* hyperbolic surfaces in the fibers of their being since the Silurian Age. The question of how humans might imitate this fleshy embodiment of a "pathological" geometry was no easy problem; in short, artisans had to learn how to embody hyperbolic math.

It turns out we can do so with crochet. Using a female-coded craft, we can generate coraline frills and ruffles that follow the conformations of hyperbolic space, realizing in yarn an idea that shook mathematics to its core and helped lead Einstein to the general theory of relativity.[7] The technique a crafter employs is to *increase* stitches. The more frequently one increases the more crenellated the form becomes, and by *varying* the rate of increase we can produce a whole taxonomy of crochet coral "creatures"—each of which may be understood as a data point in a virtual landscape of mathematical possibility (figs. 1 and 2).

To create a hyperbolic form, one begins with a line of chain stitches, then iterates the algorithm: "Crochet 'n' stitches; increase one stitch; repeat." As we increase, the form begins to bend away from Euclidean flatness, taking on an ever more pronounced curvature: first one ruffle, then two, and so on. Working with hook and yarn, the crocheter creates a model of the *hyperbolic plane*, a surface characterized by mathematicians as the geometric opposite of a sphere. While the Euclidean plane is said to have *zero curvature* and the sphere *positive curvature*, the hyperbolic plane has *negative curvature*. It's a geometric analog of a negative number.[8] Consonant with Smith's notion of vernacular natural history, this material making of non-Euclidean surfaces constitutes a form of *vernacular mathematics*—one that's been almost exclusively explored by women.

Vernacular mathematics systems involving material practices are found throughout the world and have been too little acknowledged in both the “science” and “art” domains.

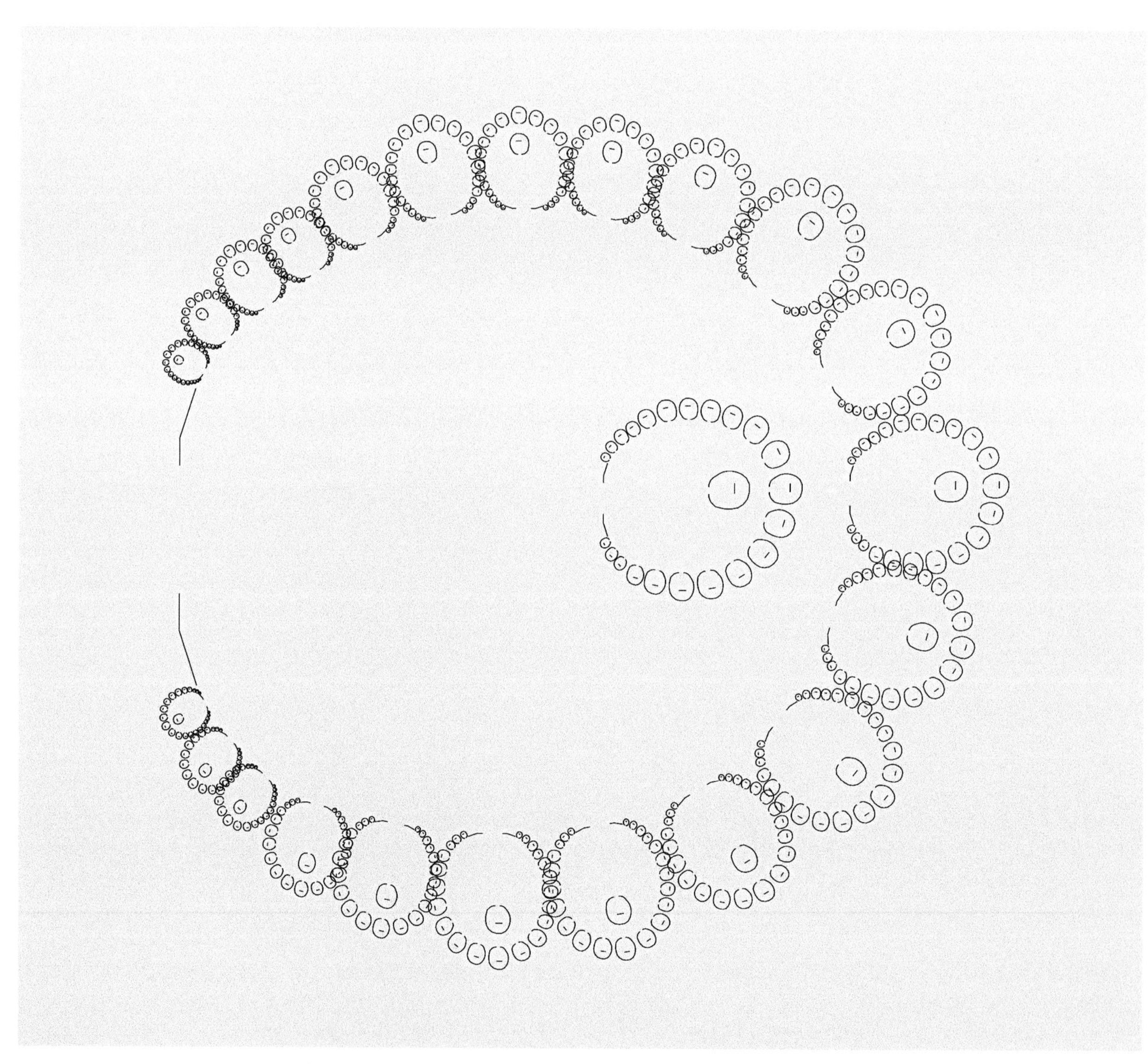

←
Figure 3: Fractal design for layout of a Ba-ila village in southern Zambia, from Ron Eglash, *African Fractals* (1999)

The domestic frontiers of hyperbolic space

The discovery of "hyperbolic crochet" is attributed to Cornell mathematician Daina Taimina, who created such models as pedagogical tools for college-level geometry classes.[9] Taimina's brilliance was to identify how a humble craft could be employed to emulate a structure mathematicians had struggled to visualize for two hundred years. With crochet, she crafted models they could *see* and *feel* and manipulate in their hands. One can even stitch lines onto such surfaces to visually demonstrate bizarre properties of hyperbolic space, such as the angles of a triangle adding up to less than 180° and the circumference of a circle measuring more than $2\pi r$.[10]

But if Taimina was the first to recognize the math embedded here she wasn't the first to construct such shapes—ladies crocheting doilies have been making hyperbolic surfaces for at least a hundred years. In the collection of doilies Christine and I own we have an exquisite piece of lacework from the nineteenth century with cascading layers of ever more crenellated hyperbolic frills. Also, a selection of 1940s pattern books for "ruffled doilies" features dozens of examples of hyperbolic edgings spelled out in stitch *algorithms* incorporating subroutines and other staples of computer-coding techniques. The "literate artisans" who wrote these patterns—and the women who reproduced the objects in their homes—had a clear understanding of how hyperbolic surfaces behave. Theirs was (and is) a mature form of material "knowledge making."

Thus, in parallel to the academic study of hyperbolic geometry going on in university math departments, wives and maids at home were also developing an understanding of non-Euclidean concepts and a rigorous language for describing such forms. Using what Smith calls "sensory tools of embodied experience," ladies crocheting doilies have long been exploring the frontiers of hyperbolic space.

Smith's project to recognize the role of artisanal practices in scientific knowledge making could also be paralleled if we consider the history of mathematics, where age-old traditions of vernacular understanding have long been overlooked. One great exemplar is the body of Islamic tiling patterns in mosques and palaces throughout the Middle East and Spain.[11] On the walls and ceilings of the Alhambra palace in Granada and other masterpieces of Islamic tessellated art, we find all the variations of tiling patterns formally categorized by European mathematicians in the nineteenth century. Thrillingly, medieval Islamic mosaicists also give us examples of *aperiodic* tiling, a *chaotic* version of tessellation that Western mathematicians didn't "discover" until the 1960s.[12] And just as Islamic artisans working with material techniques long preceded academic mathematics in comprehending tiling, so African artisans discovered *fractals* hundreds of years before Western geometers. In his splendid book *African Fractals* (1999), mathematician Ron Eglash documents how craftspeople across that continent have been incorporating fractals into textile and ceramic designs, hairstyling, and even the layout of villages for perhaps a thousand years (fig. 3).[13] Many other indigenous design techniques could be cited.[14] Vernacular mathematics systems involving material practices are found throughout the world and have been too little acknowledged in both the "science" and "art" domains.

Crochet codes and crafty cryptology

Artisanal thread-based processes can also be seen to encompass a vernacular form of *coding*. Indeed, female crafters have been deploying the apparatus of codes and algorithms for centuries. Handicrafts such as knitting, crochet, basketry, and weaving were the original *digital* technologies—*technes* created by digits—and it is one of the ironies of the computer age that the "digital" has come to connote disembodiment and divorce from the material domain when the term derives from our fingers. History records this linkage in the punch cards of early computers, born out of cards created to automate looms.

Crochet actually deploys two distinct kinds of codes: one *graphical*, the other *lexical*. In the doily patterns here, we see examples of a *spatialized* code a crafter can enact with her fingers (fig. 4). Each mark or symbol represents a set of stitches to be performed, making these images visual algorithms.[15] Beginning at the center and spiraling out, a crocheter performs the instructions the diagram describes using yarn as a medium to bring the algorithm into material form. Much as Smith's Renaissance artisans began to formalize their knowledge in written texts, so doily makers have developed a rich language for conveying the information to create intricate diatom-like objects.

In addition to this visual code, crochet instructions can be conveyed by an alphabetic code, with each stitch type described by groups of letters: "ch" for chain, "sc" for single crochet, "dc" for double crochet, and so on. This dialect of the digits is another way of representing patterns, as in the image here showing the stitch pattern for a ruffled doily (fig. 5).

Alphabetic patterns such as this are a craft equivalent of computer programs. Both employ a coded lexicon to indicate specific steps, and both utilize "subroutines," small programs-within-programs that get called on as repeats. (Subroutines in the pattern here are indicated by the * symbol.) Yet for all the power of alphabetic crochet patterns, the graphical variety has added virtues. In the pattern below, it is hard to imagine the object being created until it emerges in your hands. Who but an expert crafter would recognize the remarkable form in figure 6 as the result of such a code?

With a *diagrammatic* pattern such as those in figure 4, one knows in advance the configuration it will produce because the graphics represent a one-to-one correspondence with the structural components of the finished form. The pioneering mathematician and logician Charles Sanders Peirce referred to such images as "icons," and to him *iconicity* was the highest form of signification.[16] Peirce believed practitioners of all sciences, including math, should strive to develop iconic notations for representing knowledge, and he famously created graphical systems to describe the logic underlying computing. He took inspiration from electrical circuit diagrams and chemical diagrams, both of which lay out their component parts in a similar fashion to doily patterns (fig. 7). In all these cases, diagrams serve to make visible a logic of spatial relations—a literal *topo-logy*—thereby becoming tools to think with.

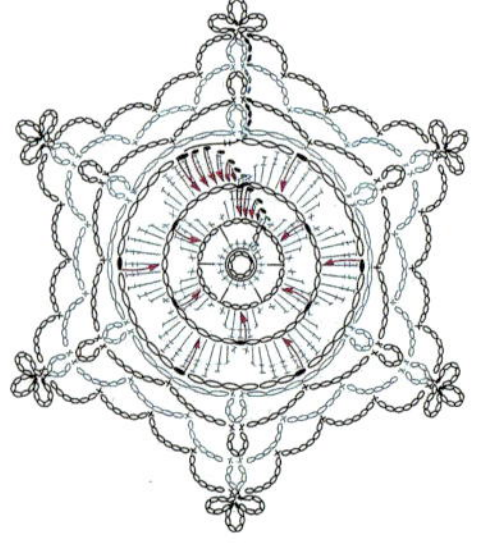

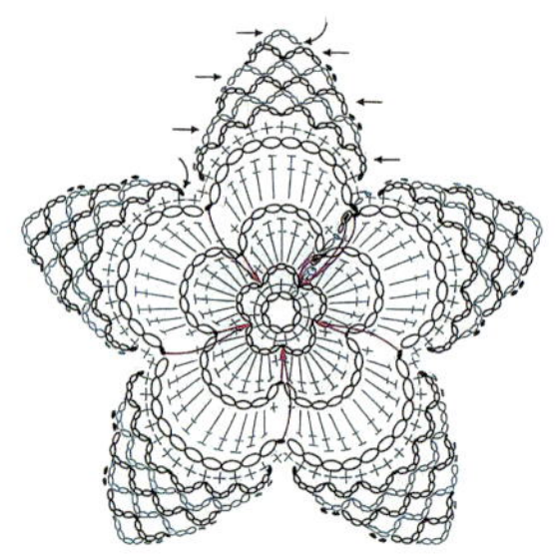

↑
Figure 4: Sarah Simons, diagrammatic crochet doily patterns

Victorian Ruffle No. 5902

Materials Required: AMERICAN THREAD COMPANY "DE LUXE" MERCERIZED CROCHET AND KNITTING COTTON, ARTICLE 346

7—300 yd. Balls White.
Steel Crochet Hook No. 7.
Doily measures about 25½ x 31 inches without ruffle.
Ch 39, d c in 7th st from hook, * ch 1, skip 1 st of ch, d c in next st, repeat from * 15 times.

2nd Row. S c into last mesh over the d c just made, * ch 25, s c in same mesh, repeat from * 6 times, ch 20, 2 s c in each of the next 7 meshes, ch 20, s c in next mesh, * ch 25, s c in same mesh, repeat from * 3 times, ch 20, 2 s c in each of the next 7 meshes, ch 20, s c in corner mesh, * ch 25, s c in same mesh, repeat from * 7 times, ch 20 and working on other side of meshes, work 2 s c in each of the next 7 meshes, ch 20, s c in next mesh, * ch 25, s c in same mesh, repeat from * 3 times, ch 20, 2 s c in each of the next 7 meshes, ch 20, s c in next mesh (corner) ch 25, s c in same mesh, break thread.

3rd Row. Attach thread in 1st loop of center group on side, s c in same space, * ch 7, s c in next loop, repeat from * 4 times, s c in 1st loop of end group, * ch 7, s c in next loop, repeat from * 8 times, s c in 1st loop of next group at side, * ch 7, s c in next loop, repeat from * 4 times, s c in 1st loop of end group, * ch 7, s c in next loop, repeat from * 8 times, join to 1st s c.

4th Row. Sl st to center of loop, * ch 10, s c in next loop, repeat from * all around, then without joining rows work 3 more rows of 10 ch loops.

Next Row. * Ch 30, s c in same loop, repeat from * 5 times, 10 s c in next loop, s c in next loop and work 6-30 ch loops in same loop, repeat from * all around, join and break thread. Attach thread in 1st long loop and work 10 ch loops over long loops and 3 ch loops between groups of long loops. Sl st to center of loop and work a 10 ch loop in each 10 ch loop. Without joining rows work 8 more rows of 10 ch loops.

Next Row. Ch 3, work 5 d c in same loop, * ch 5, 5 d c in next loop, repeat from * all around.

SCALLOP: Sl st into loop, * ch 10, s c in same loop, ch 10, s c in same loop, ch 10, s c in same loop, ch 10, s c in next loop, repeat from * all around and continue work without joining rows.

Next Row. * Ch 10, s c in next loop, repeat from * all around and repeat the last row 12 times, break thread.

↑
Figure 5: Victorian Ruffle doily pattern, from the pamphlet *Ruffled Doiles and the Pansy Doily, Star Book* (The American Thread Company). no. 59, 1948

Handicrafts such as knitting, crochet, basketry, and weaving were the original *digital* technologies—*technes* created by digits—and it is one of the ironies of the computer age that the “digital” has come to connote disembodiment and divorce from the material domain when the term derives from our fingers.

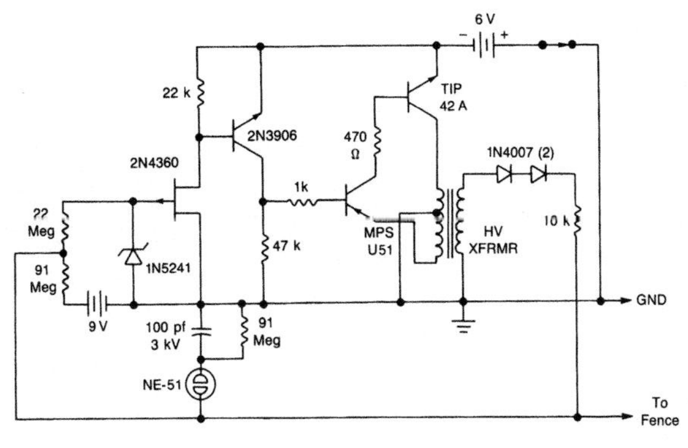

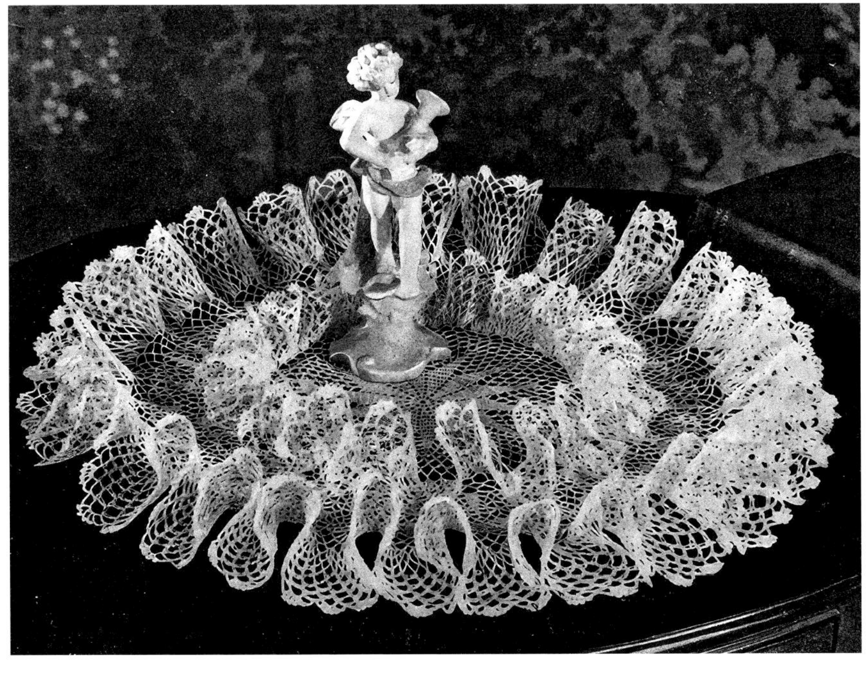

↑
Figure 6: Hyperbolic doily crafted from a pattern in *Ruffled Doilies and the Pansy Doily*

↑
Figure 7: Diagrams of an electrical circuit (top) and the chemical structure of Kevlar (bottom)

Iterate, deviate, innovate

Life itself instantiates a code: the code of DNA in the heart of living cells. And again, we find here a natural process that we crochet reef artisans strive to emulate.

Among the virtues of DNA is its propensity for *imperfect* reproduction. When a cell holding DNA replicates, malfunctions can occur; here or there a DNA "letter" may be changed, perhaps one is deleted or a new one gets added. Such "mistakes" are essential for the process of evolution, for if DNA always replicated perfectly life would lock into a groove with no new creations. Deviations at the molecular level cause mutations at the physiological level, leading ultimately to taxonomic *variety* and the whole plethora of living things. Here, as well, we crochet makers imitate nature. Every person who comes to the project begins with a simple seed that they can gradually evolve, through deviation, into more complex forms. Each crochet coral "reefer" starts with the kernel of the basic hyperbolic algorithm given above—yet perfect hyperbolic forms (like perfect spheres) are the antithesis of living things, which are never quite regular, never geometrically precise. It is this move into "imperfection" that sparks the *Crochet Reef* project to life, hefting it from the domain of pure math into a kind of fiberized organicism.[17] After learning the basic technique, every crafter is free to inject their own deviations: to add to the code or change it here and there, mimicking the DNA deviations of organic evolution.

We too *queer* the code. "Iterate, deviate, innovate" has been the motto of our project. What is it *you* can imagine that no one else has done before? Each maker is free to invent new shoots on the crochet "tree of life," new woolly "organisms" whose multiplicity imitates the diversity of living beings. By emulating the accreted variation of earthly organisms, our crochet reef community has built a library of floofy formations and brought into being an ever-evolving taxonomy of crochet coral "species." Working with codes played out through fibers, we reefers together craft an imitation of life—a visionary yarn-based ecology and true "material imaginary."

NOTES

1 Pamela H. Smith, *Ways of Making and Knowing: The Material Culture of Empirical Knowledge* (Ann Arbor: University of Michigan Press, 2014).
2 Smith, from slides delivered during a closed Zoom lecture at the National Gallery of Art, Washington, DC, April 6, 2014.
3 Smith, *Ways of Making and Knowing*.
4 Smith, *From Lived Experience to the Written Word: Reconstructing Practical Knowledge in the Early Modern World* (Chicago: The University of Chicago Press, 2022).
5 Smith, slides from National Gallery of Art lecture.
6 Delger Erdenasanaa. "Ocean Heat Has Shattered Records for More Than a Year. What's Happening?" *The New York Times*, April 10, 2024, https://www.nytimes.com/2024/04/10/climate/ocean-heat-records.html (accessed May 1, 2024).
7 The discovery of hyperbolic geometry opened the door to a wider exploration of geometric possibility and led Bernard Riemann to develop a generalized description of geometric surfaces or "manifolds." This Riemannian geometry underlies the general theory of relativity that describes the curving structure of space-time.
8 Margaret Wertheim, *A Field Guide to Hyperbolic Space* (Los Angeles: Institute For Figuring Press, 2005).
9 Daina Taimina created her first hyperbolic crochet model in 1993, inspired by a paper model created by William Thurston. Thurston's model was difficult to make and hard to manipulate; Taimina realized she could generate the same effect with yarn, making for a pliable, manipulatable surface.
10 Taimina, *Crocheting Adventures with Hyperbolic Planes: Tactile Mathematics, Art and Craft for all to Explore*, 2nd ed. (Boca Raton, FL: CRC Press, 2018).
11 Jean-Marc Castéra, *Arabesques: Decorative Art in Morocco* (Courbevoie, France: ACR Edition, 1999).
12 Metin Arik, "Mathematical Mosaics, Islamic Art and Quasicrystals," talk given at Crystallography for the Next Generation conference, Hassan II Academy of Science and Technology, Rabat, Morocco, April 23, 2015, https://www.iycr2014.org/__data/assets/pdf_file/0016/111706/Session2_Arik.pdf (accessed May 22, 2024).
13 Ron Eglash, *African Fractals: Modern Computing and Indigenous Design* (New Brunswick, NJ: Rutgers University Press, 1999).
14 For example, Polynesian sand drawings, Celtic and Chinese knots, and Indian paisley.
15 I am indebted to *Crochet Coral Reef* contributor Sarah Simons from the Center for Land Use Interpretation for these images of doily patterns from old crochet pattern books.
16 Albert Atkin, *Pierce's Theory of Signs*, in Edward N. Zalta and Uri Nodelman, eds., *The Stanford Encyclopedia of Philosophy* (Metaphysics Research Lab, Philosophy Department, Stanford University), 2010.
17 *Value and Transformation of Corals: Christine and Margaret Wertheim*, exh. cat. (Baden-Baden, Germany: Museum Frieder Burda; and Cologne: Wienand Verlag, 2022).

→
Christine Wertheim, Margaret Wertheim, and the Institute For Figuring, *Pod World: Eye Jellies*, 2022, jellyfish by Margaret Wertheim for the *Crochet Coral Reef Project*, 2005–present

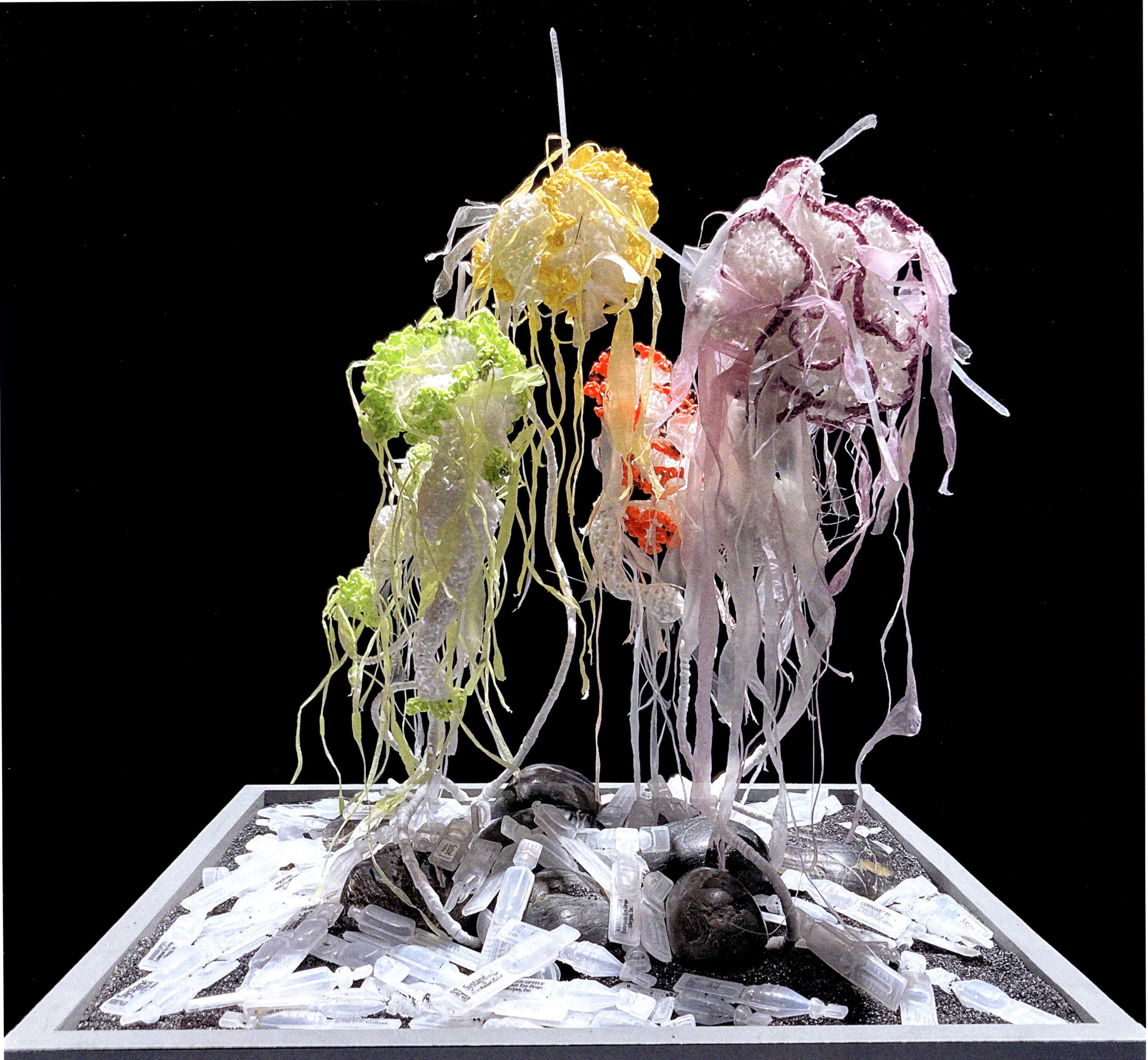

Artists

Refik Anadol
Data to Discovery
Laurie Frick
George Legrady
Rafael Lozano-Hemmer
Giorgia Lupi and Ehren Shorday
Iñigo Manglano-Ovalle
Sarah Morris
Mimi Ọnụọha
Semiconductor
Hyojung Seo
Linnéa Gabriella Spransy
Mika Tajima
Fernanda Viégas and Martin Wattenberg
Peggy Weil
Christine Wertheim, Margaret Wertheim,
and the Institute For Figuring

Refik Anadol

b. Istanbul, 1985; lives and works in Los Angeles

California Landscapes: Generative Studies (A), 2023
AI data painting
3840 × 2160 pixels, 16 minutes
Courtesy RAS – Refik Anadol Studio

California Landscapes: Generative Studies (B), 2023
AI data painting
3840 × 2160 pixels, 16 minutes
Courtesy RAS – Refik Anadol Studio

California Landscapes: Generative Studies (C), 2023
AI data painting
3840 × 2160 pixels, 16 minutes
Courtesy RAS – Refik Anadol Studio

Refik Anadol's curiosity about machine learning—provoked by such questions as "If a machine can learn, can it also dream? Can it hallucinate?"—prompts his distinctive visual language that merges data, abstraction, and immersive storytelling. Through large-scale digital walls, AI data sculptures, and architectural projections, Anadol transforms large datasets into fluid, dynamic compositions of color and texture, inviting viewers into the latent spaces of algorithmic imagination. The information sources that feed the artist's projects range from climate data to art historical archives, each reinterpreted through custom machine-learning models and presented in a variety of multidisciplinary forms.

The diversity of presentation and imagery reflects the creative potential of data-driven art. In the digital mural *Bosphorus: Data Sculpture* (2018), Anadol interpreted radar data of the Marmara Sea into a poetic visualization rendered by custom software and sound design. For his multimedia performance *Living Architecture: Casa Batlló* (2022), he drew from approximately one billion images encapsulating the visual history of Catalan architect Antoni Gaudí's archive to create a digital projection, performed in sync with sound design by Kerim Karaoglu, mapped onto the façade of Gaudí's Casa Batlló in Barcelona.

Anadol's *California Landscapes: Generative Studies* series (2023) is an exceptional stylistic departure from many of his large-scale digital works that feature sensuous, wavelike forms. Using a dataset of over 153 million pictures of California's national parks, landscapes morph, fold, and melt into one another, revealing the machine's interpretive process. In contrast to the seamless abstract aesthetics of his earlier works, Anadol allowed the algorithm's scaffolding—shimmering transitional lines—to remain visible, exposing the anatomy of the algorithmic image-making process much like turning a canvas around to show its wooden frame or brushwork on the reverse.

Anadol's exploration of data as a visual medium pushes the boundaries and assumptions of what computer programming—and to a large extent, information—can become. As Blaise Agüera y Arcas, vice president and fellow at Google Research, observed: "Like the invention of applied pigments, printing press, photography, and computers, we believe machine intelligence is an innovation that will profoundly affect art."[1] Anadol's work, in using data and AI to expand the idea of painting, sculpture, and installation art, invites us to reconsider this burgeoning technology as a creative means of expression. –cv

→
Detail of a still from *California Landscapes: Generative Studies (A)*, 2023

1 Quoted in Anadol, "A New Renaissance in Art: Refik Anadol on the AI Transformation of Art," talk given at Google I/O Dialogues on Technology and Society, May 16, 2024, 5:55, https://youtu.be/laqu7NqSlLo?si=eZbnK6RWrRu76Y5P.

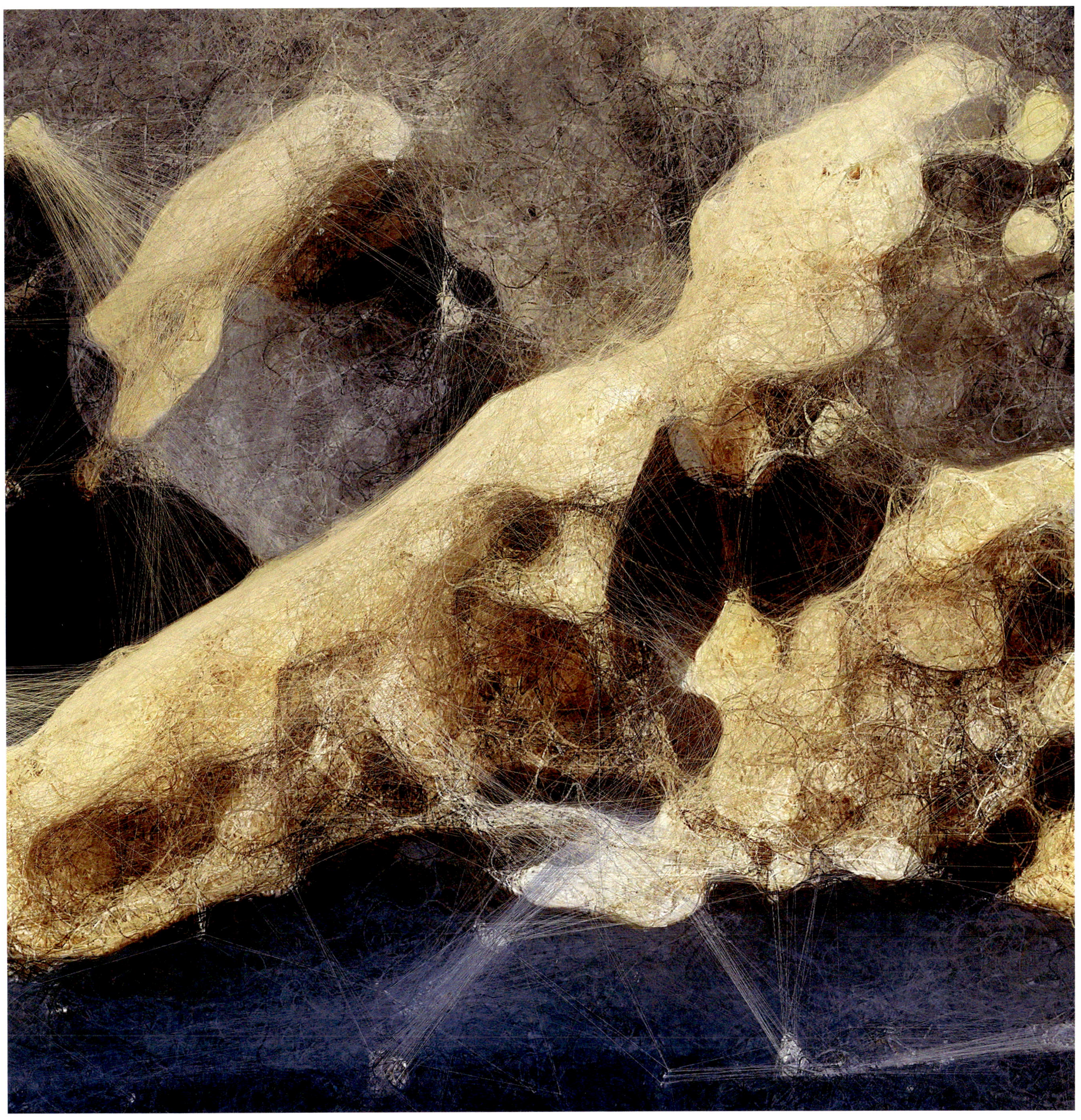

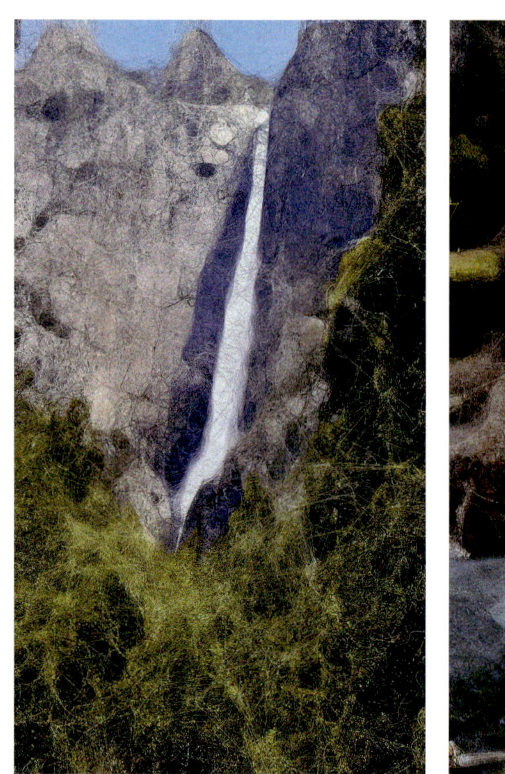
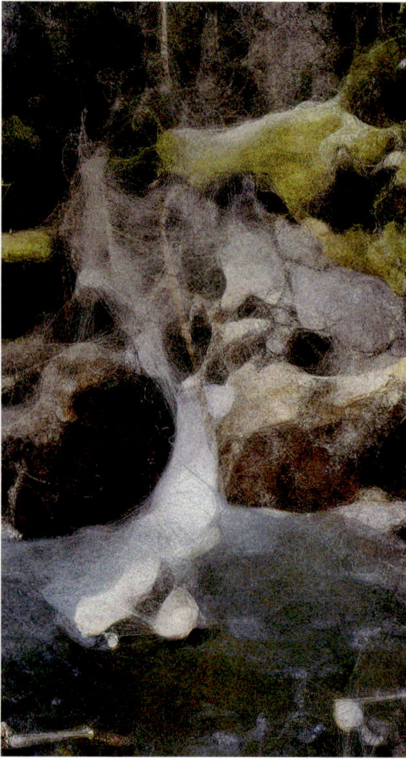
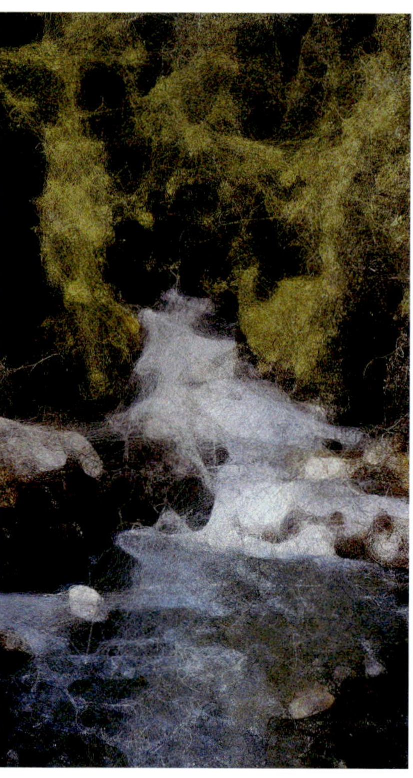

↗
Stills from *California Landscapes: Generative Studies (A)*, *(B)*, and *(C)*, 2023

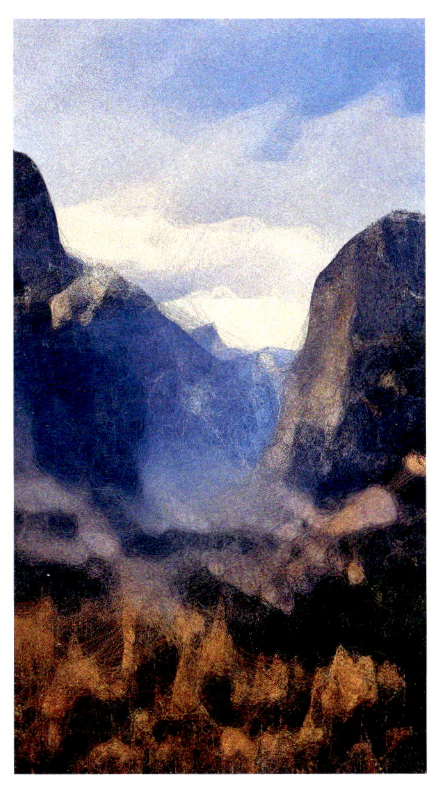

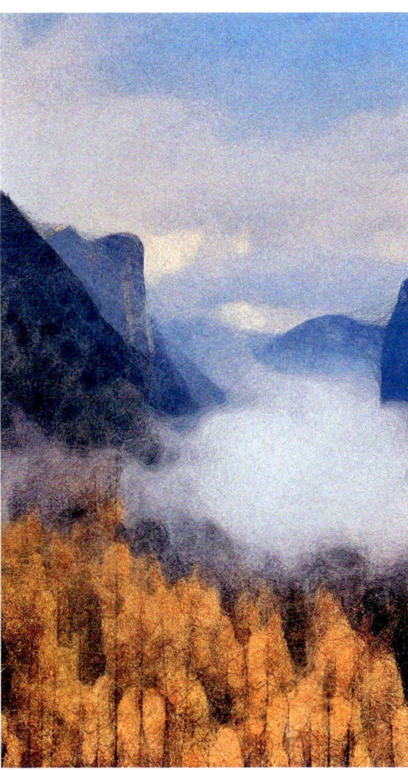

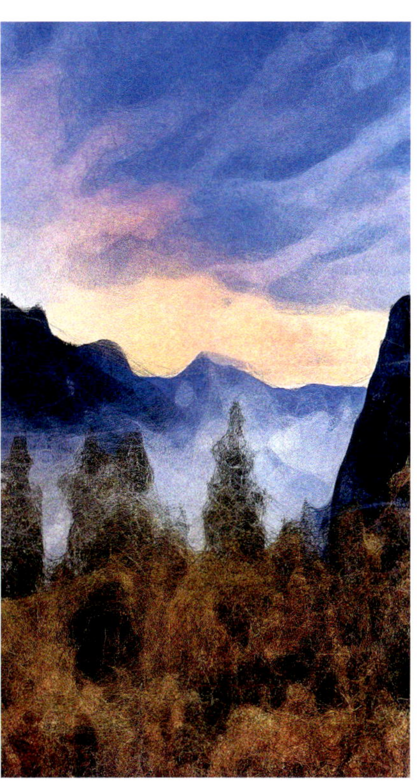

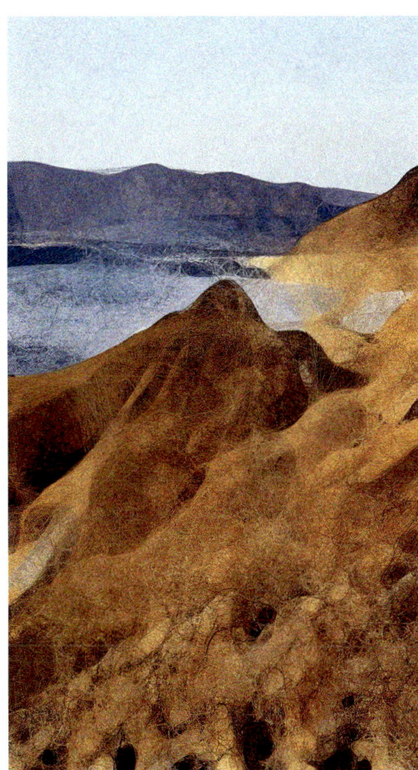

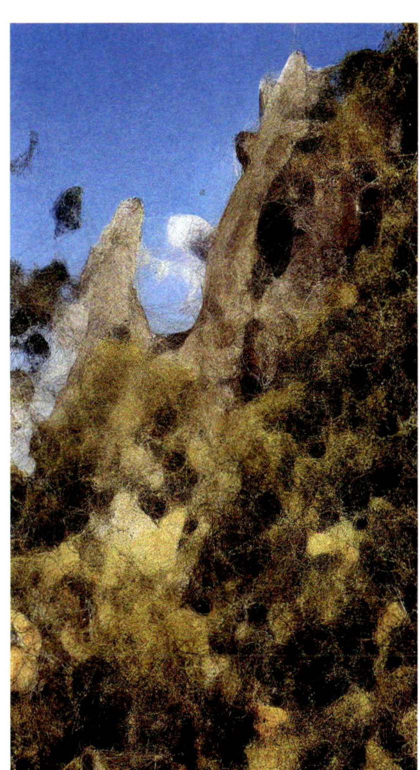

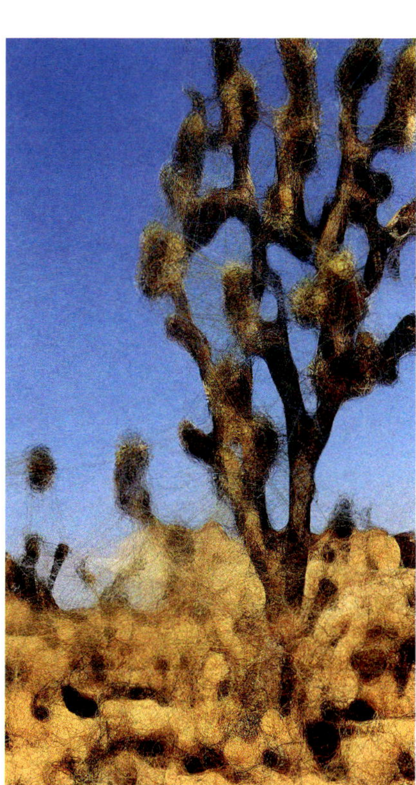

Data to Discovery Santiago Lombeyda Hillary Mushkin

Data to Discovery (founded 2013, Pasadena, CA; directors: Scott Davidoff, Maggie Hendrie, Santiago Lombeyda, and Hillary Mushkin)
Santiago Lombeyda (b. 1974, Quito, Ecuador; lives and works in Pasadena, CA)
Hillary Mushkin (b. 1969, New York; lives and works in Los Angeles and Pasadena, CA)

3DDNA (3D Genome Structure Map and Analysis), 2016–24
With Jeff Brewer (software engineer) and Ethan Mcfarlin (assistant videographer). Created with 3DDNA interactive data visualization software (2016) and developed by NASA Jet Propulsion Lab/Caltech/ArtCenter Data to Discovery Program and Guttman Lab, Caltech. D2D visualization team: Peter Polack (software engineer), Aprameya Mysore (designer), and Shixie Shi (designer). Collaborators: Mitch Guttman (professor of biology and bioengineering, Caltech) and Noah Ollikainen (Guttman Lab postdoctoral scholar)
Data visualization video
3:06 minutes
Courtesy Data to Discovery with Guttman Lab

GRVIN (Grain Assemblies Visualization and Analysis), 2018–24
With Jeff Brewer (software engineer) and Ethan Mcfarlin (assistant videographer). Created with GRVIN interactive data visualization software (2018) and developed by NASA Jet Propulsion Lab/Caltech/ArtCenter Data to Discovery Program and Andrade Lab, Caltech. D2D visualization team: Jeff Brewer (software engineer), Adrian Galvin (designer), and Pooja Nair (designer). Collaborators: Jose Andrade (professor of mechanical and civil engineering, Caltech) and Utkarsh Mital (Andrade Lab postdoctoral scholar)
Data visualization video
1:52 minutes
Courtesy Data to Discovery with Andrade Lab

Data to Discovery (D2D) is a cross-institutional design endeavor co-organized by Santiago Lombeyda, faculty (interactive design) at ArtCenter College of Design and lecturer at Caltech, and Hillary Mushkin, research professor (art and design) at Caltech. An innovative partnership across NASA/Jet Propulsion Laboratory, Caltech, and ArtCenter College of Design, D2D visualizes scientific research data through experimental interdisciplinary collaborations.[1] Recognizing that “seeing something in a new way can transform one’s understanding,”[2] the D2D team works intensively with scientists on digital models to further their research.

Two projects, *3DDNA* (2016–24) and *GRVIN* (2018–24), exemplify the critical role visuality can have in scientific research. *3DDNA* developed out of the need to visualize in three dimensions the complex folding of the human genome, the complete sequence of nucleotides that make up DNA.[3] Prior to *3DDNA*, biologists lacked ways to interact with a 3D genome model, making it “difficult to search for specific genes of interest and explore the structure of the genome surrounding that gene.”[4] 3D navigation through the genome and the ability to see the positioning of the various nucleotides provides crucial insights “to understand the relationships between genome structure and critical biological processes that occur in the cell nucleus, such as gene transcription and splicing.” Through *3DDNA*, each strand lights up when activated in a colorful mass of nucleotides resembling a ball of yarn, showing how the strand weaves through the ball and, by extension, what strands it neighbors. This multidimensional visualization enhances comprehension of genome structures in normal and cancerous cells, enabling new ideas on cancer growth that lead to advancements in cancer-targeting drugs.[5]

GRVIN provides key insights into the nearly impossible to see: the physical dynamics of granular materials such as soil, rock, and sand. While visible as a mass to the naked eye, the behavior of individual grains is practically unobservable. *GRVIN* allows engineers to see a full collection of discrete grain data on a micro level.[6] Designers and scientists created a visual model showing high-resolution contours of falling grain in three dimensions, enabling observations of movement, force, and stress across micro levels as well as the intersecting connections among particles.

D2D exemplifies the next generation of data visualization design. Embedded into research, their projects allow new ways of observing data in action and advance understanding. As research data has exponentially grown in step with digital and interactive technology, data visualization models have evolved for information to be performed rather than represented. This leads to discoveries with reverberating effects, from new cancer therapies to an enhanced understanding of our delicate ecosystem. —cv

1 Mission statement of Data to Discovery, https://datavis.caltech.edu/. Projects for collaboration are established over the fall and early winter. In the summer term, a team of selected graduate students in data visualization and design from ArtCenter work with scientists and researchers on the projects.
2 Hillary Mushkin, in conversation with the author, August 10, 2023.
3 Lorinda Dajose, “Visualization Brings Data to Life,” CalTech News, posted October 28, 2016, https://www.caltech.edu/about/news/visualization-brings-data-life-52802.
4 Dajose, “Visualization Brings Data to Life.”
5 Dajose, “Visualization Brings Data to Life.”
6 Project description of *GRVIN* on Data to Discovery website, https://datavis.caltech.edu/projects/grvin/.

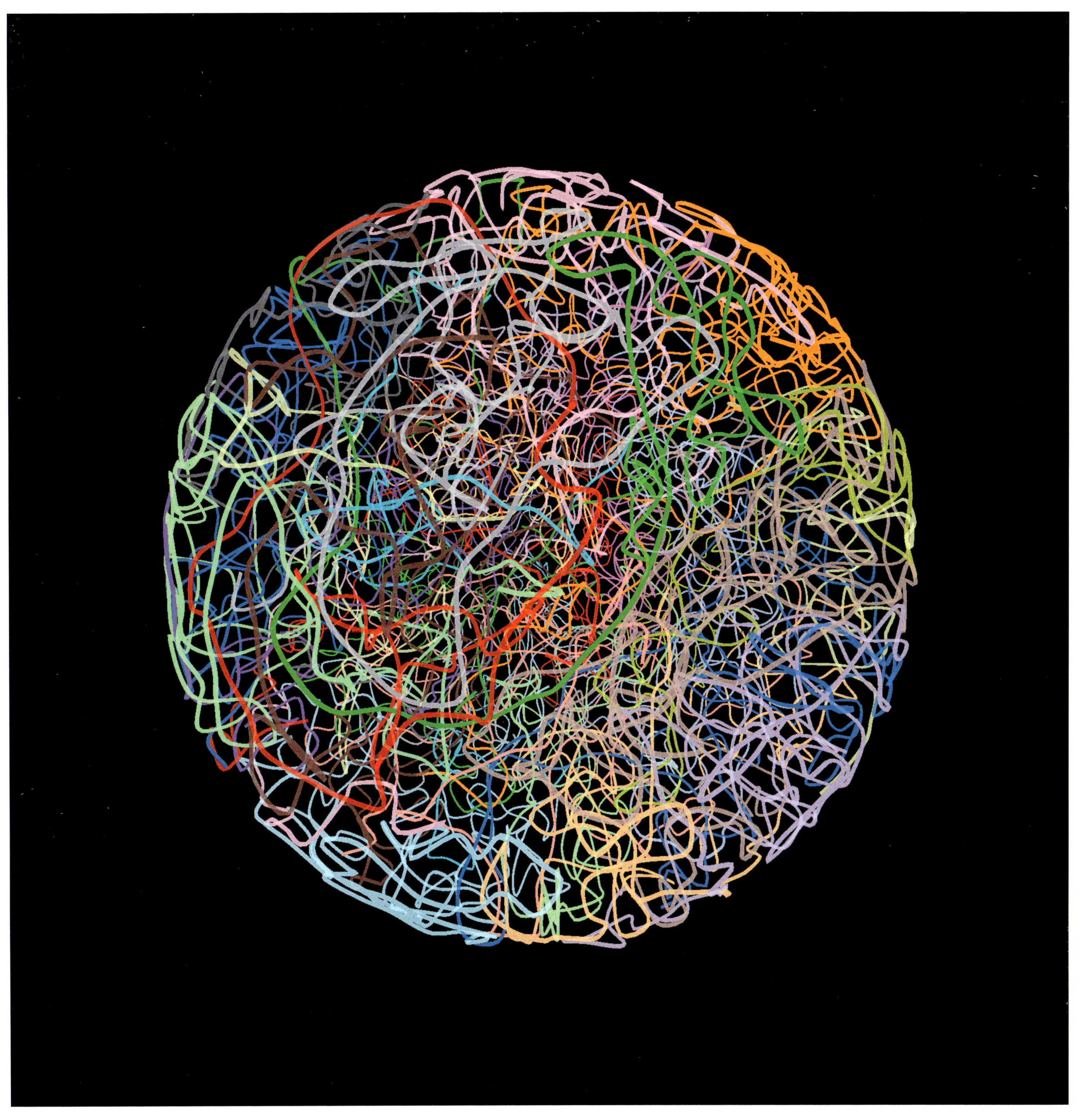

↑
Still from *3DDNA*, 2018–24

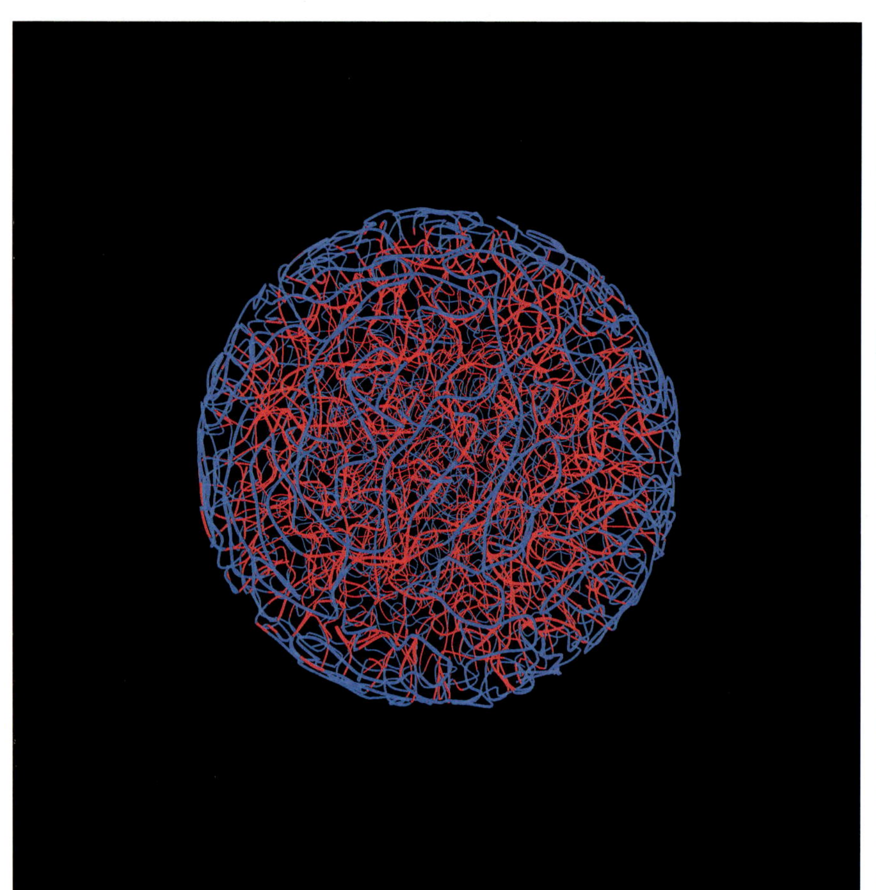

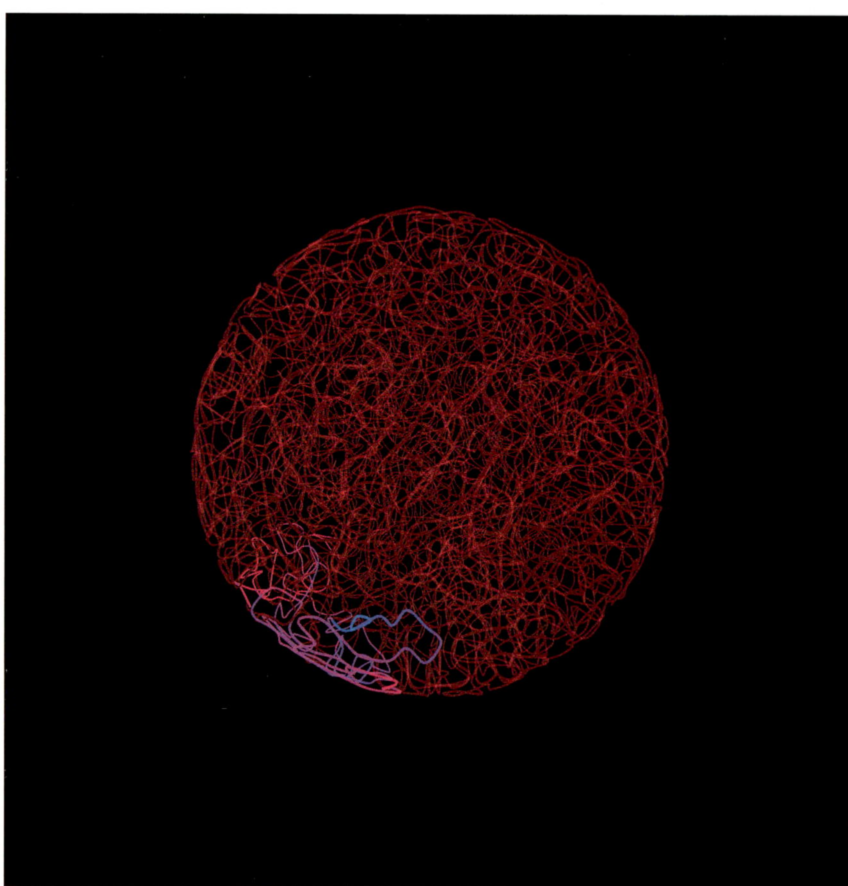

↑
Stills from *3DDNA*, 2018–24

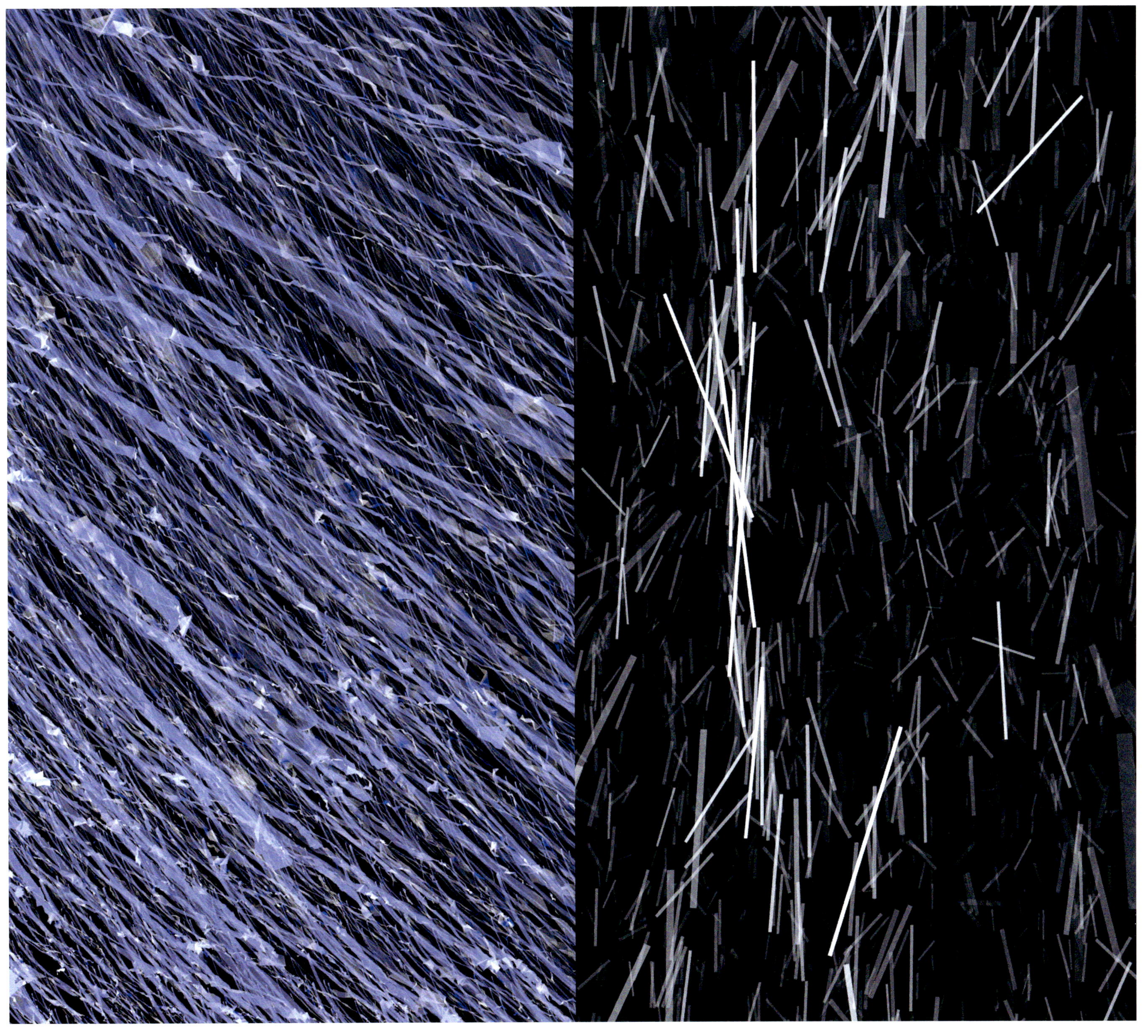

↑
Still from *GRVIN*, 2018–24

Laurie Frick

b. 1955, Los Angeles; lives and works in Austin, TX

Moodjam Intense, 2024
Abet Laminati samples on ACM panel
86 × 86 inches
Courtesy the artist

Moodjam Mild, 2024
Abet Laminati samples on ACM panel
86 × 86 inches
Courtesy the artist

With an interest in humanizing data, Laurie Frick creatively mines her own biological functions and behavioral patterns as part of her art practice. Inspired initially by the daily activity tracking of computer programmer Ben Lipkowitz and the beauty of his charts, Frick began tracking her own sleep with an electroencephalogram headband, eventually expanding the project with data from her husband's (and then others') sleep patterns. While based on computer-generated data, the resulting works, *Sleep Drawings* (2010–12), are hand drawn and colored.

For a more recent work, Frick initially mapped her moods in color swatches through Moodjam.com, a website that allows users to track their moods with colors. Intrigued, she dove deeper into the almost imperceptible changes in her moods, tracking her temperament every six seconds using a combination of methods—including heart-rate monitoring, facial recognition, and galvanic skin response—to assess her stress, nervousness, and general mood. For the works in this exhibition, *Moodjam Intense* and *Moodjam Mild* (both 2024), the artist coded her data on emotions such as happiness, anxiety, sadness, and calmness with the colors of countertop laminate samples that she had sourced during an artist residency at the Headlands Art Center near San Francisco. The resulting gridded works seem to emanate light, as the lighter tones in the center of the compositions give way to more saturated colors toward the edges. Instead of depicting the artist's outer appearance, these self-portraits use data to convey traits that take longer phenomenologically and psychologically to process; fleeting and often unconscious patterns are transformed into the visual and emphatically tactile.

In her larger practice, the artist pulls data from open-source spaces or taps into gathered information provided to her. The artist also sheds light on and personalizes data that can be uncomfortable. For *7 Stages* (2010), she was given information about 155 patients with the neurodegenerative disease amyotrophic lateral sclerosis (ALS) and the progression of their symptoms during a residency at the McColl Center in Charlotte, North Carolina. She chose to represent the patients using wood blocks, branding each with the subject's occupation and age and dyeing it a color signifying the severity of their symptoms. Thus representing the symptoms of real people suffering from a devastating disease, the blocks were arranged in a loose pyramid, some falling onto the floor, to allow the viewer to approach the data in a more experiential way than if just presented with a chart or numbers. As Frick once explained, "You can take a topic that is really tough and pull viewers in with something luscious."[1] —FW

1 "I Want My Data! With Laurie Frick," Zoom webinar presentation for Joint DataViz Meetup event, December 6, 2021, posted on YouTube December 8, 2021, https://www.youtube.com/watch?v=DoClhyHnsRU.

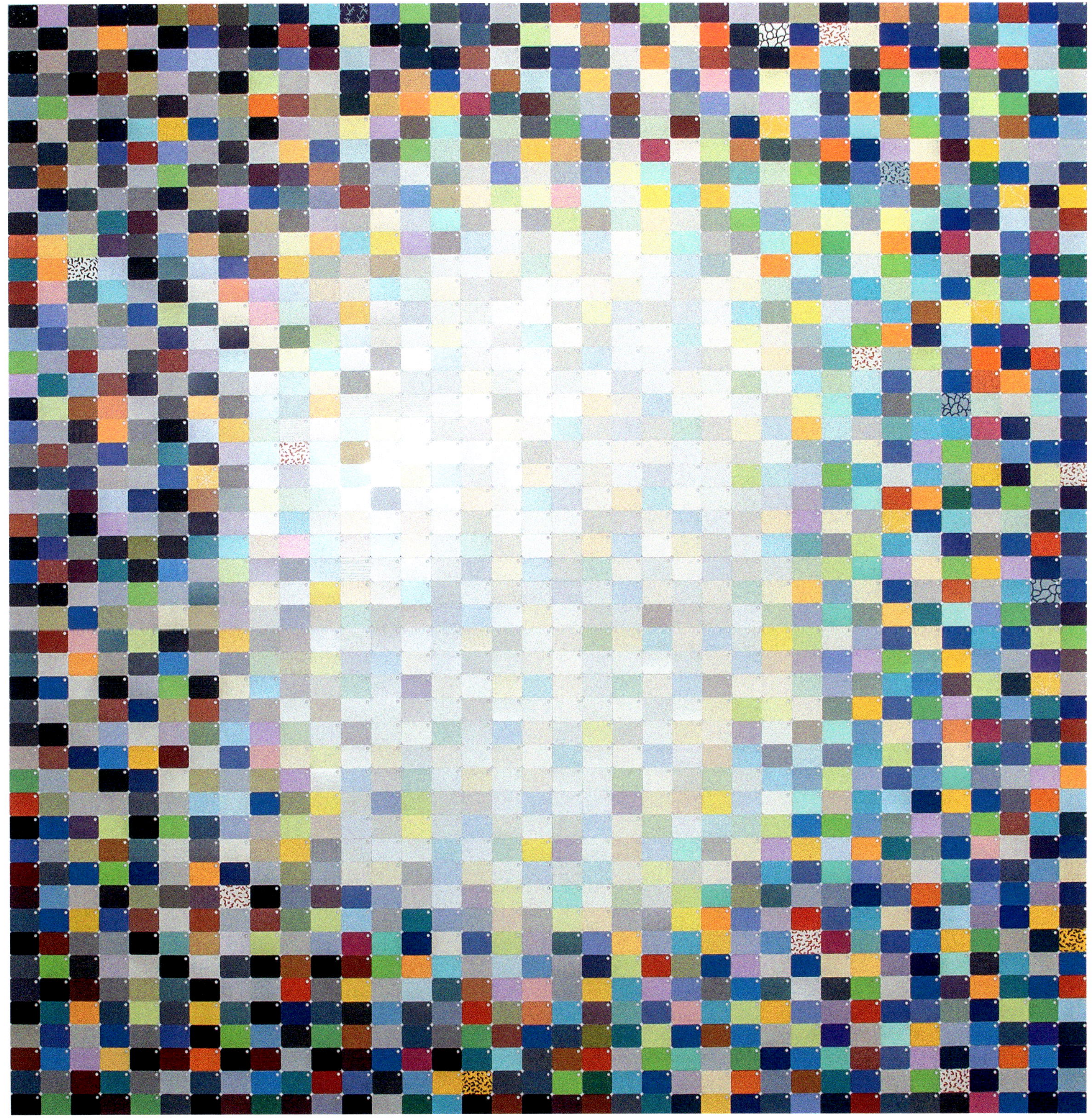

↑
Moodjam Mild, 2024

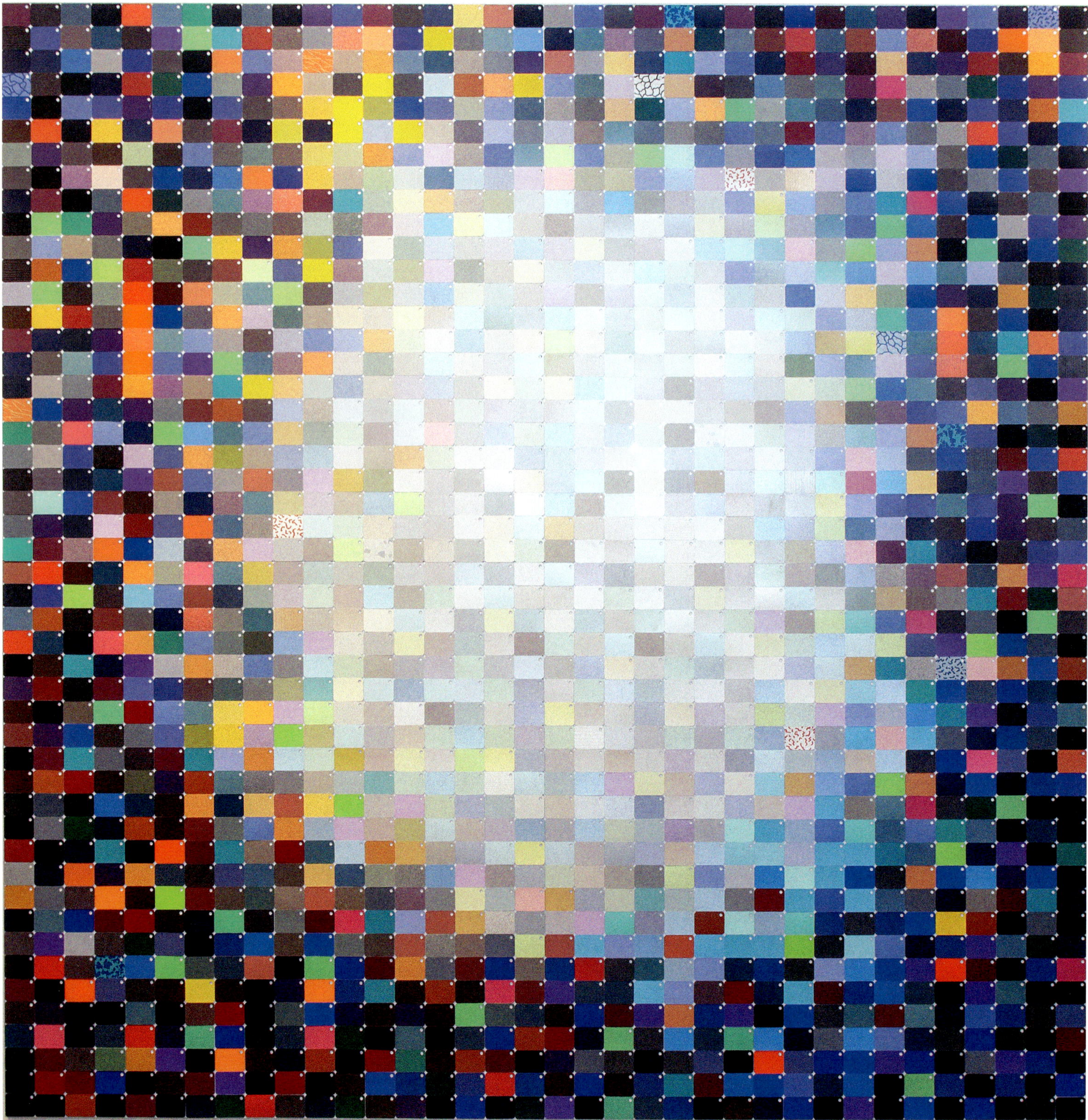

↑
Moodjam Intense, 2024

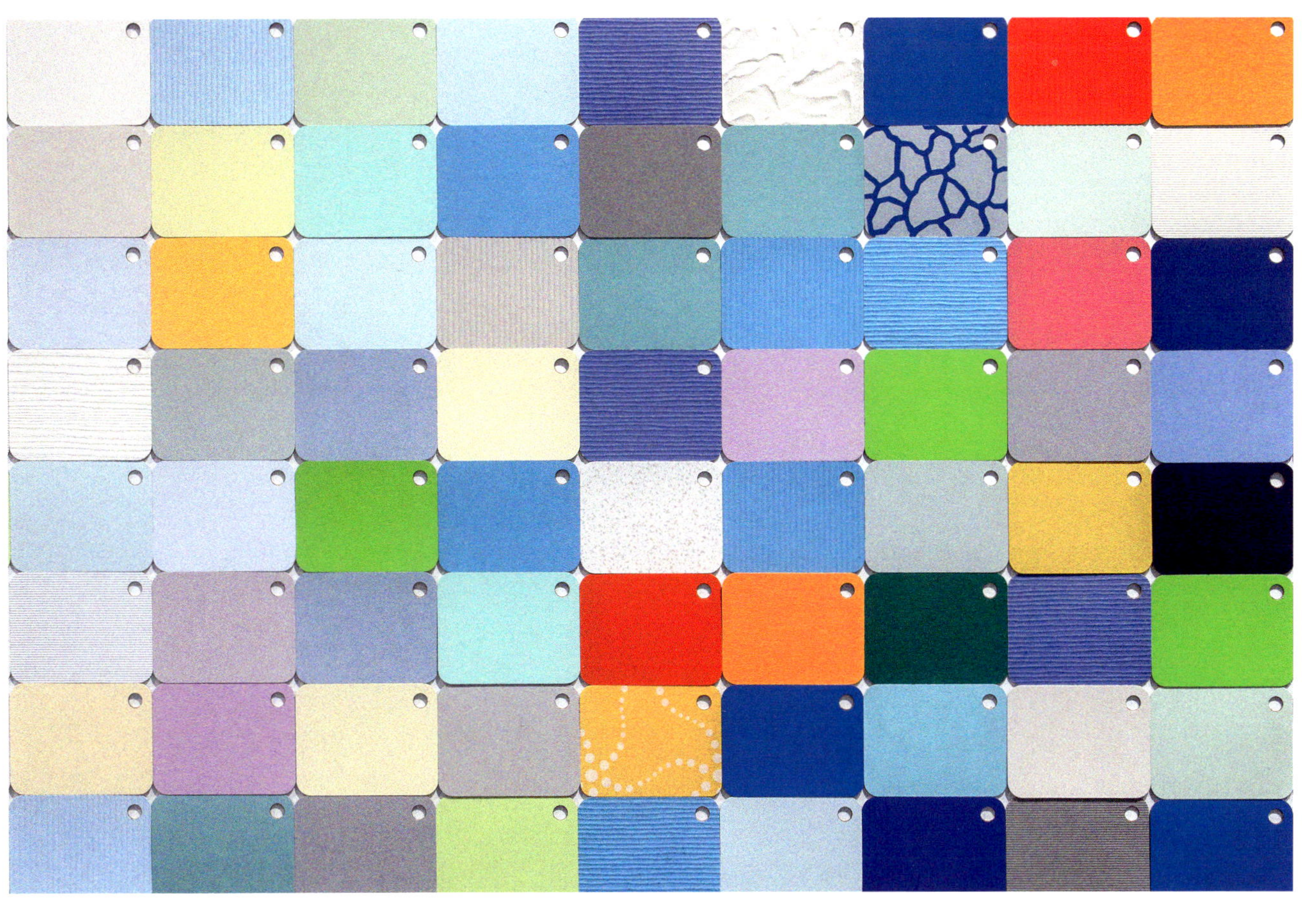

↑
Detail of *Moodjam Mild*, 2024

George Legrady

b. 1950, Budapest; lives and works in Santa Barbara, CA, and Paris

Ten works from the *Phantom Waves Series*, 2020–21
ChromaLuxe dye-sublimation prints on aluminum
30 × 40 inches each
Courtesy the artist

→
Phantom Waves Series: Linear Oscillation (top)
and *Triangular Demarcation* (bottom), 2020–21

George Legrady's practice began with documentary and conceptual photography in the early 1970s and evolved into the domains of digital photography and media from the late 80s into the early 90s. Discursive in a plethora of digital technologies, his decades-long practice has taken a labyrinthine journey into an array of prescient cultural narratives and methodologies.

Concepts and practices in the field of data visualization have been deeply ingrained in Legrady's work from very early in his career, especially regarding the collection of information. *An Anecdoted Archive from the Cold War* (1994) is a CD-ROM intertwining both personal and official documents representing the artist's upbringing in Stalinist Hungary. Taking advantage of digitization's ability to combine disparate types of information, the work established the artist as "one of the first to recognize the database as a creative medium."[1] Also heralding the twenty-first-century preoccupation with archiving, both analog and digital, is his *Pockets Full of Memories* (2001; commissioned by the Centre Pompidou, Paris), a cache of personal objects scanned and classified by museum visitors at an input station. *Making Visible the Invisible* (2005–present), a site-specific installation at the Seattle Public Library, spreads across six plasma screens installed behind the main desk in the Mixing Chamber (a large open public space dedicated to online research). The onscreen data—revealing patron checkouts of materials by the hour—are culled, reordered, and remapped through a custom statistical processing program for presentation to visitors.

Seeing the Unseeable features selections from Legrady's *Phantom Waves Series* (2020–21), a group of images created through computer code exploring, in the artist's words, "the fundamental elements of the digital photograph, which the Pixar co-founder Alvy Rae Smith ... identifies as the combination of waves, sampling and computing to result in Digital Light."[2] The series also features an equation utilizing frequency modulation—a technology familiar in the study of sound and soundwaves—that Legrady employs as an aesthetic tool.[3] "Every once in a while, I come back to this, how to use math equations to create aesthetically interesting results," Legrady has stated. "The minute you digitize a photograph it's really not a photograph anymore; it's just a string of numbers."[4]

Phantom Waves visualizes the harmonic values as frequencies intersect, forming complex patterns that are captured in still images. By manipulating oscillating frequencies applied to pixels, Legrady achieves results that could not have been realized without computation and mathematical modeling. An inspiration for this series—twentieth-century electronic music, specifically compositions by composer, architect, and engineer Iannis Xenakis—also employs frequency modulation. Regardless of their origins, these images seem to vibrate, to stutter, and to even somehow hum. Printed in a dye sublimation process in rich blacks and stark whites onto aluminum panels, the luminous, penetrating patterns of *Phantom Waves* conjure early modernist experimental films such as Oskar Fischinger's *Spirals* (1926) and Op art paintings such as Bridget Riley's mesmerizing geometries from the early 1960s. Simultaneously, these works stand alone as embodiments of a vast range of references and an infinite realm of possibility. —JJ

1 Sjoukje van der Meulen, "Database Art and Design: Pioneering Strategies in the Arts towards Collecting and Archiving," *Stedelijk Studies Journal* 10 (2020), https://stedelijkstudies.com/journal/database-art-and-design/.
2 George Legrady, email to the author, October 13, 2024.
3 Legrady has repeatedly returned to the equation, taken from the 1986 *Scientific American* article "Computer Recreations" by A. K. Dewdney, rewriting the computer code in varying ways.
4 Debra Herrick, "George Legrady's Phantom Waves, new algorithmic art," *The Current* (University of California, Santa Barbara), March 3, 2023, https://news.ucsb.edu/2023/020861/making-waves.

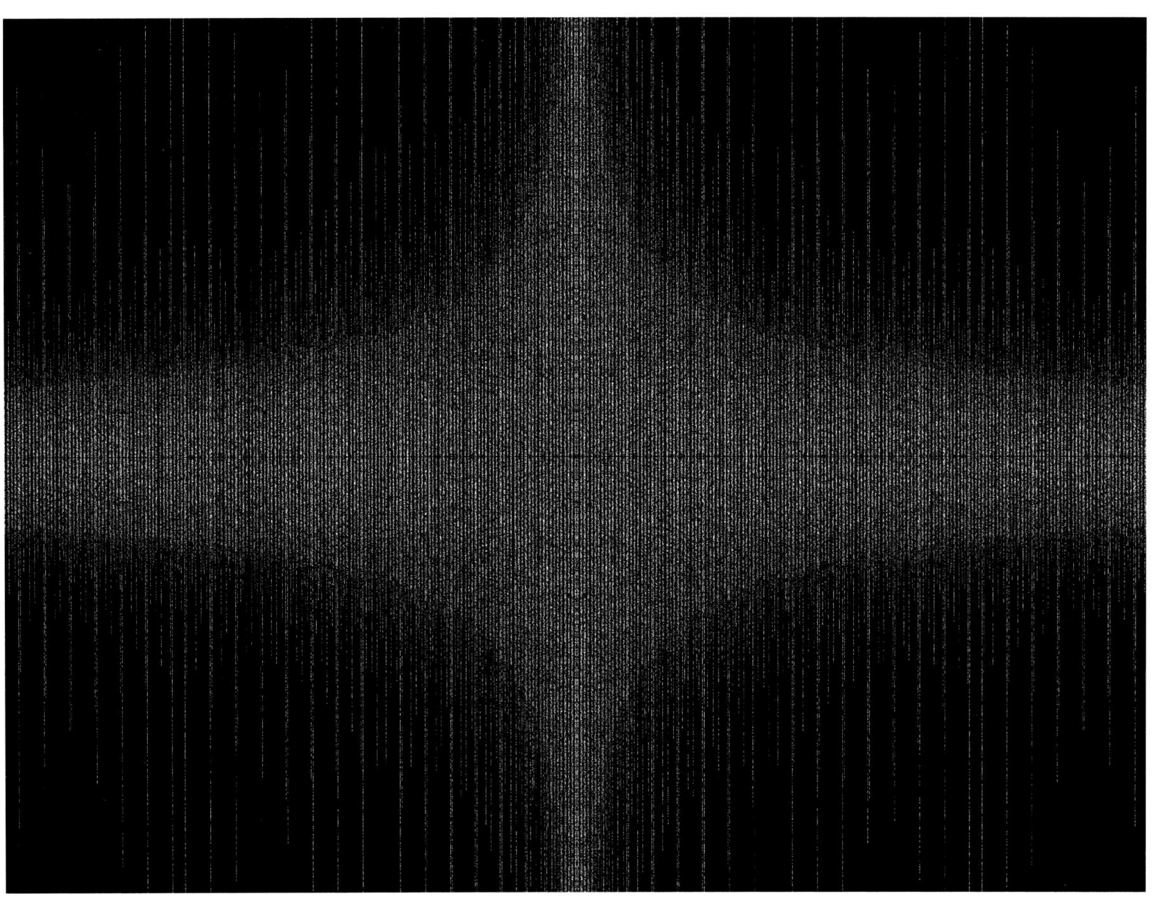

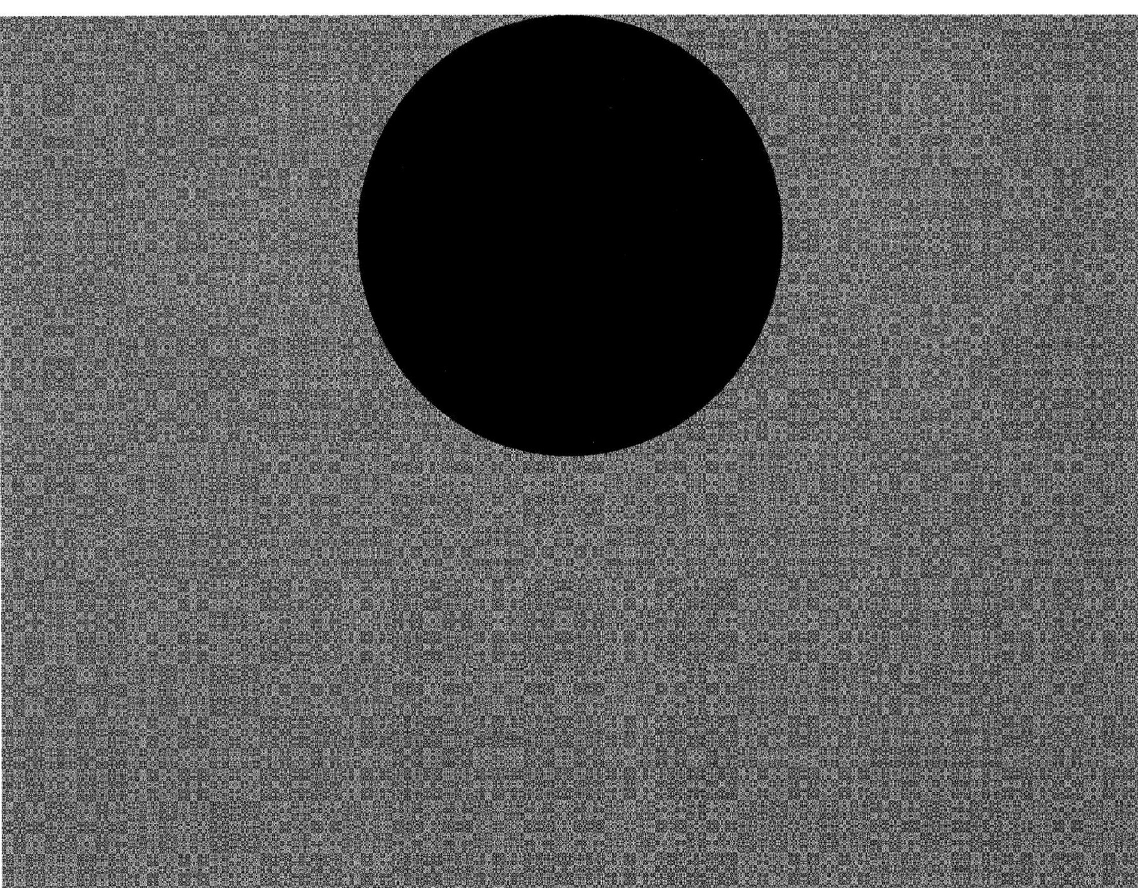

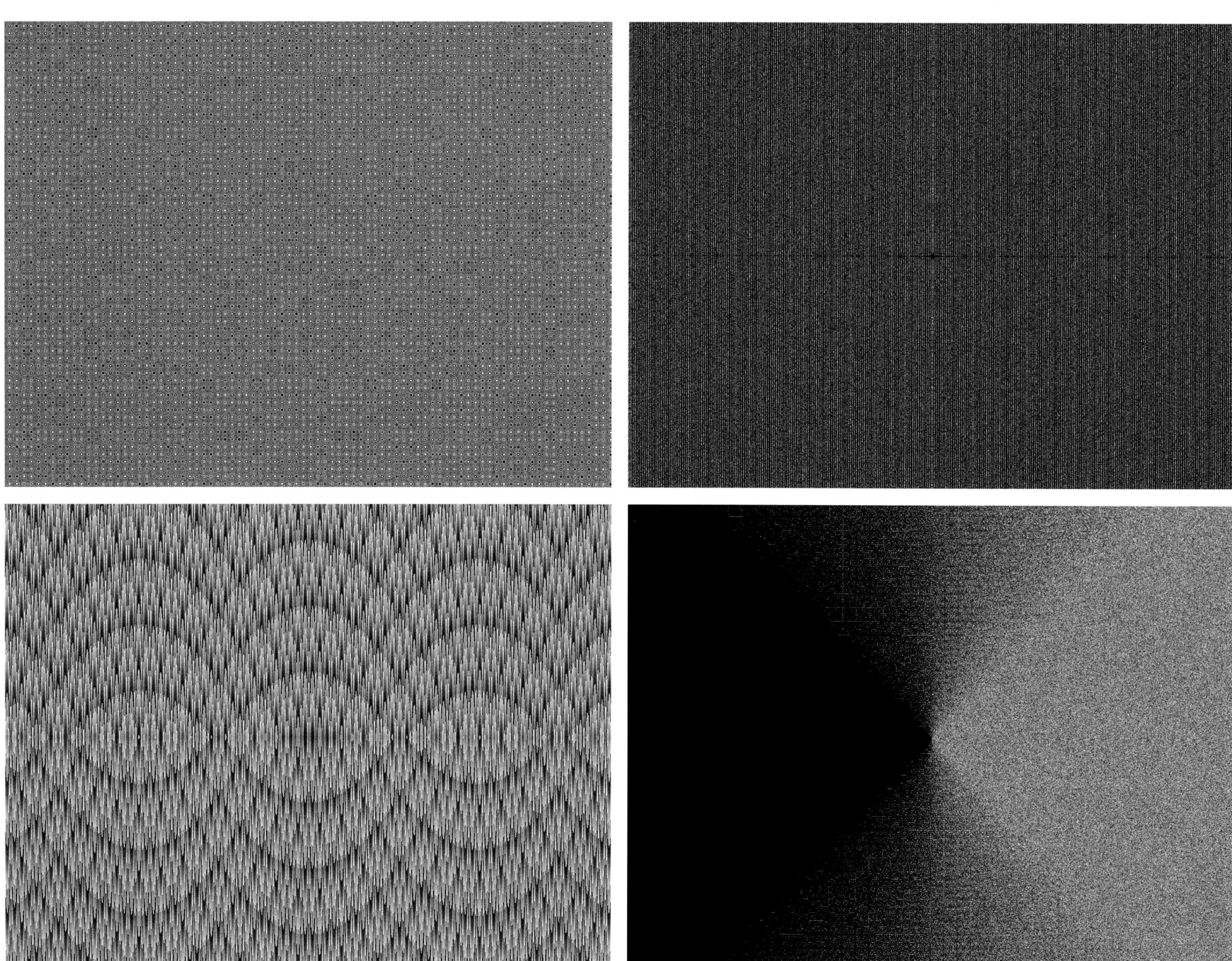

↑
Clockwise from top left: *Phantom Waves Series: Irregular Oscillation*, *Linear Oscillation 2*, *Cascade*, and *Mid-Point Synthesis*, 2020–21

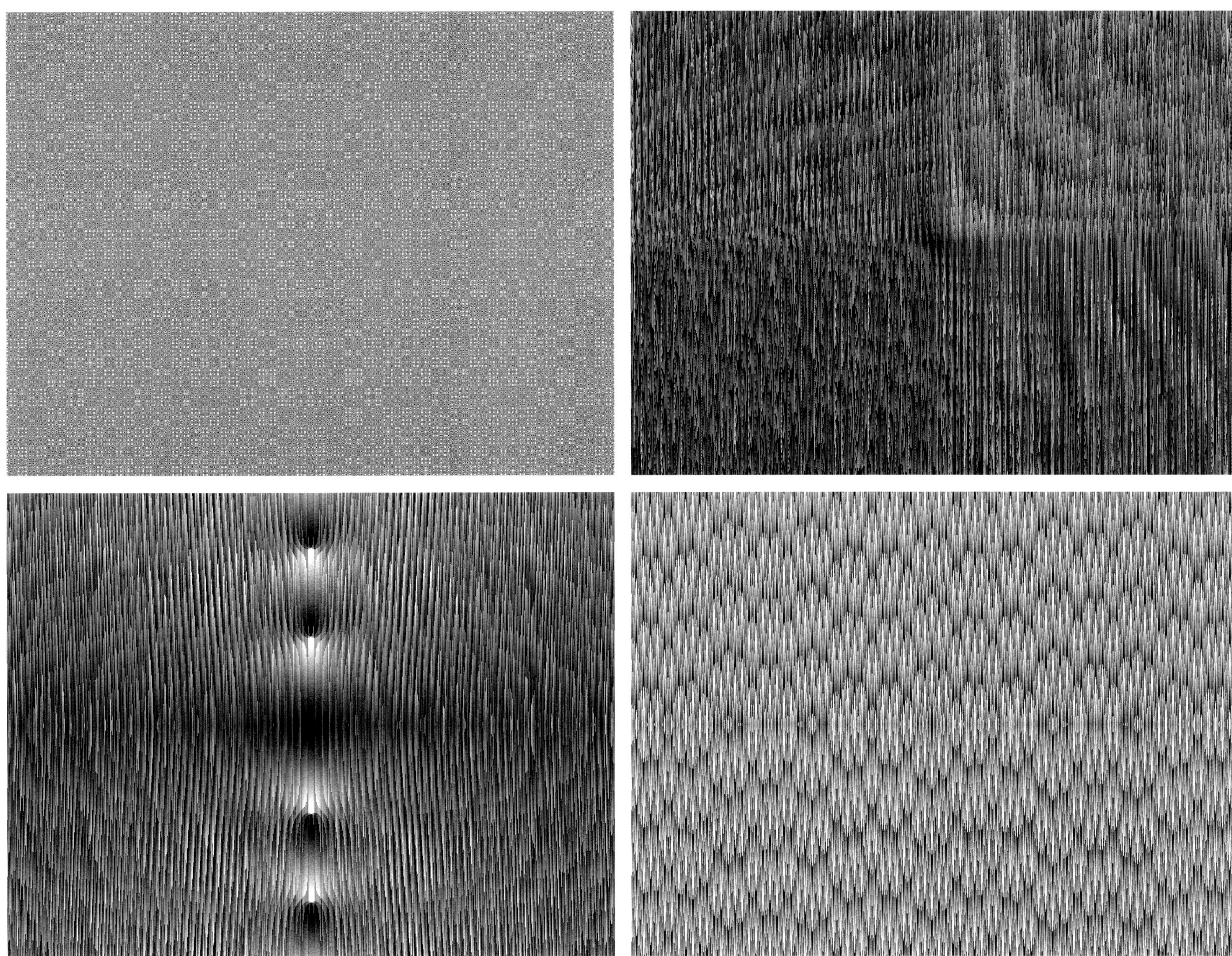

↑
Clockwise from top left: *Phantom Waves Series: Oscillation Grid*, *Bristle Anistrophy*, *Wave Fracture 2 Vertical*, and *Cascade Jaggy*, 2020–21

Rafael Lozano-Hemmer

b. 1967, Mexico City; lives and works in Montreal

Hormonium (Text Stream 8), 2022
Custom-generative code and computer 4k display
Dimensions variable
Courtesy of the Collection of Arkive

Rafael Lozano-Hemmer harnesses an array of sophisticated technologies to explore and coalesce socio-political histories and scientific phenomena. Informed by architecture and performance and employing digital tools such as computerized surveillance, robotics, and artificial intelligence, his installations most often take the form of sleekly electronic, dimly lit installations. In many ways the artist's works variously spotlight the viewer, becoming test sites for and about humankind while calling attention to matters simultaneously individual and communal. Hospitable in temperament, his works effectively eliminate any perceived barriers that may prevent observers from engaging and interacting, while also subtly introducing alternative approaches to issues that differentiate each of us from the other.

Lozano-Hemmer's education in chemistry and early experience in a molecular-recognition laboratory set the stage for his artwork, which employs sophisticated software and surveillance technologies. Data and its characteristics run rampant through the distinct algorithms driving each work, beginning with one of his earliest, *Surface Tension* (1992), an interactive installation where, in the artist's words, "a giant human eye follows the observer with Orwellian precision."[1] Accentuating the characteristics of datasets—namely, their ubiquity as well as our collective incomprehension of their presence and power—is *Zero Noon* (2013), a digital clock displaying real time by drawing on hundreds of different reference systems. Generating the time for this small yet prescient work is a menu of daily statistics culled from the government, *Harper's Magazine*, academic studies, and many other sources that viewers may select or, in some cases, even suggest.

Revisiting Lozano-Hemmer's ongoing reference to the human in its empirical, biological, and even philosophical forms is *Hormonium (Text Stream 8)* (2022). This work is part of his *Text Stream* series—single monitor works presenting new algorithmic text springs (animated texts) from select sources, ranging from literary tomes by figures such as the French poet Stéphane Mallarmé *(Recurrent Mallarmé (Text Stream 1)* [2018]) to scientific essays, including the writings of Charles Babbage and Ada Lovelace *(Babbage Lovelace (Text Stream 5)* [2019]).

Hormonium (Text Stream 8) utilizes abbreviations of the names of human hormones: E (for estrogen), GH (for growth hormone), TSH (thyroid-stimulating hormone), and so on. Manifested as an ocean, its waves breaking upon a shallow shore, the myriad acronyms roll in with the surf, spilling, crashing, and dissipating into particles, or airborne letters, upon impact. As such *Hormonium* reimagines human biological rhythms that surge, overlap, flow back, reemerge, and disintegrate. Simulating the span of a life in real time, the hormones change depending on the time of day, month, or year, evolving as time goes on. Markers of the specific age of the work, along with its circadian, ultradian, and infradian rhythms, are registered, also in real time, along the lower edge of the monitor. Currently three years old, the work reveals mostly growth hormones, as would a toddler of the same age. When the work reaches ninety years of age, the determined span of its lifetime, the work will reset. A demonstrable harmony of generative art and biology, *Hormonium* embodies the complex bonds between nature and science, the individual and the common. Modest in scale yet epic in resonance, this work is paradoxically lucid and profound. —JJ

→
Detail of *Hormonium (Text Stream 8)*, 2022

1 Project description of *Surface Tension* (1992) on the artist's website, https://www.lozano-hemmer.com/surface_tension.php.

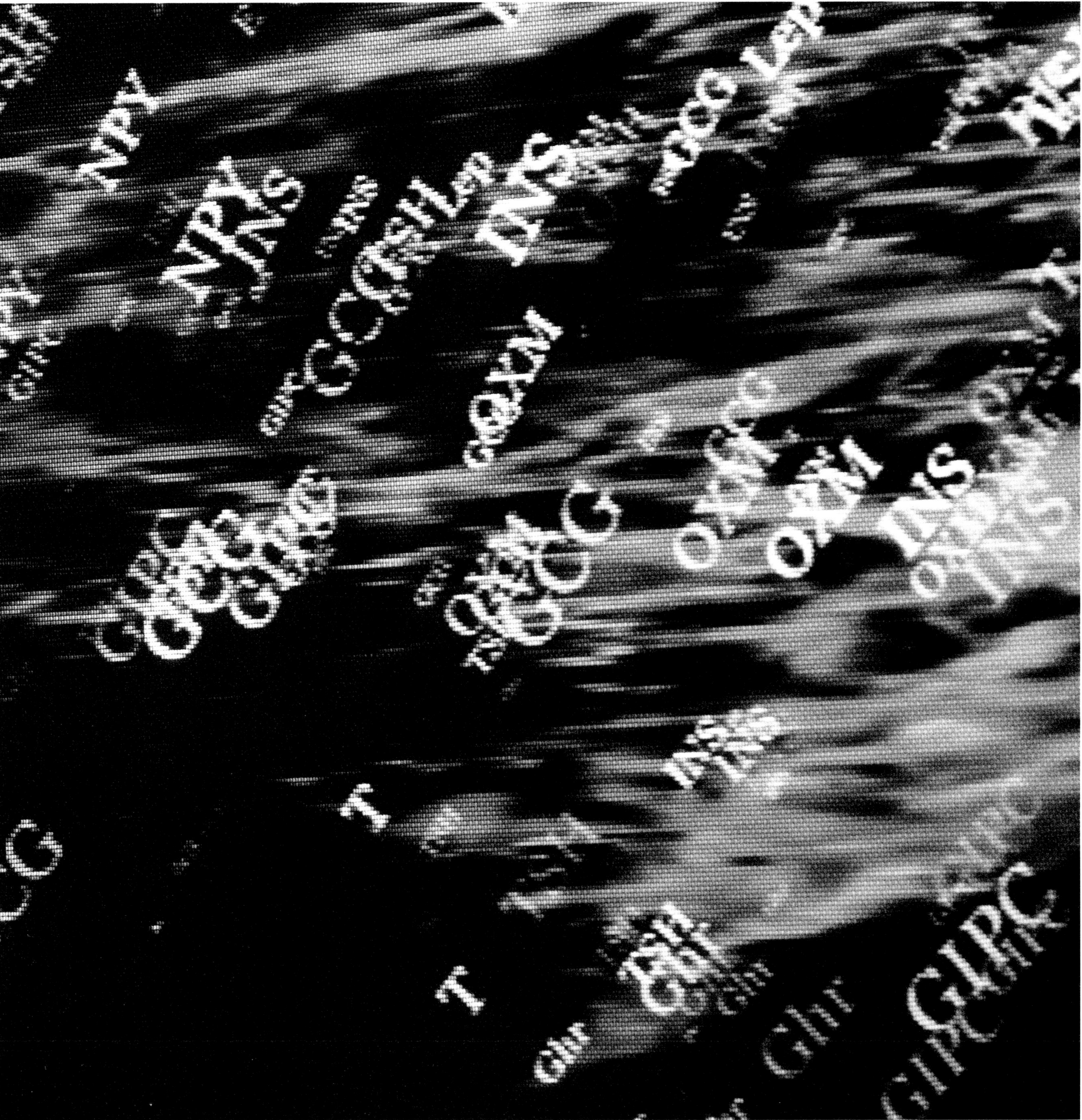

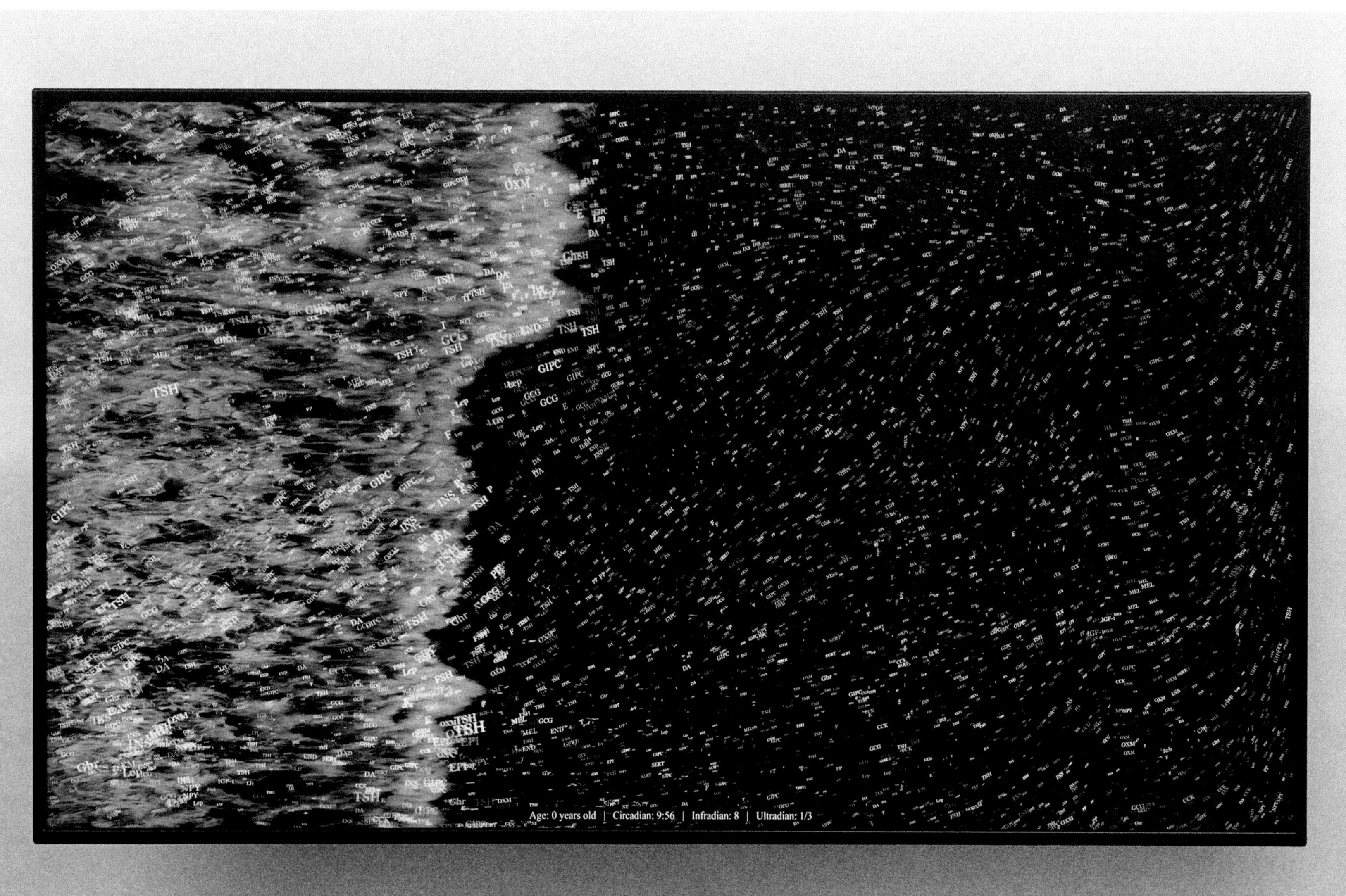

↑
Stills from *Hormonium (Text Stream 8)*, 2022

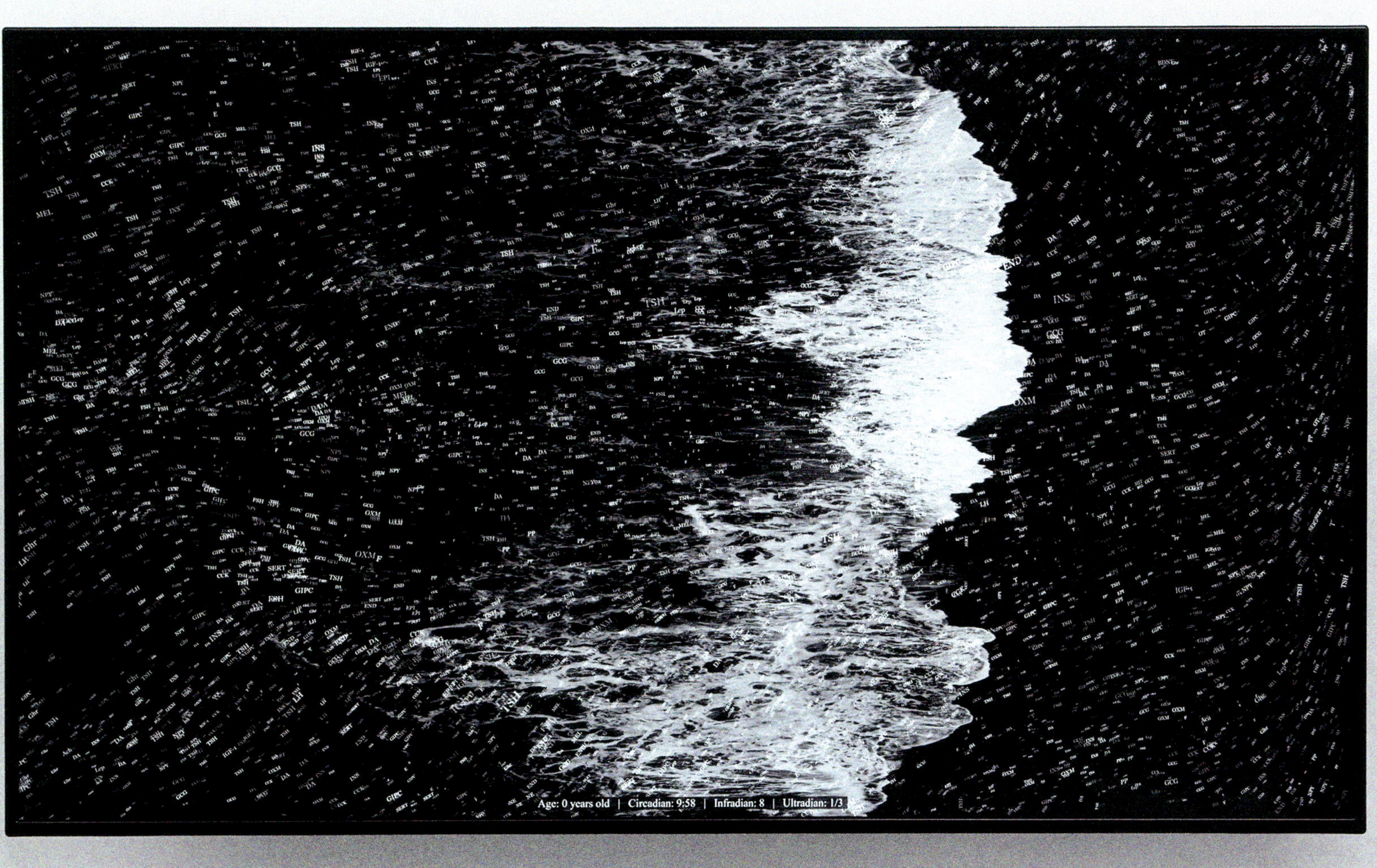
Age: 0 years old | Circadian: 9:58 | Infradian: 8 | Ultradian: 1/3

Giorgia Lupi
Ehren Shorday

Giorgia Lupi (b. 1981, Modena, Italy; lives and works in New York)
Ehren Shorday (b. 1982, New Hope, Pennsylvania; lives and works in Brooklyn, NY)

Incroci (Crossings), 2022
Black paint on raw canvas
100 paintings, 15 × 14 inches each; 75 × 280 inches overall
Courtesy of Fondazione Merz

→
Detail of *Incroci (Crossings)*, 2022

Incorporating one hundred paintings, *Incroci (Crossings)* is an exploration of human connections through data. Originally commissioned by Fondazione Merz for the 2022 group exhibition *Ordo naturalis, ordo artificialis*,[1] the installation piece developed through data visualization designer Giorgia Lupi's and artist Ehren Shorday's shared interest in the structure of communities. An advocate for what she calls "data humanism," Lupi designs data information to affirm and convey humanity rather than obscure or abstract lived experiences. The designer's ideas complement Shorday's ongoing investigations into community structures, labor systems, and how technology affects our sense of value.

The project evolved from the duo's observation that "each person's life may be unique and different, but when seen together, these distinct paths begin to form patterns."[2] For *Incroci*, Lupi and Shorday issued an open call on their social media accounts, asking strangers to share five dates (day/month/year) representing significant life moments, from the day of their birth up to the present. (The project was conducted during the Covid-19 pandemic, giving new weight to the question of what could be construed as a "significant life moment.") Out of 1,400 responses, one hundred were compiled into datasets and translated into "data portraits," each painting featuring five rising and falling black lines. According to the project key provided, "Each black line represents one date, connecting the day (along the left vertical side) with the month (horizontal side) with the year (on the right vertical side, divided according to the time span from a person's birthday to the present)."[3] The lines in each canvas piece, installed in a grid across five rows, seemingly echo one another, as similarities and rhythms develop into patterns along the grid. When the data is viewed within the context of these lines, the information takes on greater meaning as it reveals a previously unseen, shared history of memorable days.

Incroci exemplifies the ways in which data visualization is evolving beyond providing aesthetic scaffolding for data research by realizing subtext within datasets. As an information designer, Lupi has observed that the "more ubiquitous data becomes, the more we need to experiment with how to make it unique, contextual, intimate. The way we visualize is crucial because it is the key to translating numbers into concepts we can relate to."[4] This experimentation extends to the conscious use of the term "data portraits" by the collaborators, as it deliberately frames the visualized dataset as an object of aesthetic consideration. The repositioning of data in this context opens up ways of seeing information beyond numerical value and function toward a means of personal artistic expression. –cv

1 Presented in 2022 at Zisa Arti Contemporanee, Palermo, Sicily.
2 Giorgia Lupi, "Incroci—Art Commission for Fondazione Merz," giorgialupi.com/incroci.
3 Lupi, "Incroci."
4 Lupi, "Data Humanism: The Revolutionary Future of Data Visualization," *Print* 70 (2016), posted January 30, 2017, https://www.printmag.com/article/data-humanism-future-of-data-visualization/.

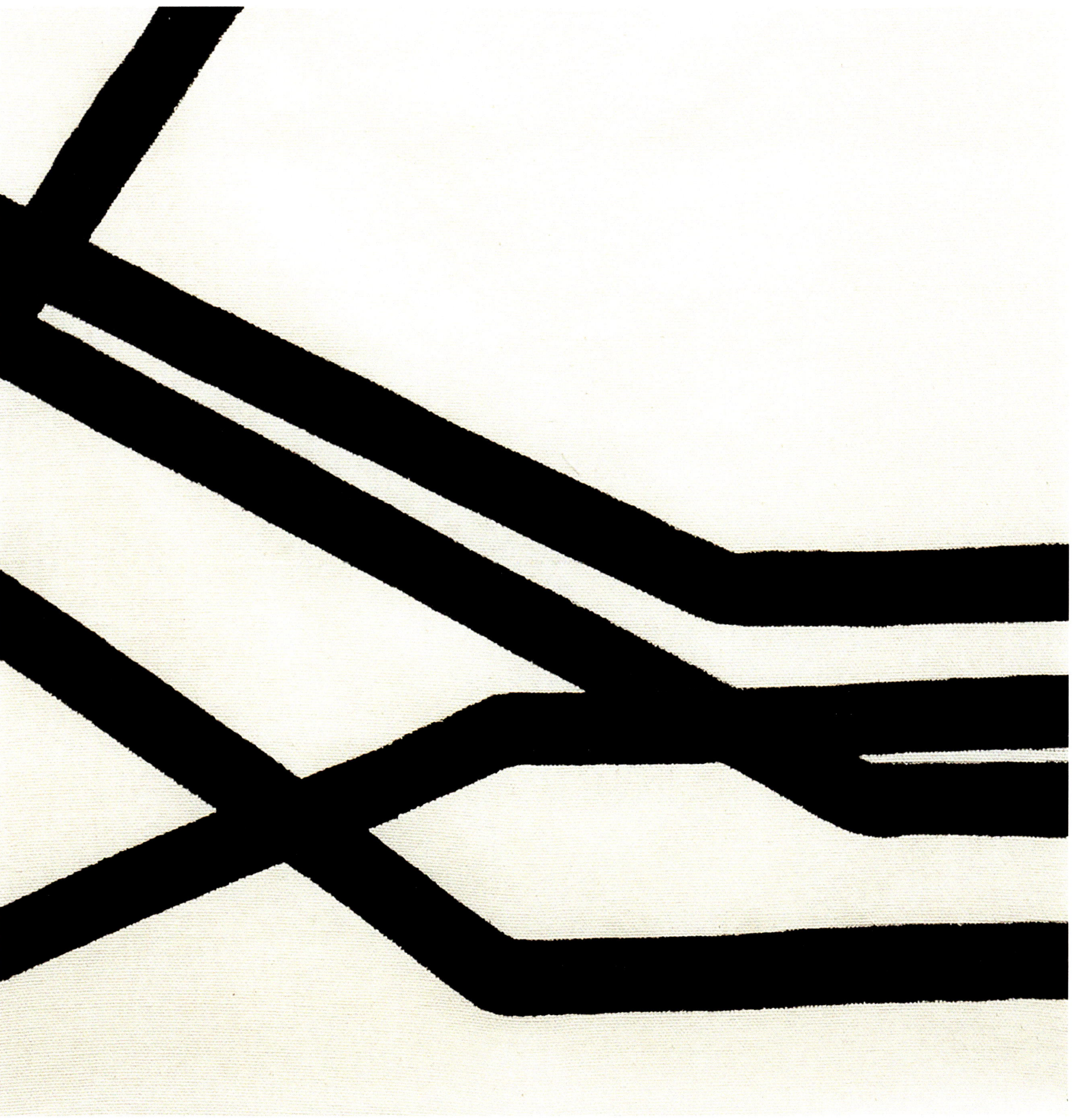

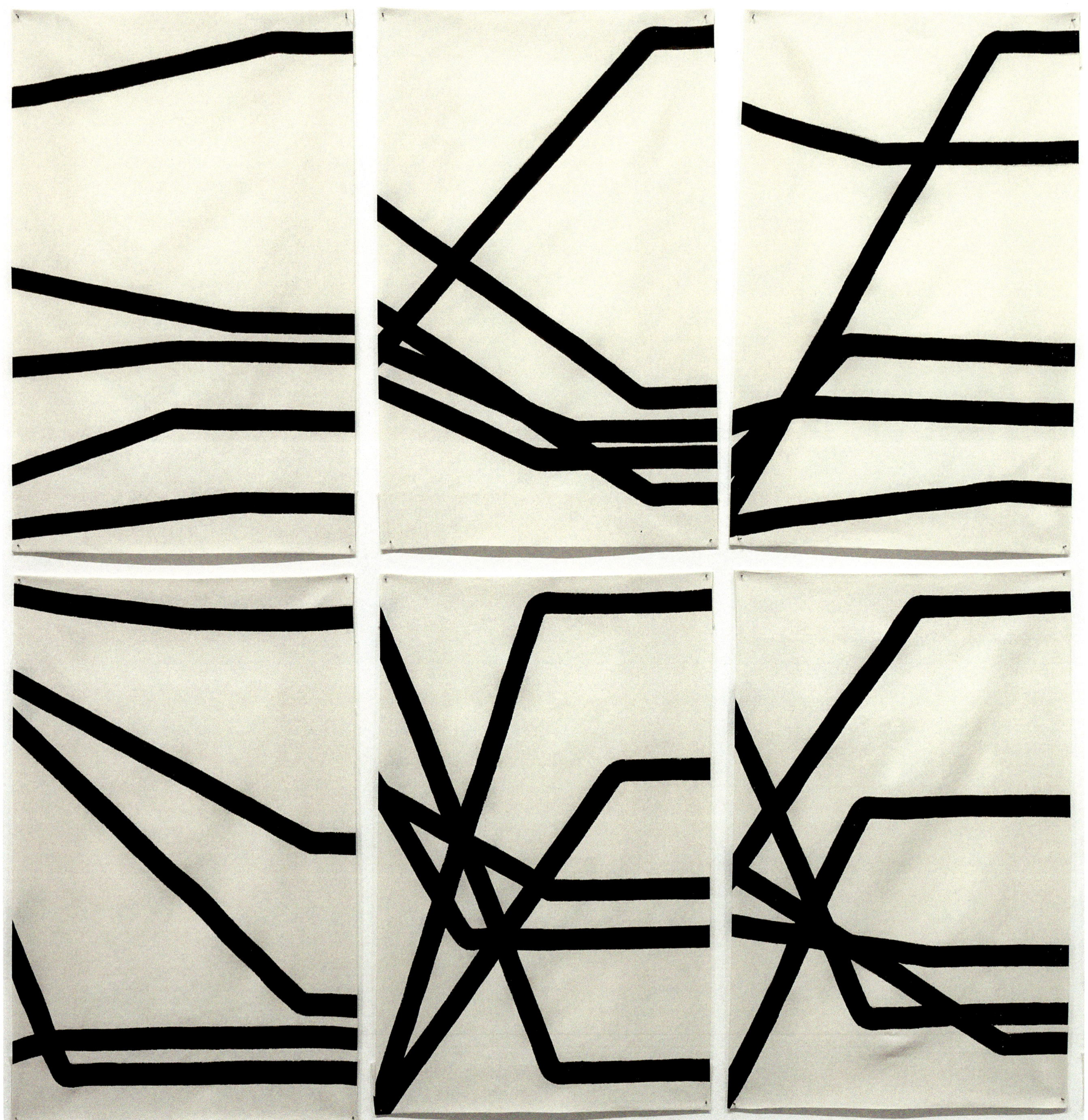

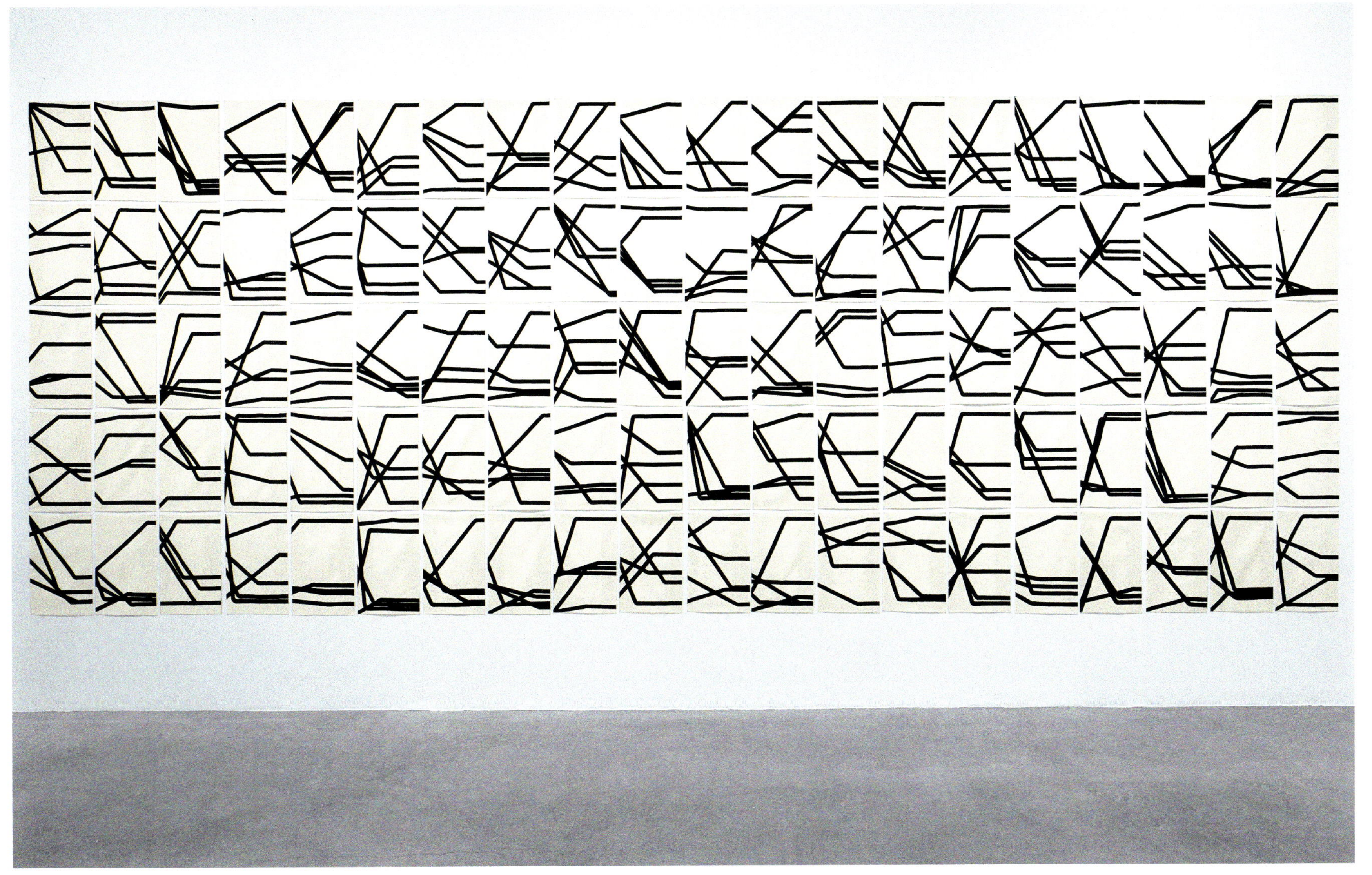

↑
Installation views of *Incroci (Crossings)*, 2022

Iñigo Manglano-Ovalle

b. 1961, Madrid; lives and works in Chicago

Lu, Jack and Carrie (from *The Garden of Delights*), 1998/2017
Archival pigment prints
Triptych: 61 × 24 inches each panel; 61 × 76 inches overall
Courtesy the artist

Storm Prototype: Cloud Prototype No. 2, 2006
Fiberglass and titanium alloy
57 1/4 × 96 5/8 × 60 1/2 inches
Courtesy the artist

Storm Prototype: Cloud Prototype No. 4, 2006
Fiberglass and titanium alloy
62 × 102 × 57 1/4 inches
Courtesy the artist

Iñigo Manglano-Ovalle is recognized for a wide-ranging, multifaceted practice that takes form in sculptures, photography, and video. Ranging in scale from modest to monumental, his works are the result of years of research and achieved working in collaboration with creatives, inventors, and technicians in a vast range of scientific fields. The impetus of his work lies firmly in the social sciences, whether concerned with examining natural and manmade systems, exposing racial and ethnic inequities, or grappling with ethical challenges presented by modern technologies.

Lu, Jack and Carrie (1998/2017) is a colorful triptych of digital prints. The abstractions are images of DNA samples utilized in genomic mapping. *The Garden of Delights*, the series from which this work derives, features samples from forty-eight participants: the artist selected sixteen individuals, each of whom, in turn, invited two others to be featured in the resulting triptychs. Inspired by art historical genres such as Spanish *casta* paintings—late eighteenth-century works illustrating a rigid, race-based colonial hierarchy—this series questions the persistence of socially constructed identity. Titled after Hieronymus Bosch's infamous triptych, Manglano-Ovalle's homage carries the melancholy and horror exuding from the late fifteenth century work: an indelible harbinger of humanity's fate.

In a myriad of ways, Manglano-Ovalle's series of DNA works is iconic in the context of contemporary artists utilizing data and in the history of data visualization, considering that the helical model of the DNA molecule marks a major advancement in representing three-dimensional objects.[1] As an example of typology and genealogy, Manglano-Ovalle's series serves as a charged reference to current and alternative notions of family and issues regarding racial and health profiling. Applying the latest DNA imaging tools available at the time they were made, the works manifest technological advancements in scientific imaging as well as new media in contemporary art. As the earliest works in *Seeing the Unseeable*, they set the stage for not only the artist's own subsequent investigations of data, but also an era that would yield increased attention toward data by many other artists and designers.

Expanding on explorations of ethnicity and race, the artist later pursued the phenomenon of migration to another type of incident altogether: the atmospheric. Manglano-Ovalle's *Storm Prototype: Cloud Prototype Nos. 2* and *4* (2006) are hovering spectral forms manifesting in three-dimensional form the analysis and compilation of real weather data. In 2002, climatologists at the Department of Atmospheric Sciences at the University of Illinois, Urbana-Champaign, tracked a powerful storm system as it entered Illinois from Missouri. Manglano-Ovalle and architect Douglas Garogalo subsequently translated this data into fiberglass and titanium alloy foil based on the delineations of the storm in the moments prior to eruption. A miniscule fraction of the size or effect of an actual storm cloud, the sculptures nevertheless convey a heightened sense of disturbance, their swollen mirrored forms appearing fluid and elusive. Produced around the same time as a large-scale series of "icebergs"—skeletal forms derived from data describing large floating masses of ice—these works represent the compulsory flow of nature, whether revealed in the sky and ocean or over land, impervious to international boundaries. "What I want to represent," the artist states, "is how the world represents itself to us."[2] —JJ

1 B. Schneiderman, "The Eyes Have It: A task by data type taxonomy for information visualizations," 1996 IEEE Symposium on Visual Languages (Piscataway, NJ: IEEE, 1996), 336–43. https://doi.org/10.1109/VL.1996.545307.
2 Profile on Iñigo Manglano-Ovalle, Christopher Grimes Projects website, https://www.cgrimes.com/inigo-manglano-ovalle.

→
Storm Prototype: Cloud Prototype Nos. 2 and *4*, 2006

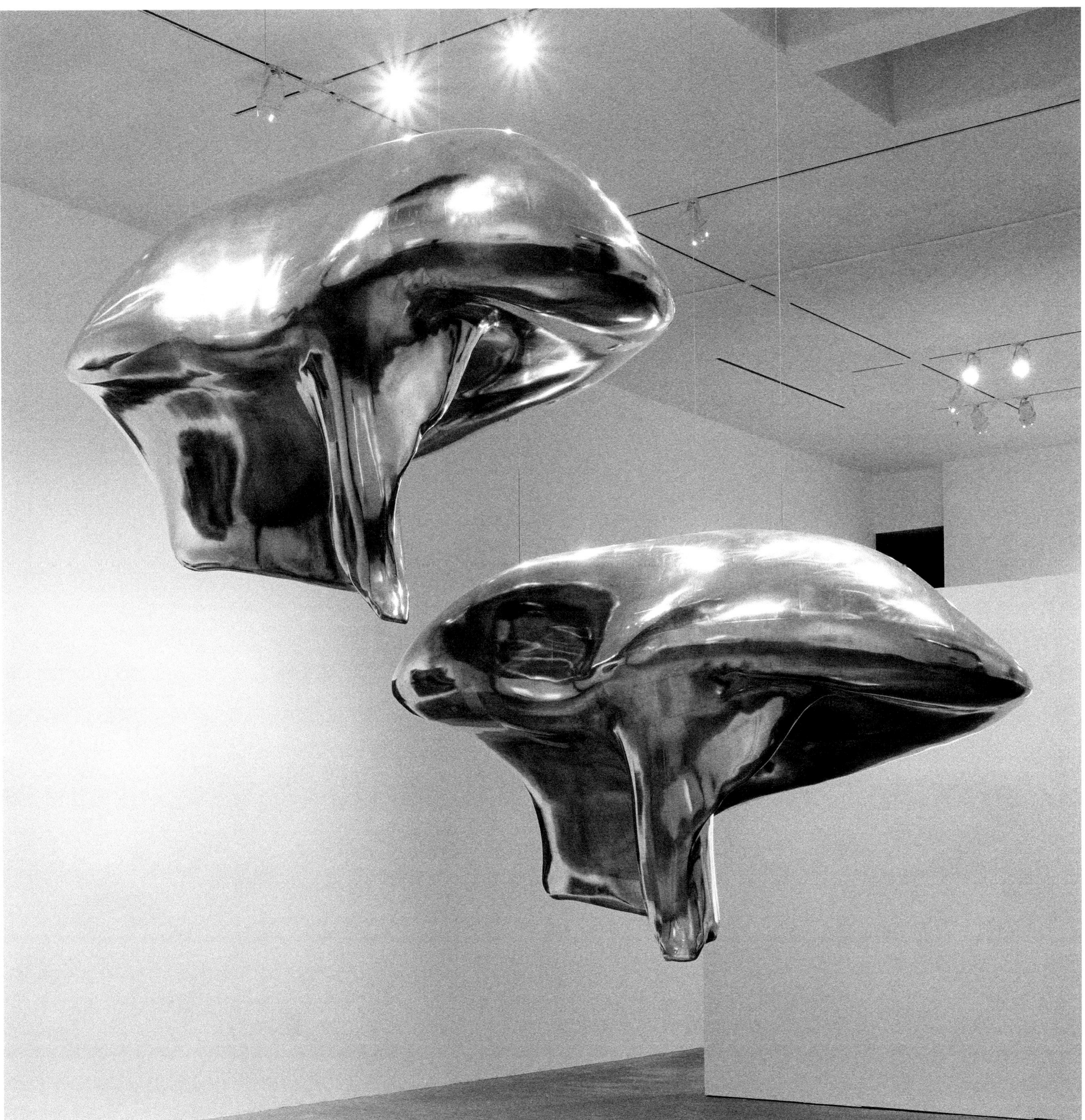

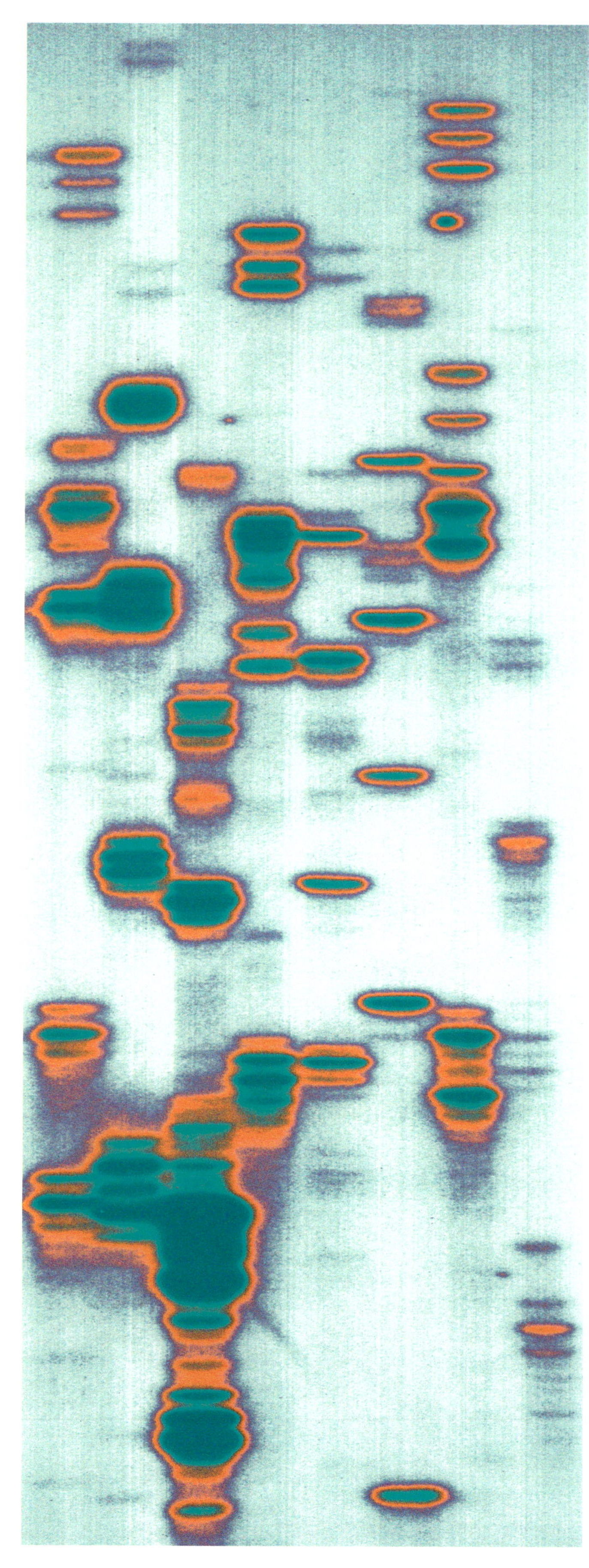

→
Lu, Jack and Carrie (from *The Garden of Delights*), 1998/2017

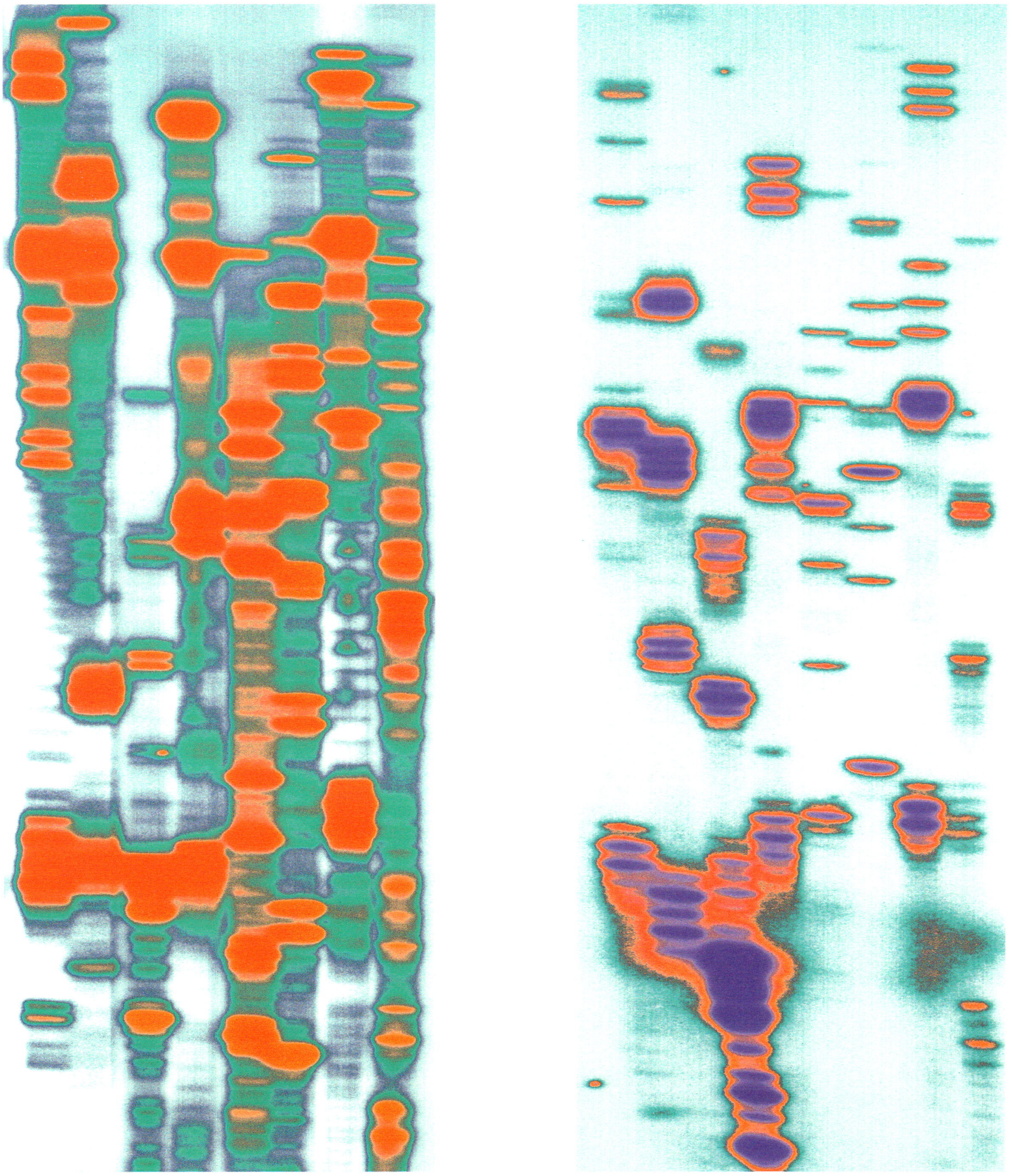

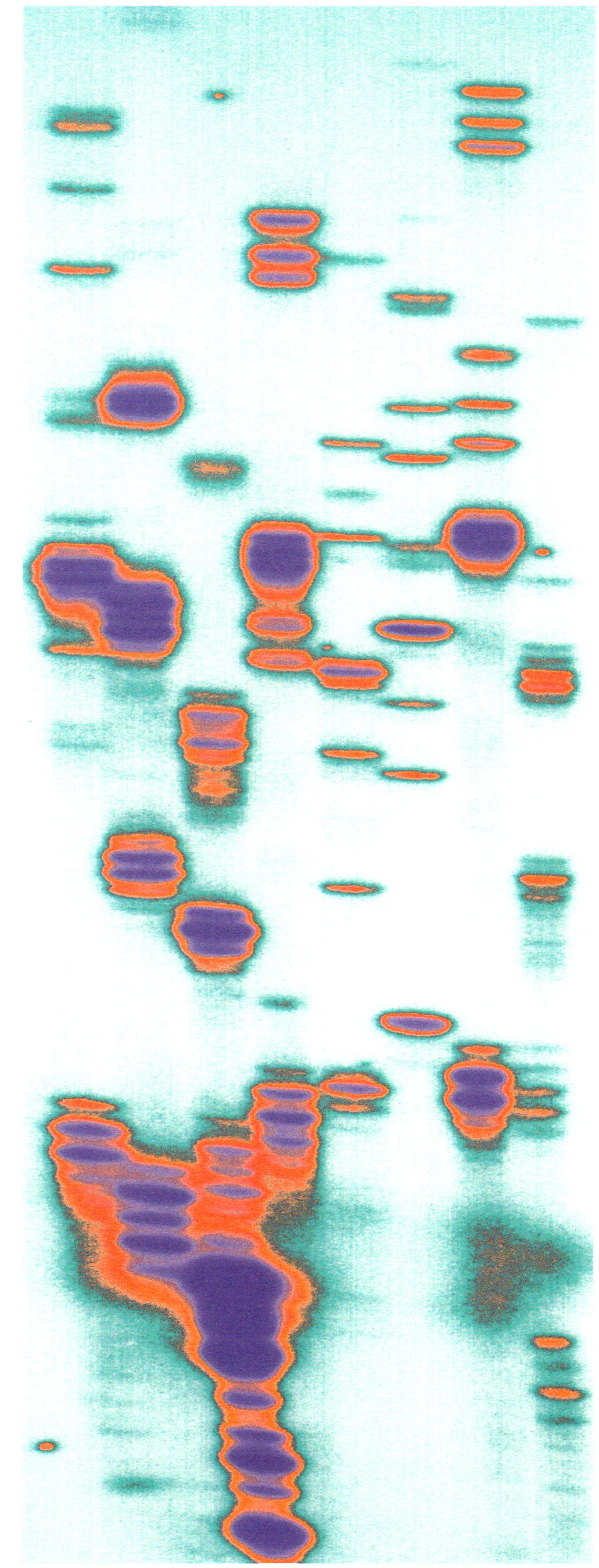

Sarah Morris

b. 1967, Sevenoaks, UK; lives and works in New York

Deviancy is the Essence of Culture [Sound Graph], 2018
Household gloss paint on canvas
48 × 48 inches
Courtesy the artist and Petzel Gallery, New York

Property Must Be Seen [Sound Graph], 2020
Household gloss paint on canvas
60 × 60 inches
Courtesy the artist and Petzel Gallery, New York

You Cannot Keep Love [Sound Graph], 2020
Household gloss paint on canvas
60 × 60 inches
Courtesy the artist and Petzel Gallery, New York

Sarah Morris creates films, paintings, and sculptures based on an expansive range of sources, including architectural spaces, graphic logos, transportation system diagrams, GPS technology, and urban movement patterns. She has said, "I want to map what is going on, these situations we find ourselves in—both physically and philosophically."[1] For the *Sound Graph* paintings (2017–20), she turned to her recent explorations of sound, language, and speech. Taking data from personal audio files—habitual recordings she makes of conversations and noise fragments from various sources—she transformed them into glossy and dynamic hard-edge paintings. Unlike other painters working in geometric abstraction, however, Morris is distinct not just for her visually pulsating compositions but for her works' highly rigorous and complex levels of cultural relevance.

Morris's interest in incorporating sound into her paintings began when she conceived the film *Finite and Infinite Games* (2017), titled after the cult philosophy and numbers theory novel by James P. Carse (1986). The title of Morris's *Deviancy is the Essence of Culture [Sound Graph]* (2018) references Carse's text and recalls not only the author's meditation on life as a contest of games but also Morris's endeavor to code, decode, and recode existing constructs into something entirely new. While it may be improbable to detect the source of her painting *You Cannot Keep Love [Sound Graph]* (2020), a simple search of the phrase reveals an unending scope of possibilities, from pop music choruses to contrived ad slogans and spiritual idioms less likely extracted from print than a daytime talk show. It is precisely this explorative interplay of structural archetypes, along with the seemingly endless possibilities of her syncopating geometries, that also points us back to her larger oeuvre while also provoking our own imaginations.

Morris has said, "the paintings are as much about visual perception as they are about audio, because there is this element of distraction and movement and the idea of a painting that can splinter and become another painting."[2] She has also referred to paintings as indexical, in the sense that "a painting can be an index for all of the paintings I've done and all the paintings I'm going to do."[3] While many of the canvases have shapes and colors that repeat, each has a rhythm and pattern that is unto itself. As such these works represent the generative—in art and many other areas—but also, more specifically, a fragment of a larger self-generating system, remaining open and acknowledging if not inviting further action, interpretation, and transmutation. It is in this way that we may understand Morris's paintings as energetic expressions of both the microscopic and the macroscopic and, more significantly, as spaces that represent limitless permutations of the literal and metaphoric. —JJ

→
Deviancy is the Essence of Culture [Sound Graph], 2018

1 Sarah Morris, in Taylor Dafoe, "'I View All Space as Public': Sarah Morris Explains Why Nothing Is Off Limits in Her New Paintings and Films," Artnet.com, May 23, 2019, https://news.artnet.com/art-world/sarah-morris-interview-1554886.
2 Morris, in "I View All Space as Public."
3 Morris, interviewed by Philippe Parreno, *Interview*, posted March 9, 2017, https://www.interviewmagazine.com/art/sarah-morris.

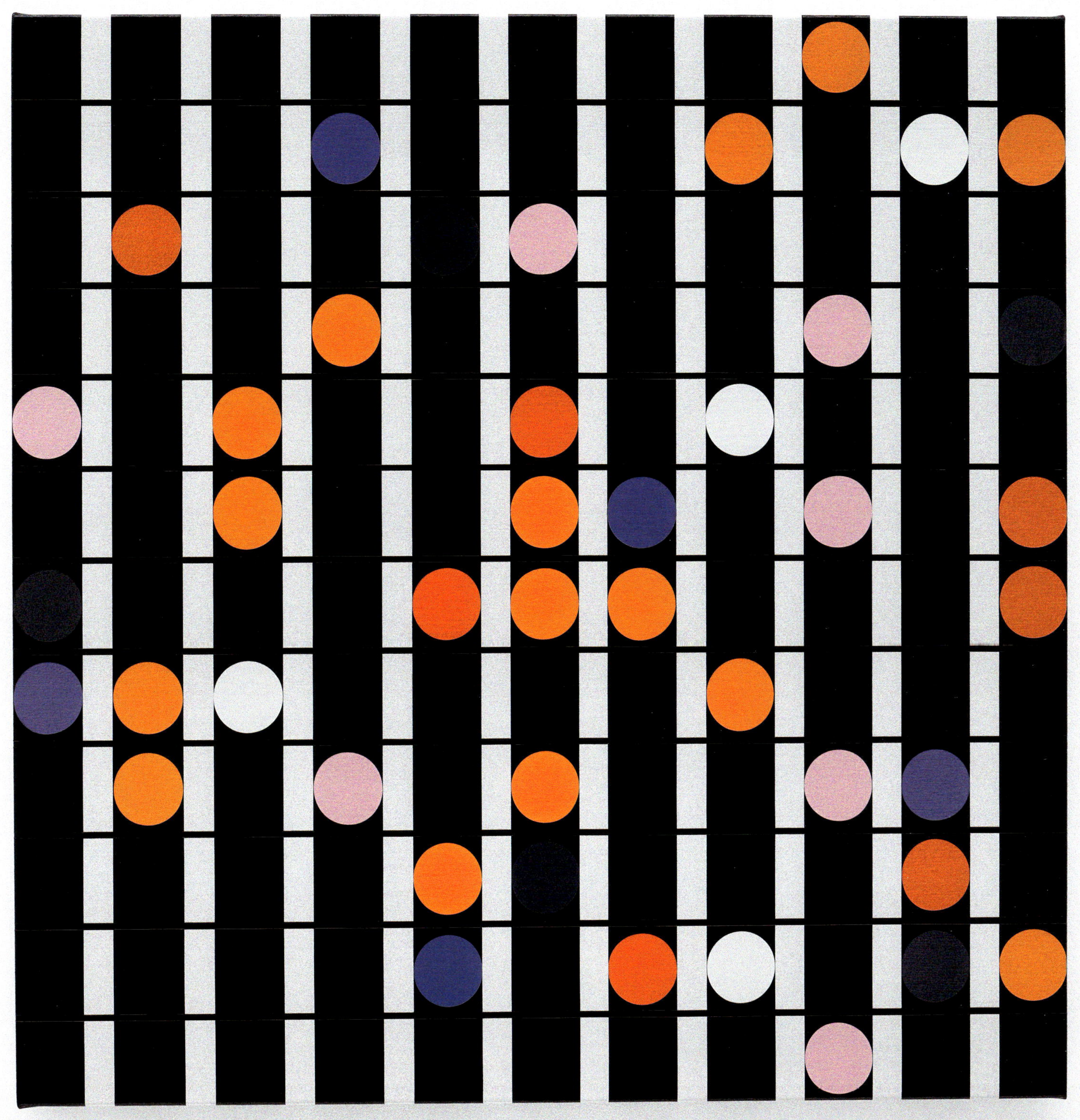

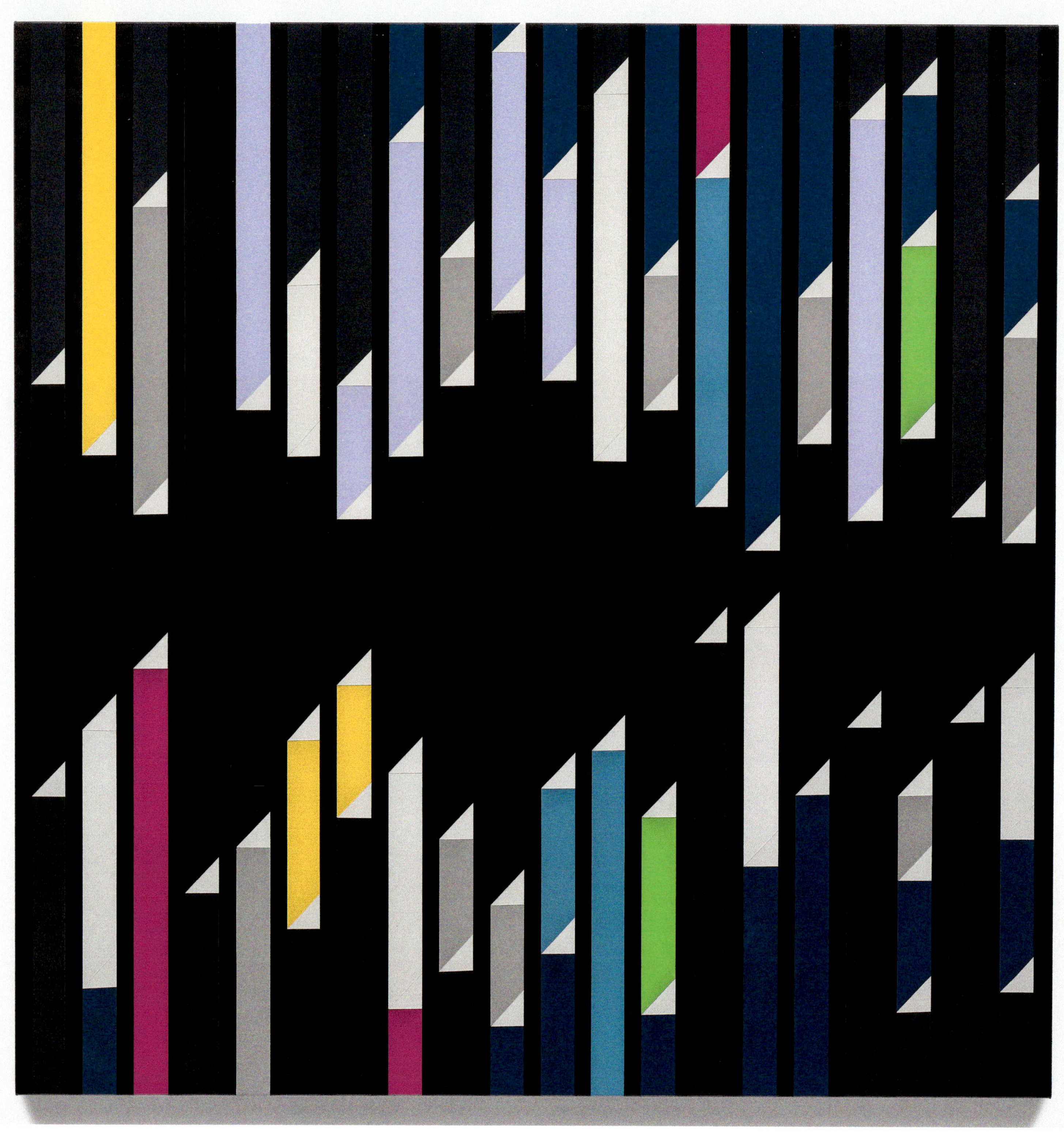

↑
Property Must Be Seen [Sound Graph], 2020

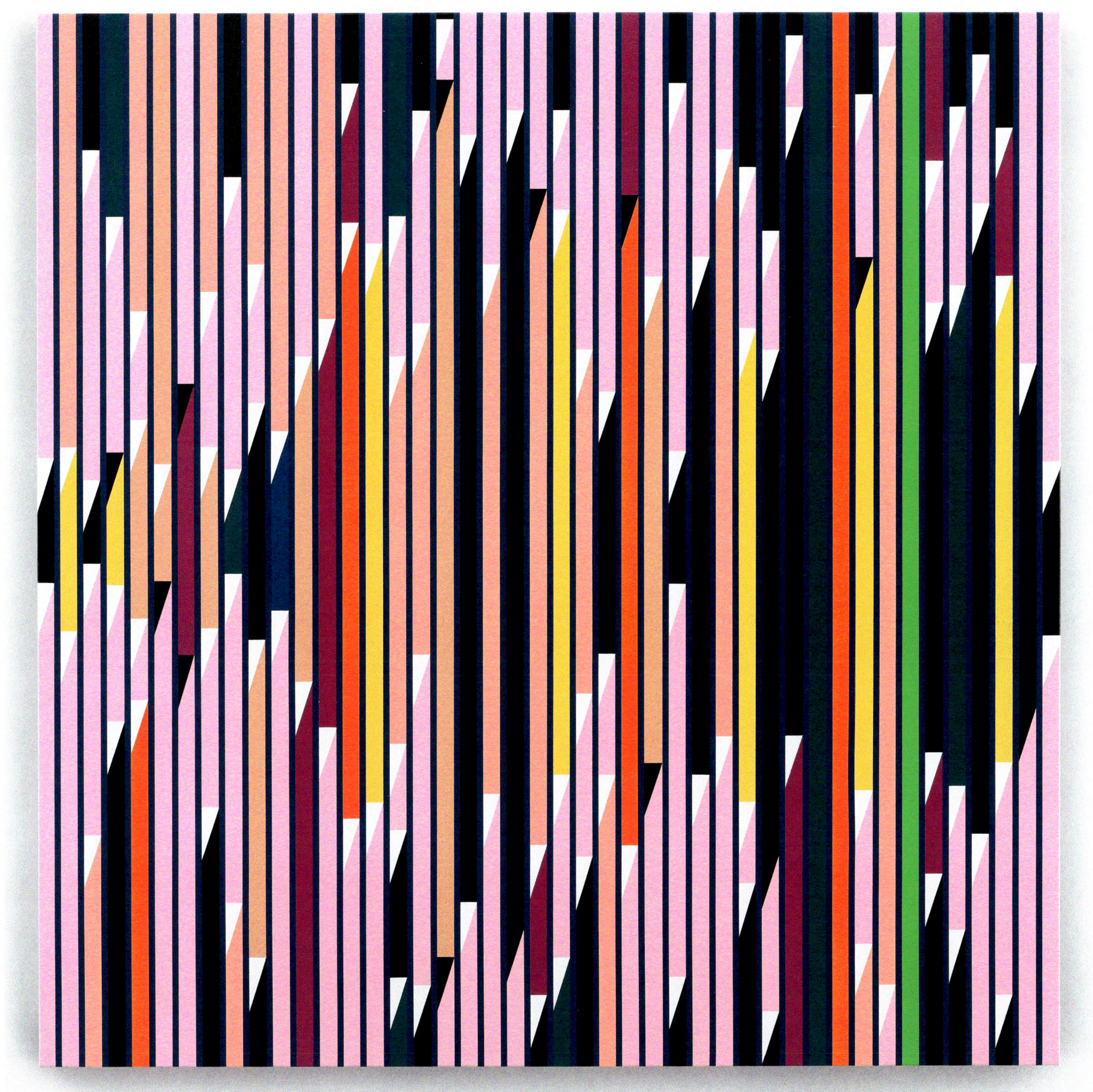

↑
You Cannot Keep Love [Sound Graph], 2020

Mimi Ọnụọha

b. 1989, Parma, Italy; lives and works in Brooklyn, NY

The Library of Missing Data Sets, 2016
Steel filing cabinet and folders
22 1/2 × 20 × 16 inches
Courtesy the artist

The Library of Missing Data Sets v 2.0, 2018
Powder-coated steel filing cabinet and folders
22 1/2 × 20 × 16 inches
Courtesy the artist

The Library of Missing Data Sets v 3.0, 2021
Steel filing cabinet and folders
18 1/2 × 15 3/8 × 19 3/4 inches
Courtesy the artist

In Absentia Series, 2019
Risograph print on paper, edition 1 of 3
Six prints, 20 1/4 × 14 1/4 inches each, framed
Courtesy the artist

Mimi Ọnụọha's practice focuses on the ramifications of hidden, repressed, or obfuscated information on society and situates the Black body squarely in relation to the ongoing technological revolution. She examines the relationships of organizing systems and practices that aim to codify society and the individuals who "fall between the margins or live between categories" of those systems. While data-collecting algorithms claim to provide comprehensive information, the vastness of knowledge hides data-driven forms of inequity in what Ọnụọha terms "algorithmic violence."[1] Revealing the conditions surrounding invisible data, she "aim[s] to trouble assumptions baked into the beliefs and technologies that mediate our existences."[2]

Ọnụọha's *The Library of Missing Data Sets* (2016–21) features three filing cabinets filled with empty file folders. Each folder is tabbed with labels such as "Publicly available gun trace data" and "Cause of June 2015 black church fires," challenging the notion of data as seamlessly complete bundles of information and bringing awareness to the repercussions of suppressed information that purposely lies hidden or untracked. Writer Nina Knaack describes this piece as "a tangible repository for the overlooked elements in a society saturated by uneven data and information poverty. It also implies that what we disregard divulges more than what we attend to."[3] The tactility of the viewer's rifling through the empty files physicalizes the sense of data that cannot be known.

In Absentia (2019) presents six risograph prints in the style of African American sociologist W. E. B. Du Bois's infographics that were presented at the Paris World's Fair of 1900. Ọnụọha visually quotes Du Bois's data visualization models to reference his comprehensive sociological research on Black rural life in Alabama from 1898 to 1905. Funded by the Department of Labor, the research was ultimately pulled from publication because it was deemed too controversial. *In Absentia* starts with this absence of tracked data and "asks what happens when data is made to disappear by those who seek to obscure the intertwined workings of racism and power."[4] As Ọnụọha states, "When structural workings of racism meet the distancing power of quantification, both combine to freeze us in place."[5]

Ọnụọha's current project, *Ground Truths* (2023–25), developed from the discovery of a mass grave in her hometown of Sugar Land, Texas. The remains of ninety-five people were traced to the violent nineteenth-century practice of convict leasing. Using information about the "Sugar Land 95" as a pattern rather than an isolated case, Ọnụọha developed a machine-learning model to determine which other counties across Texas contain convict-leasing–era mass burial sites. She is now creating a docu-fictional film about the project, interrogating the "structures of unknowability"[6] that allowed the grave to exist, unknown, for so long. –cv

→
The Library of Missing Data Sets v 2.0, 2018 (top), and detail of *The Library of Missing Data Sets*, 2016 (bottom)

1 Mimi Ọnụọha, "Notes on Algorithmic Violence," GitHub, published February 7, 2018, https://github.com/MimiỌnụọha/On-Algorithmic-Violence/.
2 Ọnụọha, "unofficial" bio on the artist's website, https://mimionuoha.com/about.
3 Nina Knaack, "The Artists Who Rewired Web2," Right Click Save, posted July 6, 2023, https://www.ninaknaack.com/blog/artists-who-rewired-web2.
4 "In Absentia (2019)," work description on artist's website, https://mimionuoha.com/in-absentia.
5 "Natural: or Where Are We Allowed To Be," work description on artist's website, https://mimionuoha.com/natural-where-are-we-allowed-to-be.
6 Ọnụọha, conversation with the author, November 2022.

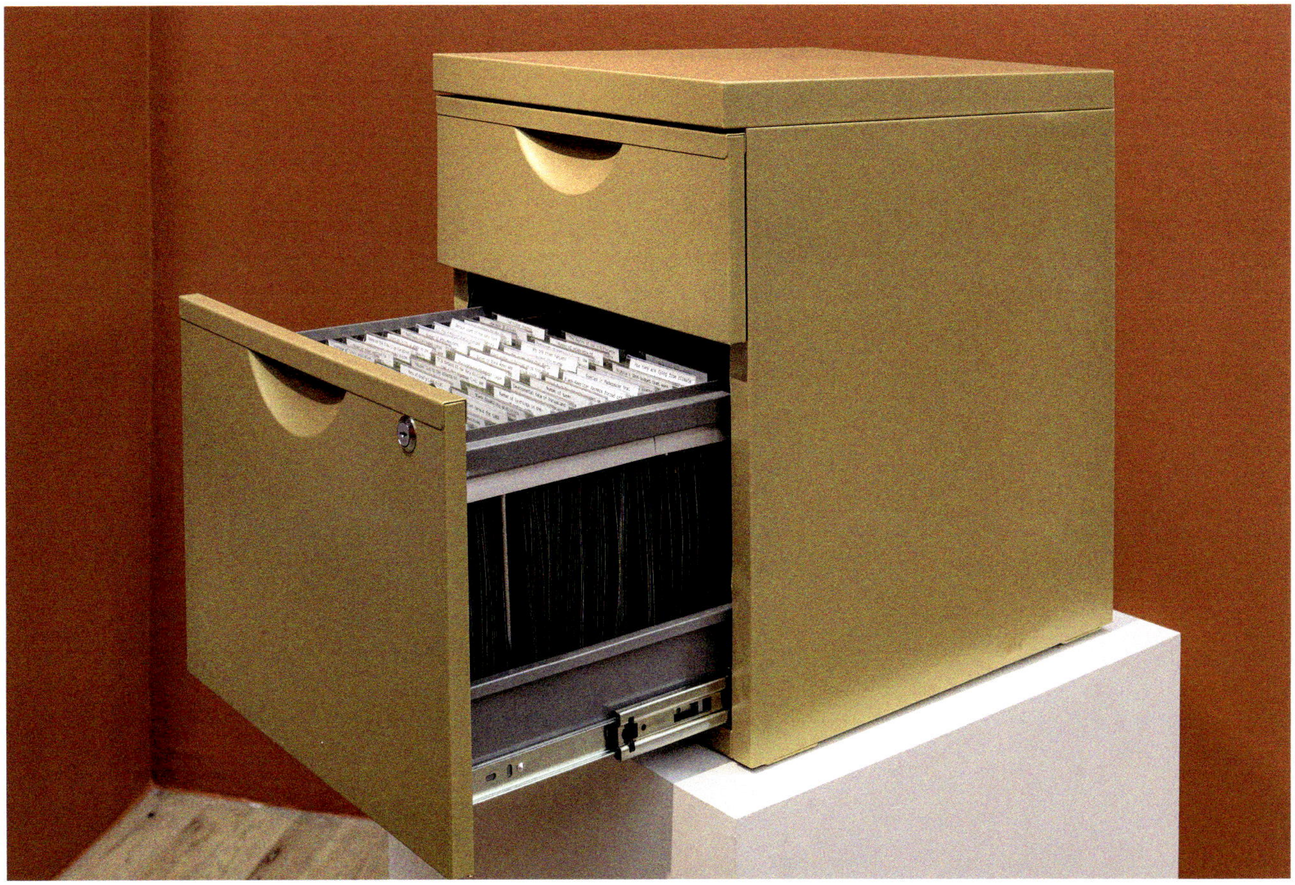

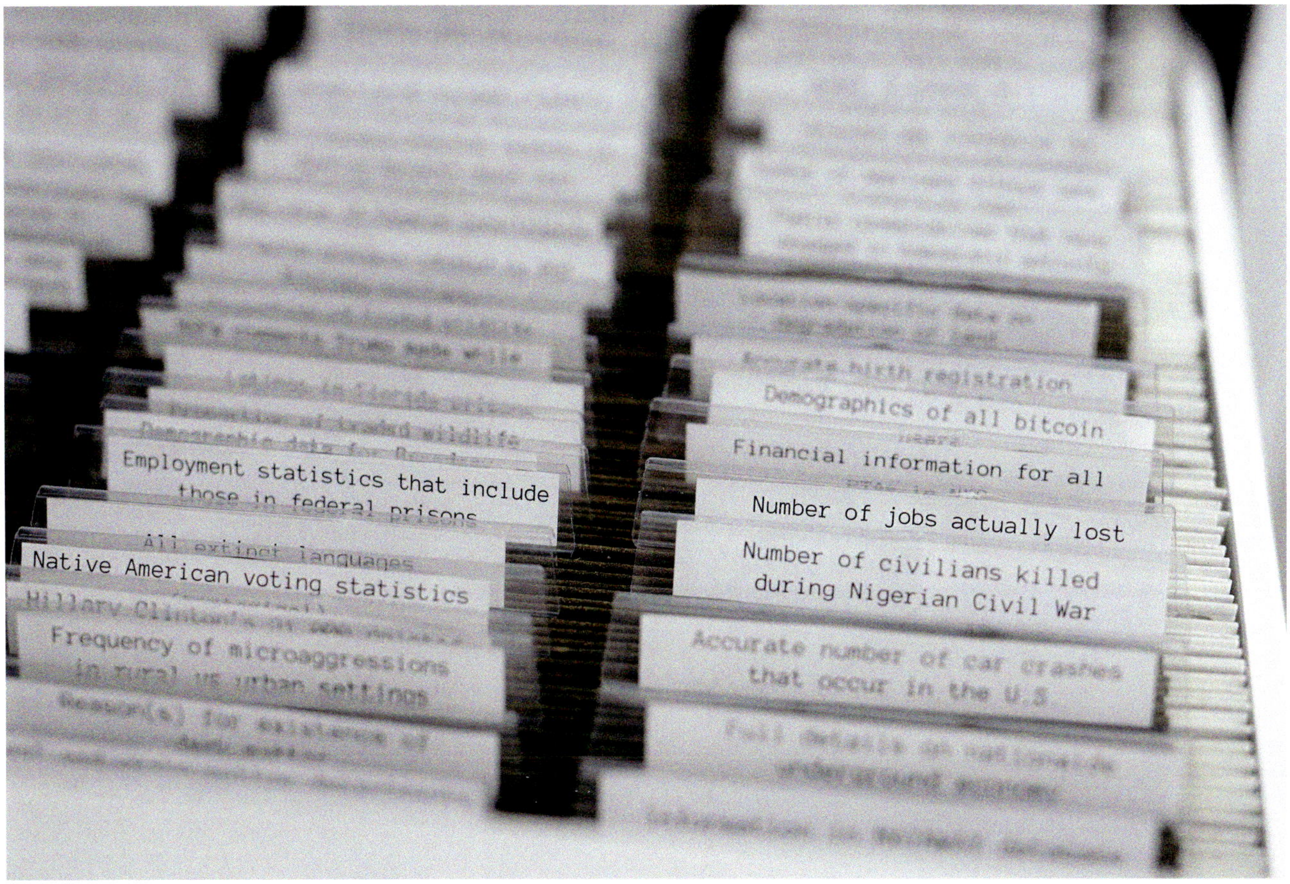

Employment statistics that include those in federal prisons
All extinct languages
Native American voting statistics
Frequency of microaggressions in rural vs urban settings
Demographics of all bitcoin users
Financial information for all
Number of jobs actually lost
Number of civilians killed during Nigerian Civil War
Accurate number of car crashes that occur in the U.S

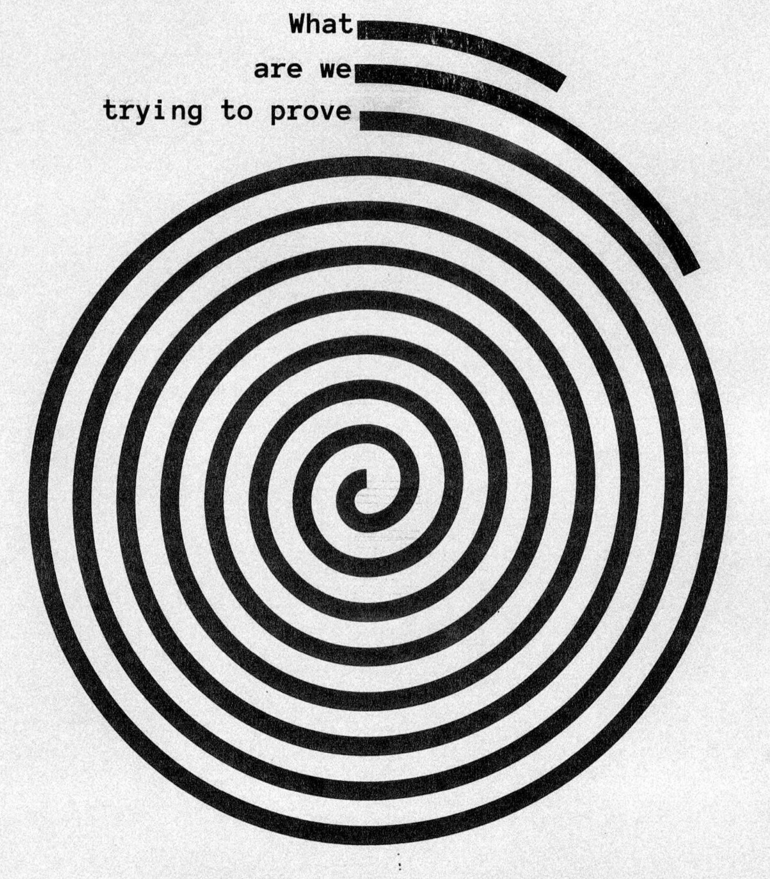

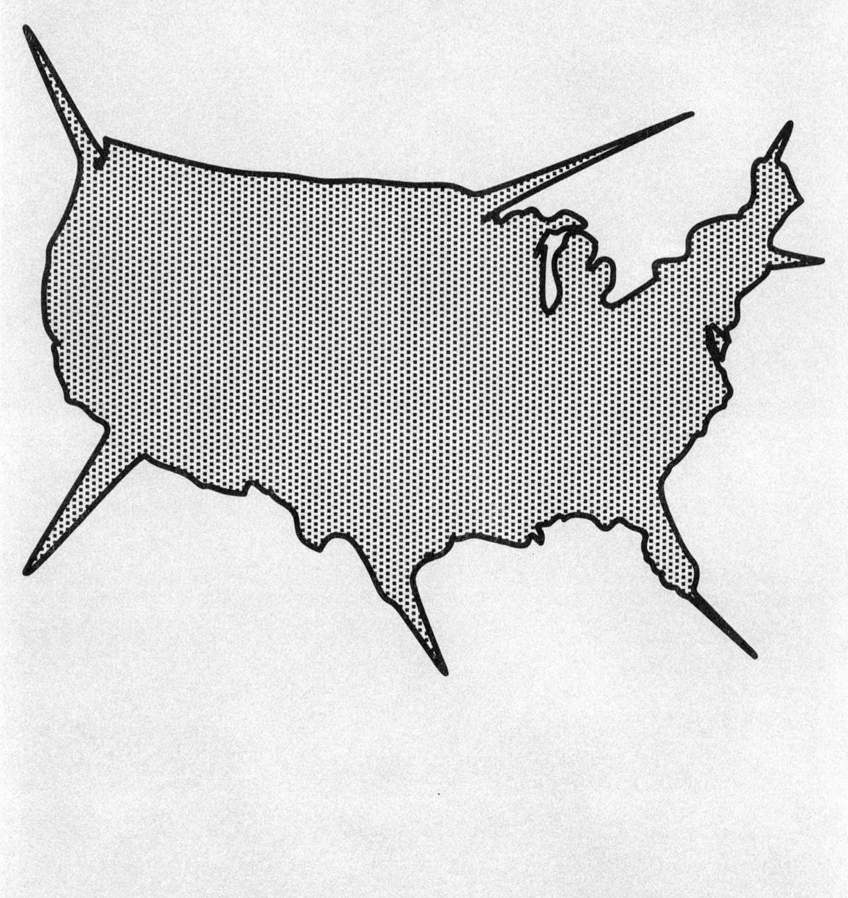

↑
In Absentia Series: The Great Impossibility (left) and *Geography of Domination* (right), 2019

It Could Never Be Large Enough

A space for truths that cannot be shown

This Land Is Your Land

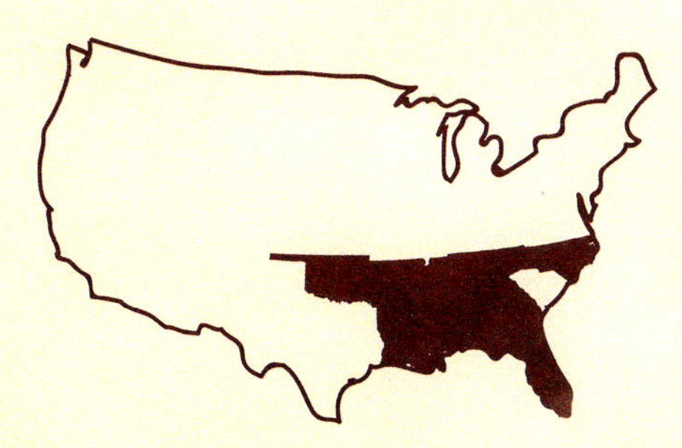

Indian
Removal
Act
1830

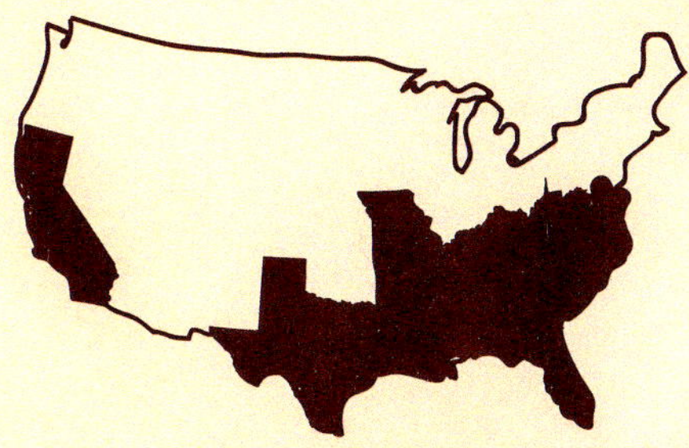

Convict
Leasing
1870

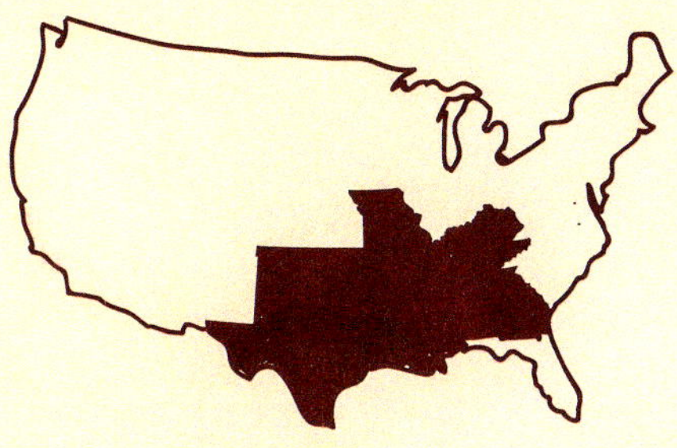

Highest
Incarceration
Rates
2019

↑
In Absentia Series: It Could Never Be Large Enough (left) and *This Land Is Your Land* (right), 2019

Semiconductor

Semiconductor (founded 1997, Brighton, UK)
Ruth Jarman (b. 1973, Southampton, UK; lives and works in Brighton, UK)
Joe Gerhardt (b. 1972, Oxford, UK; lives and works in Brighton, UK)

Spectral Constellations, 2022
Generative animations on LED mosaics
Three parts: 30 1/4 × 30 1/4 × 4 3/4 inches; 22 5/8 × 30 1/4 × 4 3/4 inches; and 30 1/4 × 22 5/8 × 4 3/4 inches
Courtesy the artists

Semiconductor, a collaboration between Ruth Jarman and Joe Gerhardt, explores ways of experiencing nature mediated through the languages of science and technology, often inspiring awe or wonder in viewers. For over twenty-five years these two artists have been collaborating with physicists and scientists around the world. Working in sound, film, installation, and sculpture, they have been at the forefront of data visualization since the early 2000s. They are particularly drawn to imperfections in the technological mediation between objects of study and the devices used to record data. Jarman once described their creative process as embracing "the errors, noise, or artefacts which are an ordinary part of the [scientific] capturing process as a way to remind us of the presence of a human observer."[1]

In 2018, Semiconductor presented the immersive, 360-degree installation *HALO* at Art Basel. The project was built on their 2015 artist residency at Switzerland's European Organization for Nuclear Research (CERN), home of the Large Hadron Collider and its ATLAS particle physics experiment, as well as their visit to Audemars Piguet, the famous Swiss watchmaker. HALO's cylinder structure featured a screen displaying animated graphics that triggered the array of 360 piano strings forming the outer wall of the sculpture. Data from sixty ATLAS collisions, which happen close to the speed of light, was used to program the visual display as well as the small hammers striking the piano strings to create sounds. Mónica Bello, the head of arts at CERN who curated the project, describes *HALO* as diving "into another reality. In a way, it's a time machine ... that confronts us with the paradox of time as a social construct."[2]

For the series of LED mosaics *Spectral Constellations* (2022) included in *Seeing the Unseeable*, Jarman and Gerhardt used data gathered from three young stars. The work employs spectroscopic readings of the light wavelengths from each of the stars "as a physical material, translating it into rings of light which resemble the gradated discs of planetary and stellar formations."[3] The mosaics not only animate light that we would not be able to see but also bring attention to how light interacts with matter. The colored LED lights pulsate and change in spherical forms in a series of generative animations, creating an almost hypnotizing effect. As astro-physicist Dr. Aurora Sicilica-Aguilar explained, the data from these young stars would have been overlooked, as scientists were originally looking for planets but could not see them through the "mess" of pulsating energy from the young stars.[4] With *Spectral Constellations*, Semiconductor emphasizes the consideration of data that is often overlooked, using this aesthetic material in their works to evoke the sublime of the unseeable in nature. —FW

1 Richard Bright, "Exploring the Material Nature of Our World and How We Experience It; Interview with Richard Bright, Ruth Jarman and Joe Gerhardt," *Interalia Magazine*, July 2019.
2 Taylor Dafoe, "How Artist Duo Semiconductor Turned Subatomic Data Into a 'Chiming Time Sculpture' for Art Basel," Artnet, June 13, 2018, https://news.artnet.com/art-world/semiconductor-audemars-piguet-1300586.
3 Semiconductor, text about *Spectral Constellations* (2022) on the artists' website, https://semiconductorfilms.com/art/spectral-constellations/.
4 Semiconductor, film about *Spectal Constellations* on the artists' website, https://semiconductorfilms.com/art/spectral-constellations/.

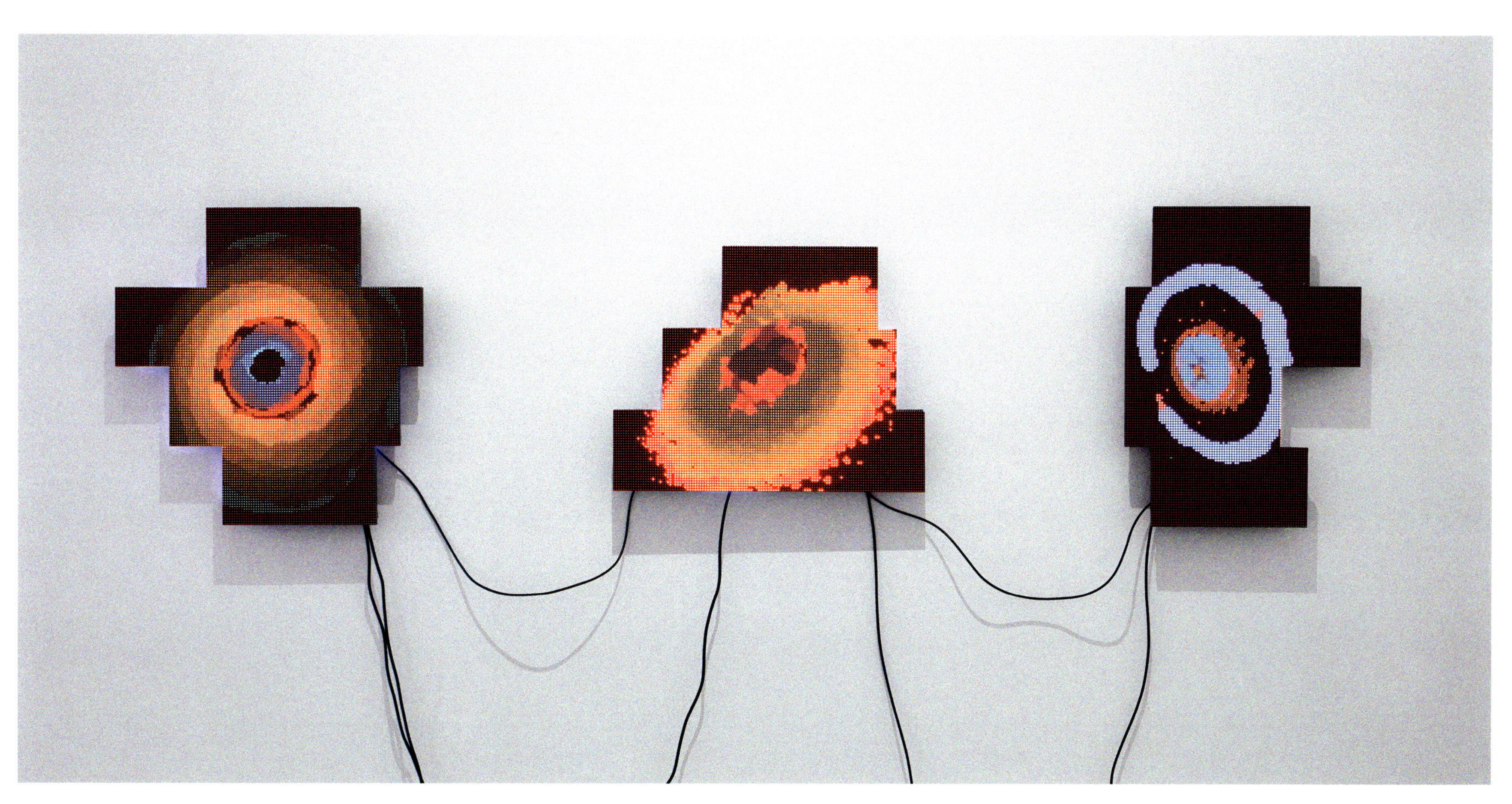

↑
Spectral Constellations, 2022

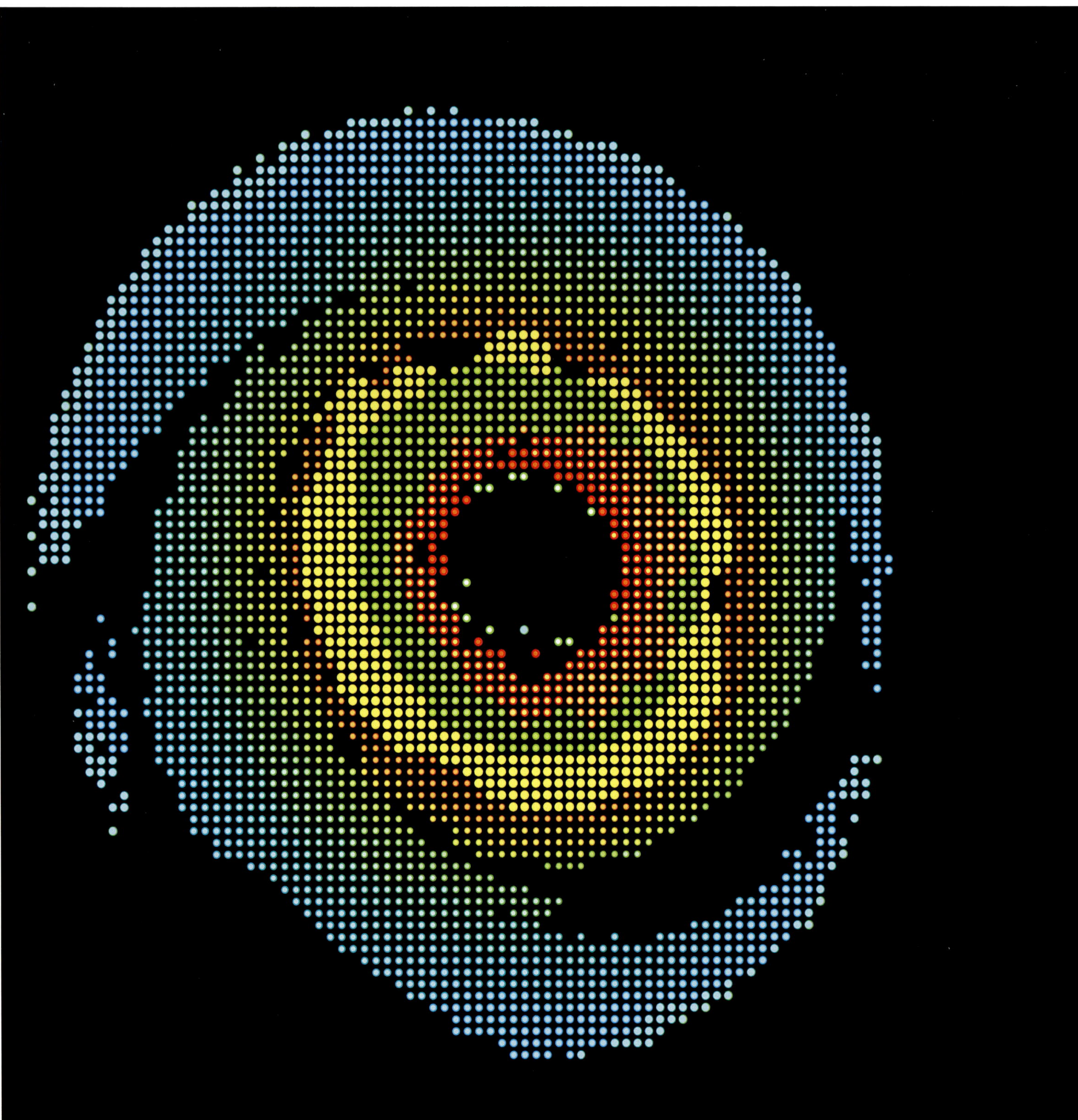

↗
Details of *Spectral Constellations*, 2022

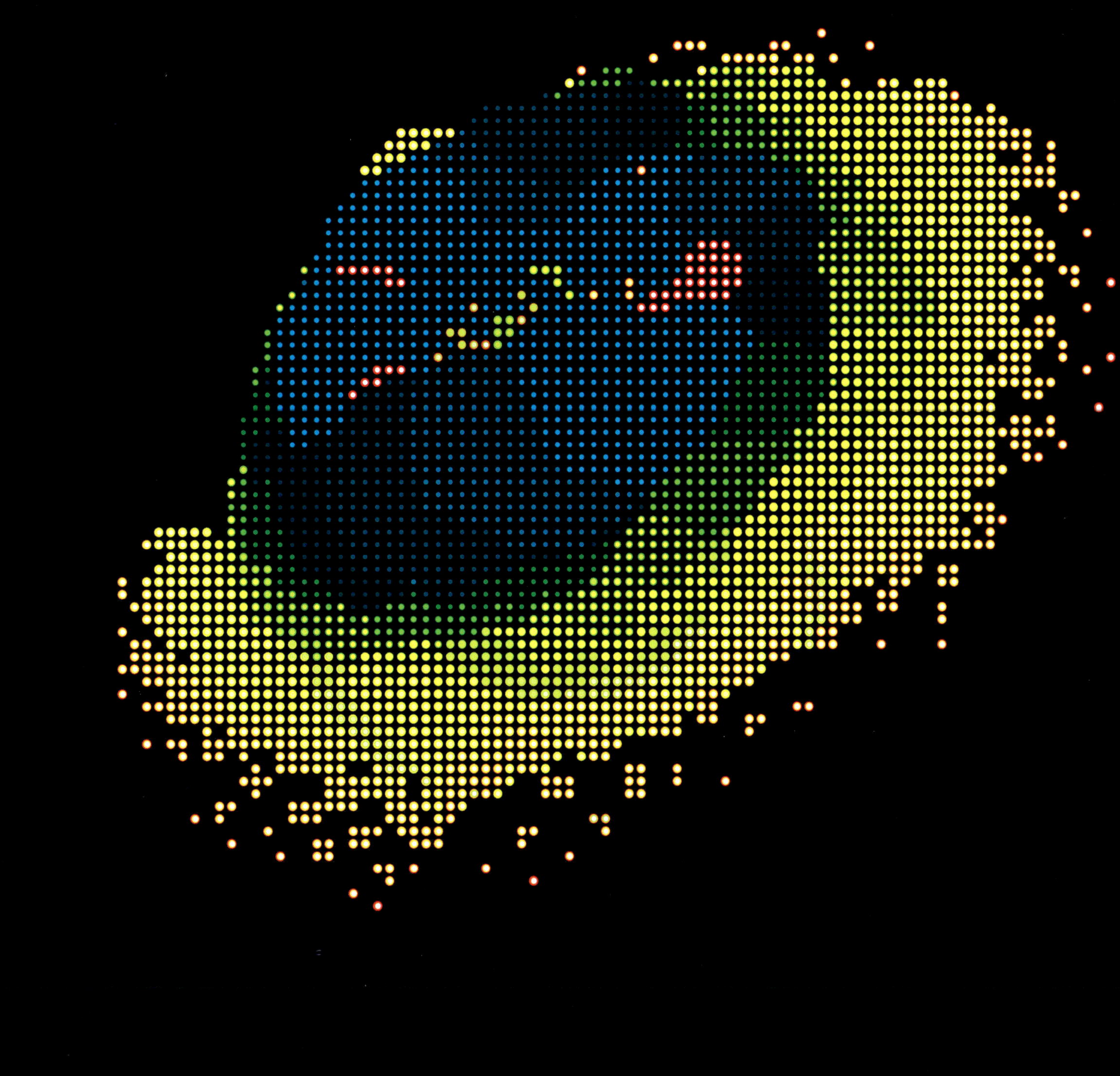

Hyojung Seo

b. Seoul, 1972; lives and works in Seoul

Singapore Weather Data Drawing: Windspeed, 2022
Video
24 second loop
Courtesy the artist

Singapore Weather Data Drawing: Wind Direction, 2022
Video
24 second loop
Courtesy the artist

Singapore Weather Data Drawing: Temperature, 2022
Video
24 second loop
Courtesy the artist

We live in the age of metadata, where the breadth of information is so vast that it becomes untenable and abstract. For digital artist and designer Hyojung Seo, this condition has provided an opportunity to transform data into an artistic medium: "I believe that as digital production technologies become more advanced, new forms of artwork will emerge and blur the lines between digital and physical artworks, broadening access to art and allowing people to experience it in various ways."[1] Her video series *Singapore Weather Data Drawing* reconsiders data visualization, broadening its mission to reinterpret data for a more playful and evocative understanding. While they generally represent information, the videos also stand as abstract digital artworks and propose an alternate avenue of understanding data.

Considered by the artist as a natural portrait of Singapore, the works translate weather data over five years (2018–22). What is singular about Seo's drawing method is her use of digital industry tools for alternative means. For this series of data drawings, the artist used Perlin noise, an algorithm often used to create organic textures in digital games and effects. Seo's experimentation with the algorithm to create abstract imagery is indicative of a larger cultural shift in how the creative community is reconsidering the use of data. Additionally, her use of the term "drawing" to indicate the aesthetic framework from which to consider the images opens ways of seeing data as an artform.

Three works from the series form a digital triptych in this exhibition; installed across three monitors, each one presents wind data across Singapore. The movement within each video is determined by the collected data, which is fed through Perlin noise to reinterpret the wind in a more whimsical and experiential manner. Each piece conveys its subject through a playful design, such as undulating lines resembling a swaying horizontal bar graph (*Windspeed*), spiky sea urchin–like patterns that retract and extend their spines as they move across the monitor (*Temperature*), and windmilling lines dotted across horizontal graphs to resemble a dancing musical score (*Wind Direction*).[2] This visual loosening of data presents weather statistics through a visual *feel* rather than more conventional data visualization design, evoking billowing bedsheets drying on a clothesline or the tickling sensation as a breeze moves over skin. The movement and shapes designed by Seo expand comprehension of the information as living, organic forms and provide an alternate means of interacting with data in our lives, not just as aggregate information for utilitarian use but as a visual experience that opens the possibility of data and coding as "an invisible experience itself [that] could become a new art form."[3] –cv

1 Instagrafite and Seohyo, "Seo Hyojung is a South Korean artist who works with technology and movement," image 6, Instagram post, May 2, 2024, https://www.instagram.com/p/C6fXBqJLUK-/.
2 In *Windspeed*, the length of each rectangular bar represents speed. Each urchin-like form in *Temperature* represents data over a ninety-day period, with the spines illustrating the highest temperature of the day. In *Wind Direction*, the angle of the lines when stilled represent the primary wind direction of the day, while the thickness of the lines indicate the strength of the wind speed.
3 Instagrafite and Seohyo, "Seo Hyojung," Instagram post, May 2, 2024, image 2, https://www.instagram.com/instagrafite/p/C6fXBqJLUK-/?img_index=1.

→
Detail of still from *Singapore Weather Data Drawing: Wind Direction*, 2022

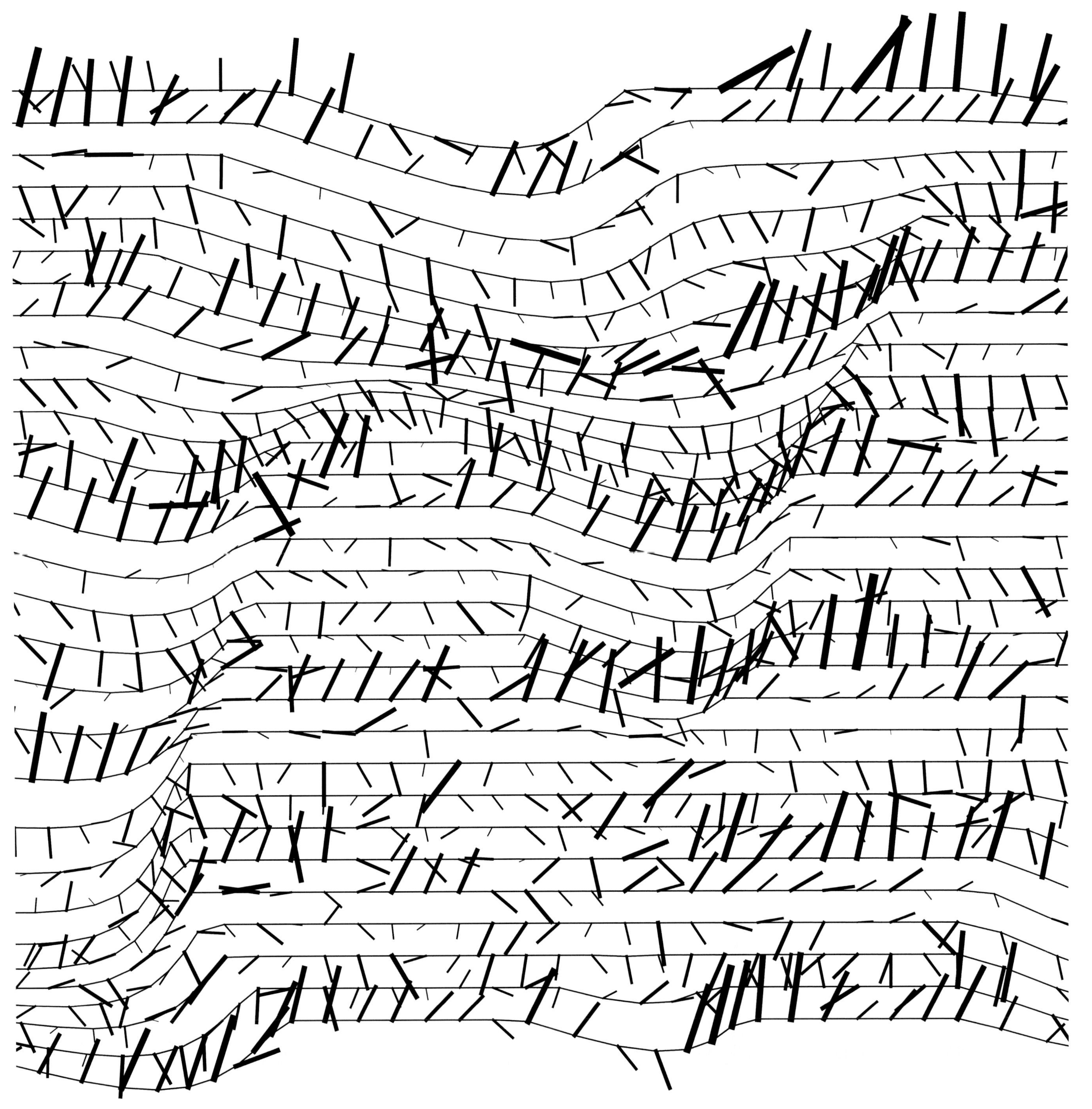

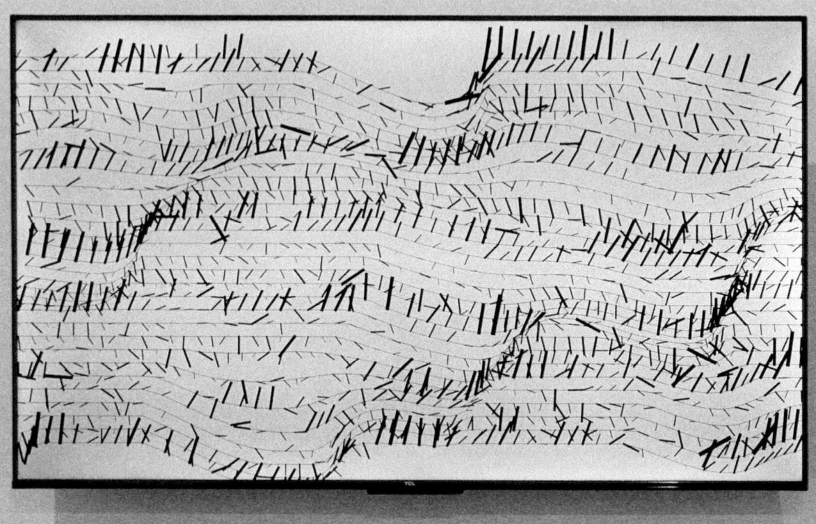

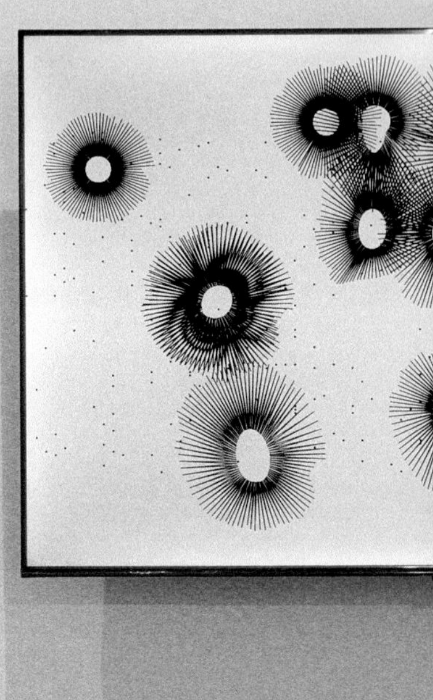

↑
From left to right: *Singapore Weather Data Drawing: Wind Direction*, *Temperature*, and *Windspeed*, 2022

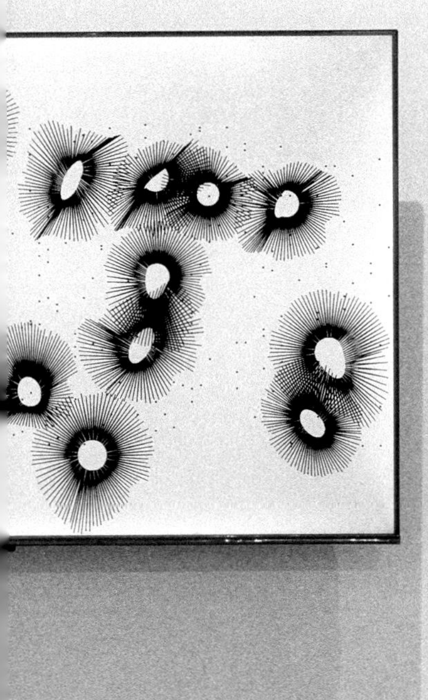

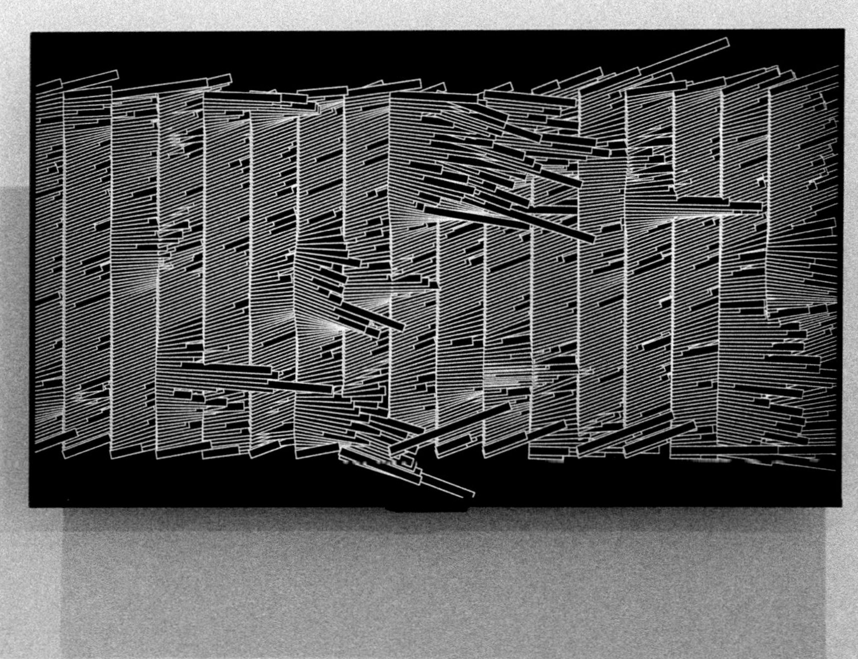

Linnéa Gabriella Spransy

b. 1976, Oconomowoc, WI; lives and works in Los Angeles

Prime Mover, 2019
Acrylic on canvas
84 × 132 × 3 inches
Courtesy of the artist

Prime Mover 0, 2023
Acrylic on canvas
84 × 132 × 3 inches
Courtesy of the artist

→
Prime Mover 0, 2023 (top), and *Prime Mover*, 2019 (bottom)

Described by the artist as "procedural abstractions," the works in this exhibition by Linnéa Gabriella Spransy present an alternative to what can be considered as data-driven art. While terms such as data and generative art are often used to describe digital-based imagery, the artist's painting method goes to the heart of data and data visualization: number patterns. Spransy considers number patterns, such as the Fibonacci sequence that can found in nature, an essential aspect of our visual constructs. As the artist states, "Humans are code-finders. We search for patterns. We give them names. The naming of the thing makes it visible. Naming brings about realities. Language is powerful and dangerous for artists, who always flirt on the outskirts of recognition."[1]

In her *Prime Mover* painting series, Spransy visualizes an intimate working relationship between artist and numbers. The paintings have a structural framework of lines patterned by prime number sequences. Solid lines are painted to represent the first five prime numbers (2, 3, 5, 7, and 11). From this accumulated form on the canvas, the chaotic environment in which the pattern is forced to grow is laid down. After the paint dries, she starts another pattern of prime numbers that grows around and within these intrusions. This push and pull of structure and chaos creates a field of balance and counterbalance, an ebb and flow between the artist and the numbers. This constancy of patterning through prime numbers elicits a personification of the digits as they adapt, move, and reconstitute.

Spransy approaches numbers as somewhat alive, on their own terms. As writer Brian Volck describes, "She compares this to the life of a forest that is devastated by wildfire, grows back, and then is flooded, only to grow once again. As a biological system, the forest strives to maintain its integrity, responding as it can to changing and periodically cataclysmic environmental factors."[2] The artist further elucidated this parallel of numbers to organic forms in a series of drawings on mylar. The *Mylar Drawings* are constructed along similar prime number patterns that accumulate and grow into branch-like forms from a spinelike column (the origin points of the number sequence). The artist cuts around these branches and, as the mylar naturally curls inward, the work takes on the shape of an oceanic life form, its unfurling edges left to freely hang along its support.

Both the *Mylar Drawings* and *Prime Mover* works reveal characteristics in the number patterns that surround us but go unnoticed. Our world evolves through numbers; patterns lie at the foundation of everything. While Spransy's work lies in some ways at the edges of what is traditionally construed as data, her investment in number patterns goes to data's core. –cv

1 Brian Volck, "System and Chaos: The Art of Linnéa Spransy," *Image*, no. 89 (Summer 2016), https://imagejournal.org/article/system-chaos-art-linnea-spransy/.
2 Volck, "System and Chaos."

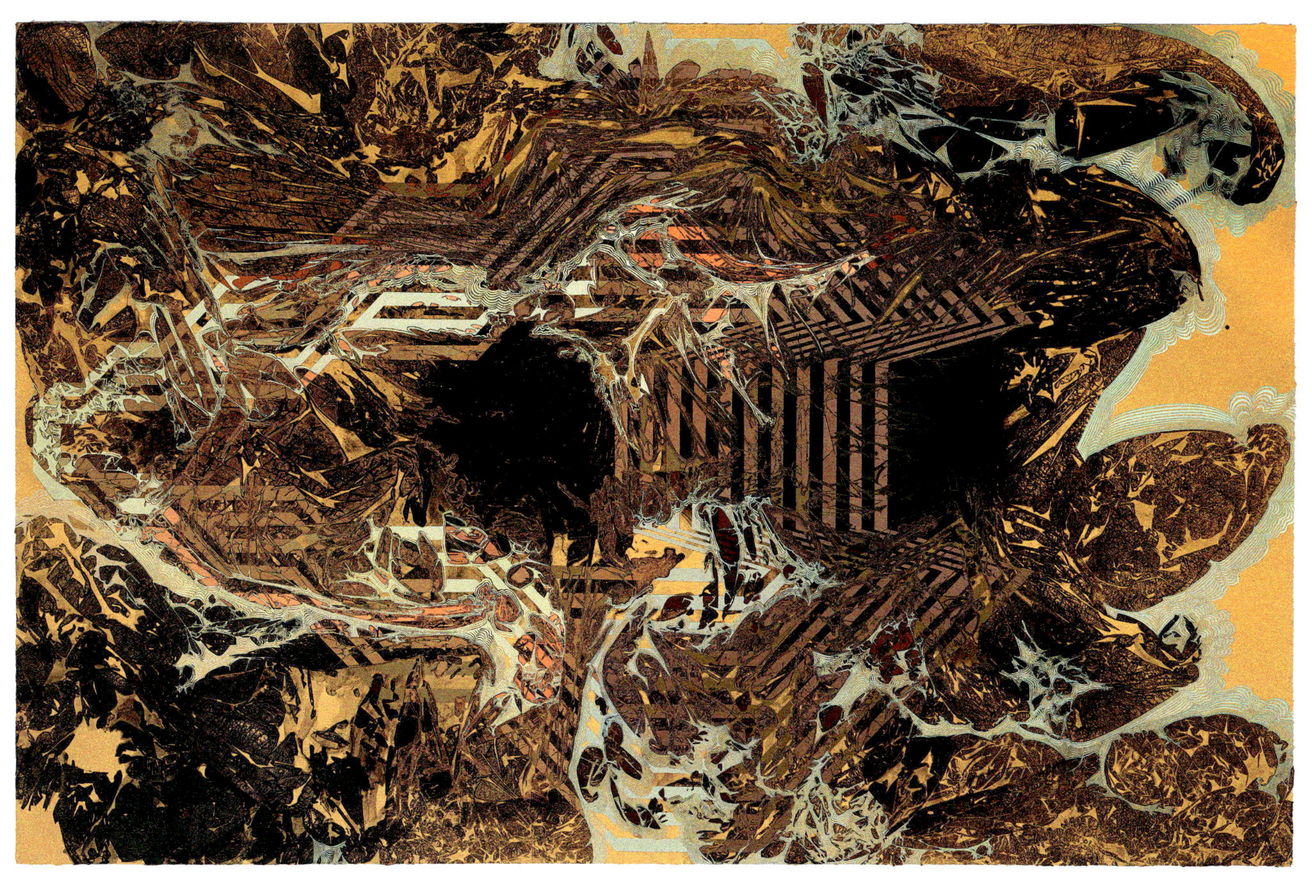

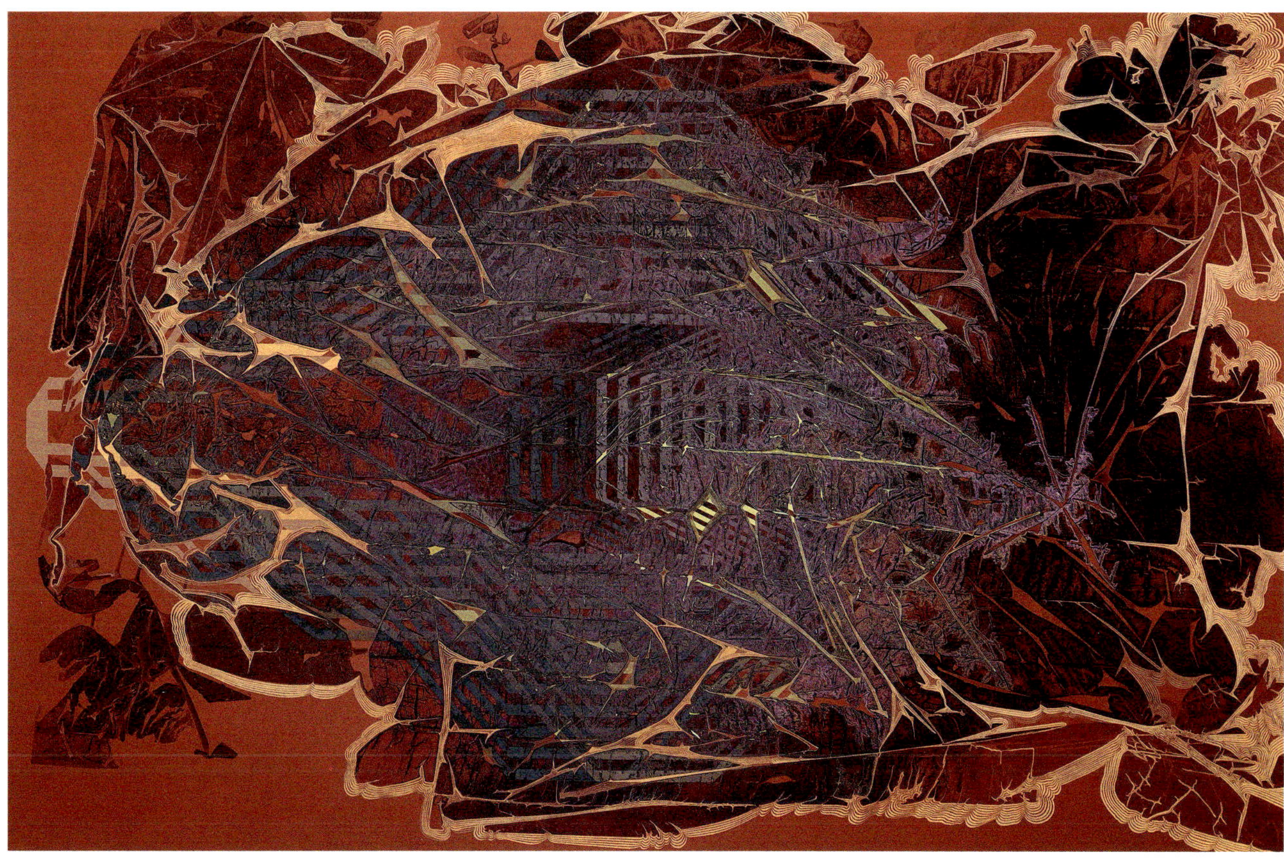

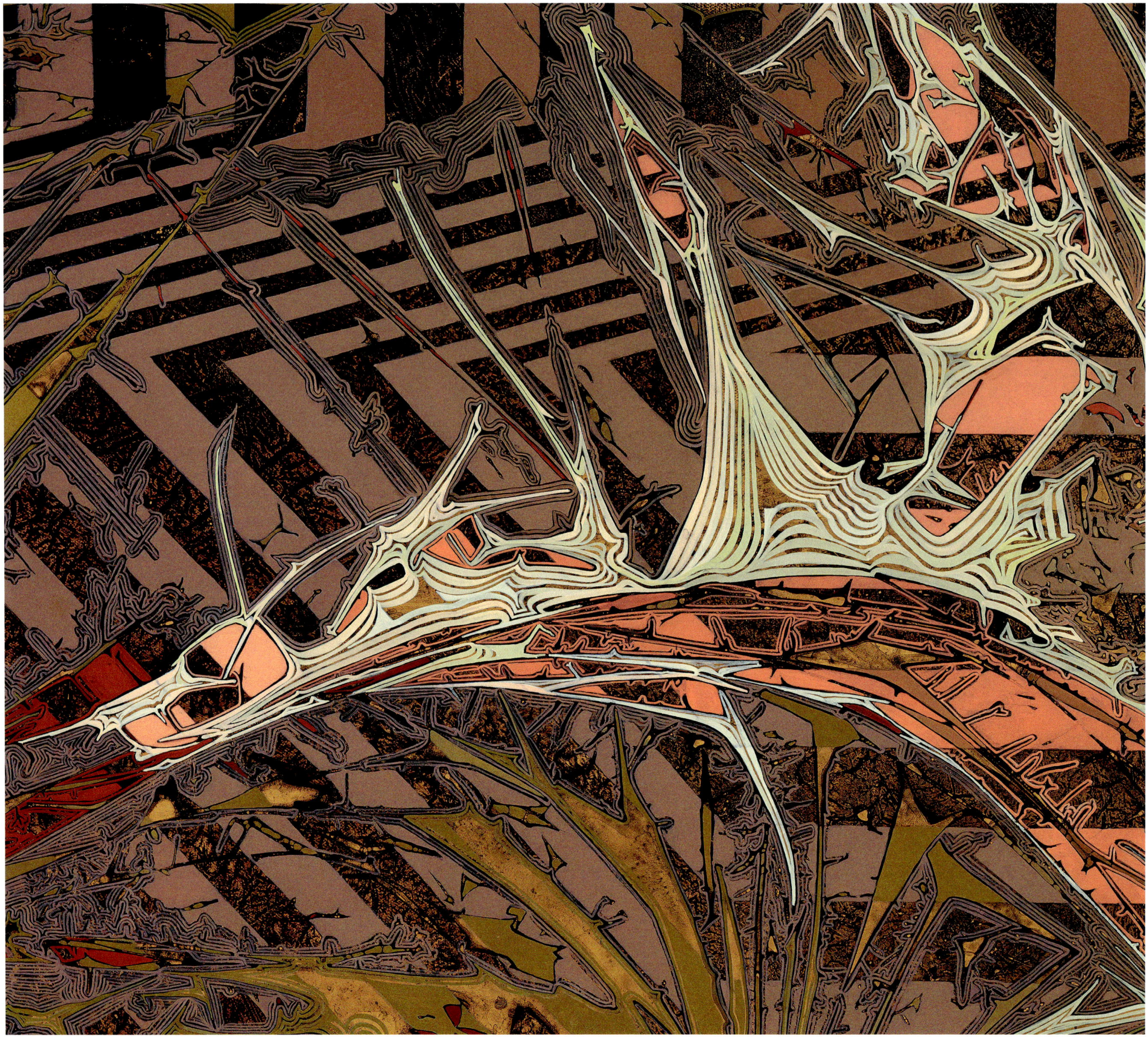

↑
Detail of *Prime Mover 0*, 2023

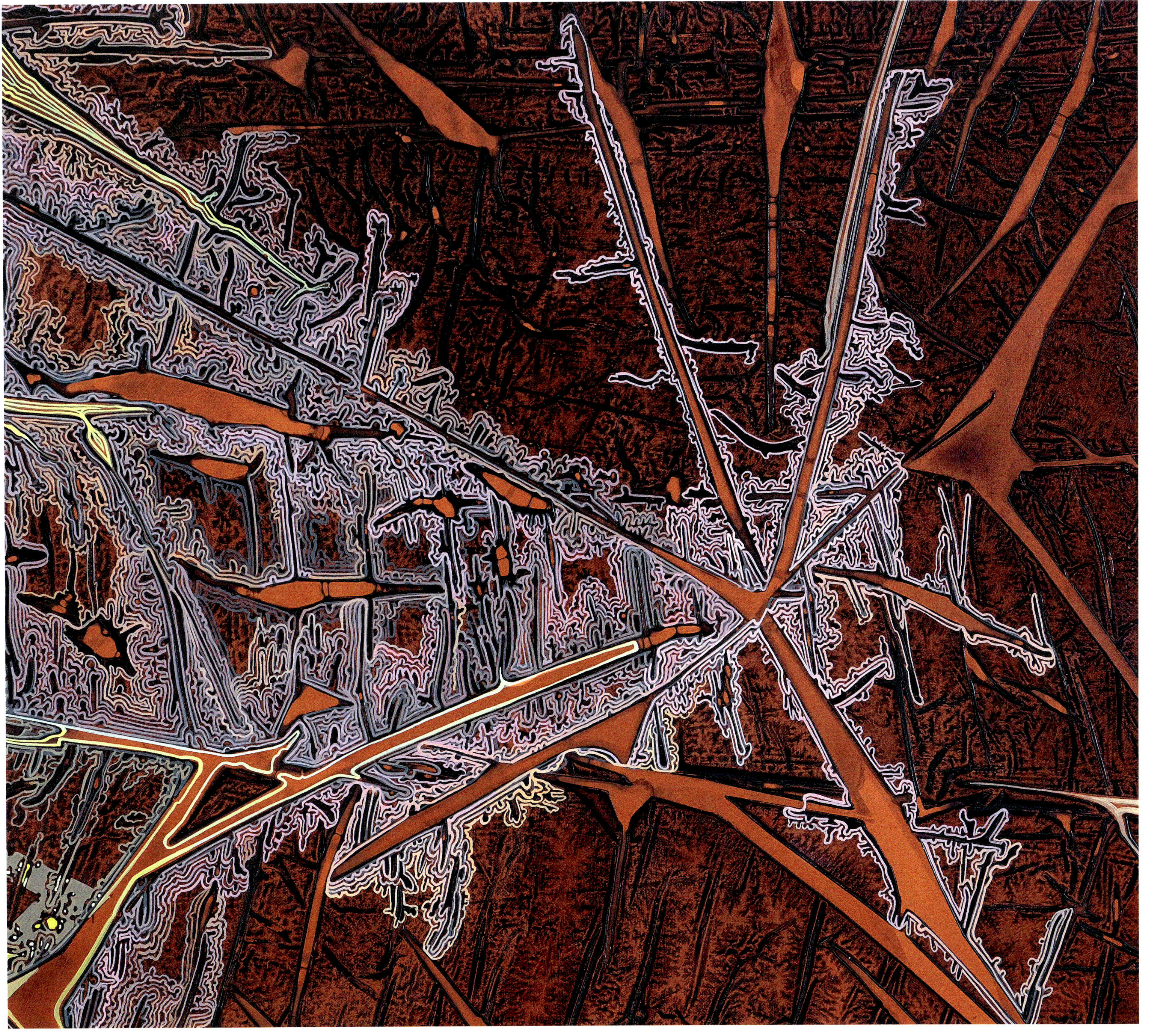

↑
Detail of *Prime Mover*, 2019

Mika Tajima

b. Los Angeles, 1975; lives and works in New York

Archive of Feelings (January 1, 2023, United States of America) #127, Los Angeles, 2023
Non-fungible token
24 seconds
Courtesy of Mika Tajima, Proof, and Pace Gallery

Archive of Feelings (January 1, 2023, United States of America) #142, Memphis, 2023
Non-fungible token
24 seconds
Courtesy of Mika Tajima, Proof, and Pace Gallery

Archive of Feelings (January 1, 2023, United States of America) #144, New York City, 2023
Non-fungible token
24 seconds
Courtesy of Mika Tajima, Proof, and Pace Gallery

Mika Tajima has long examined the intersection of humans and technology, from tracing the role of human labor in digital technology to investigating the forms and collection of psychographic data.[1] Her multidisciplinary art practice leans toward a form of intervention as she reframes our relationship to technology through unconventional means. Her digital work *Archive of Feelings (January 1, 2023, United States of America)* addresses twin aspects of data: its intangibility (especially as it becomes more abstract due to its propensity to metastasize) and the very real ways it impacts society and our lives. Presented in this exhibition as a video series, the works were originally produced as non-fungible tokens (NFTs).[2]

Archive of Feelings developed out of Tajima's *Human Synth* series (2019), which uses a custom sentiment-analysis algorithm to process text-based social media data into ephemeral, undulating plumes of digital smoke. These works capture data from X (formerly Twitter) feeds for emotive expressions shared at a specific time, date, and location, generating a form of data visualization that leaves open interpretive possibilities. The data hidden within the smoke trail resists the usefulness that is often prized in monetization strategies, and that refusal leaves the work open to examine "the ways that, as data is increasingly customized, the boundaries of agency, identity, and privacy are obscured."[3]

Archive of Feelings captures emotive, text-based data from three cities—New York, Memphis, Los Angeles—posted on the eve of 2023 and reconstitutes them into aggregated sentiment, each region represented by a digitally animated column of smoke that sensuously dances in vibrant colors. Presented on monitors for this exhibition, the work offers a time capsule snapshot, arresting the fleeting nature of social media "tweets" while also providing a sense of the heightened emotions that characterize New Year's Eve, the quintessential signifier of endings and new beginnings. As Tajima explained, "I think of mood as a medium itself and data is an abstraction of that. I am interested in how our senses and psyche are targeted, whether this is through the physical, visual and spatial or through new forms of technology that are ubiquitous in our daily lives."[4]

By using the data that is collected by corporations and the consumer algorithms to induce individuals to view, purchase, and invest in their brands, Tajima simultaneously presents a critique and a reflection of our human condition in this postcapitalist age of mass consumerism. The very thing that in many ways reduces us as consumers is what the artist uses to reclaim our humanity; emotive words shared across social media, which are harvested and used in many ways to further our compulsive buying sprees, are conveyed in a metaphorical transitional state—undulating plumes of smoke that are at once sensual and fragile. –cv

→
Still from *Archive of Feelings (January 1, 2023, United States of America) #127, Los Angeles*, 2023

1 Psychographic data is the information that describes an individual's lifestyle, values, and personality traits, which is especially valuable to corporations in grouping people into consumer categories and tracking their online habits.
2 These short videos gifs are sold through a collaborative agreement between Pace Verso (the digital art subset of Pace Gallery) and Proof, a leading NFT art-collecting community. As NFTs, one thousand *Archive of Feelings* gifs were available for purchase.
3 Mika Yoshitake, "Mika Tajima," Pace Gallery website, www.pacegallery.com/artists/mika-tajima/.
4 Christa Terry, "Mood Is Her Medium," *The Observer*, January 9, 2024, https://observer.com/2024/01/mood-is-her-medium-mika-tajima/.

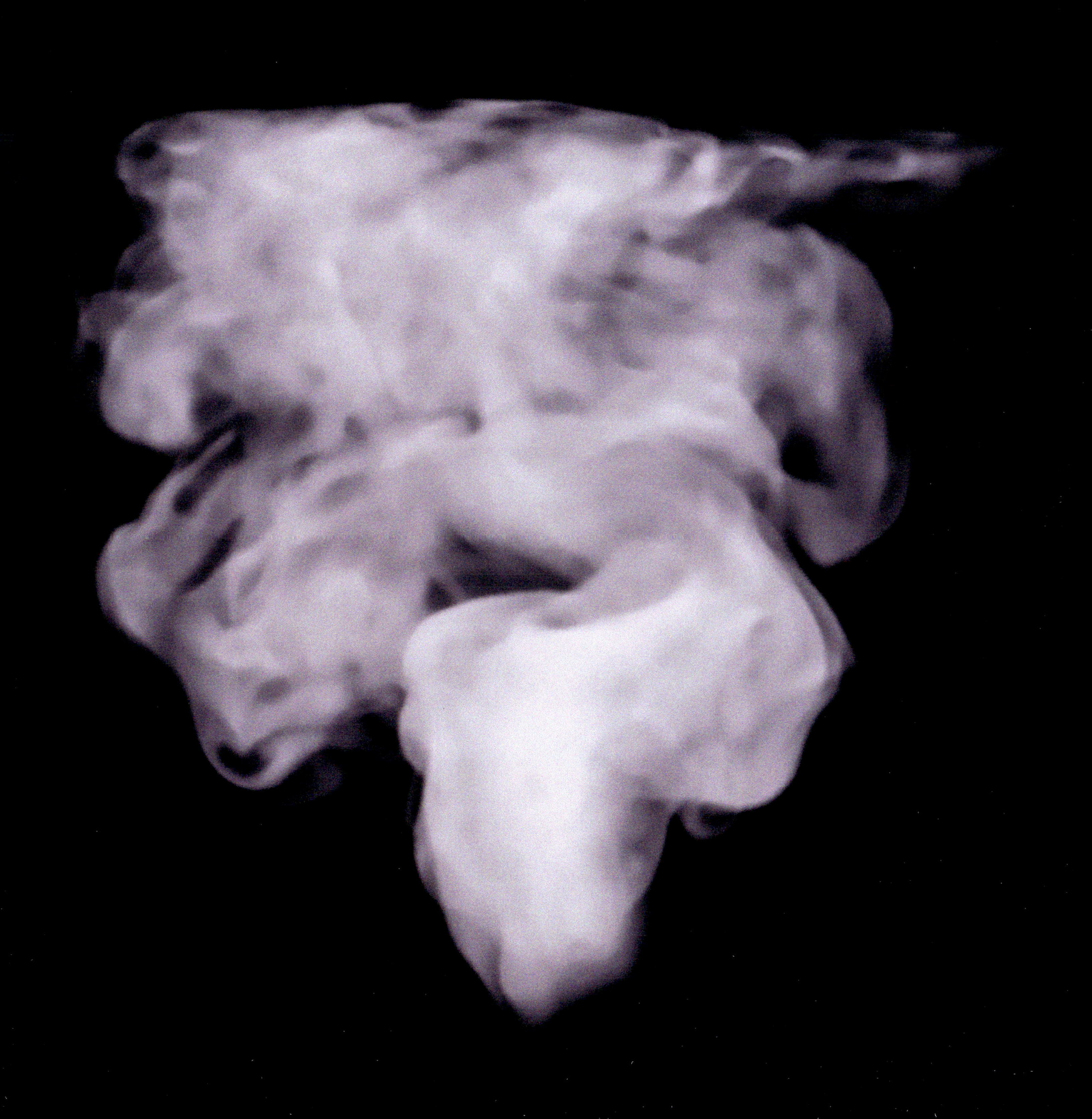

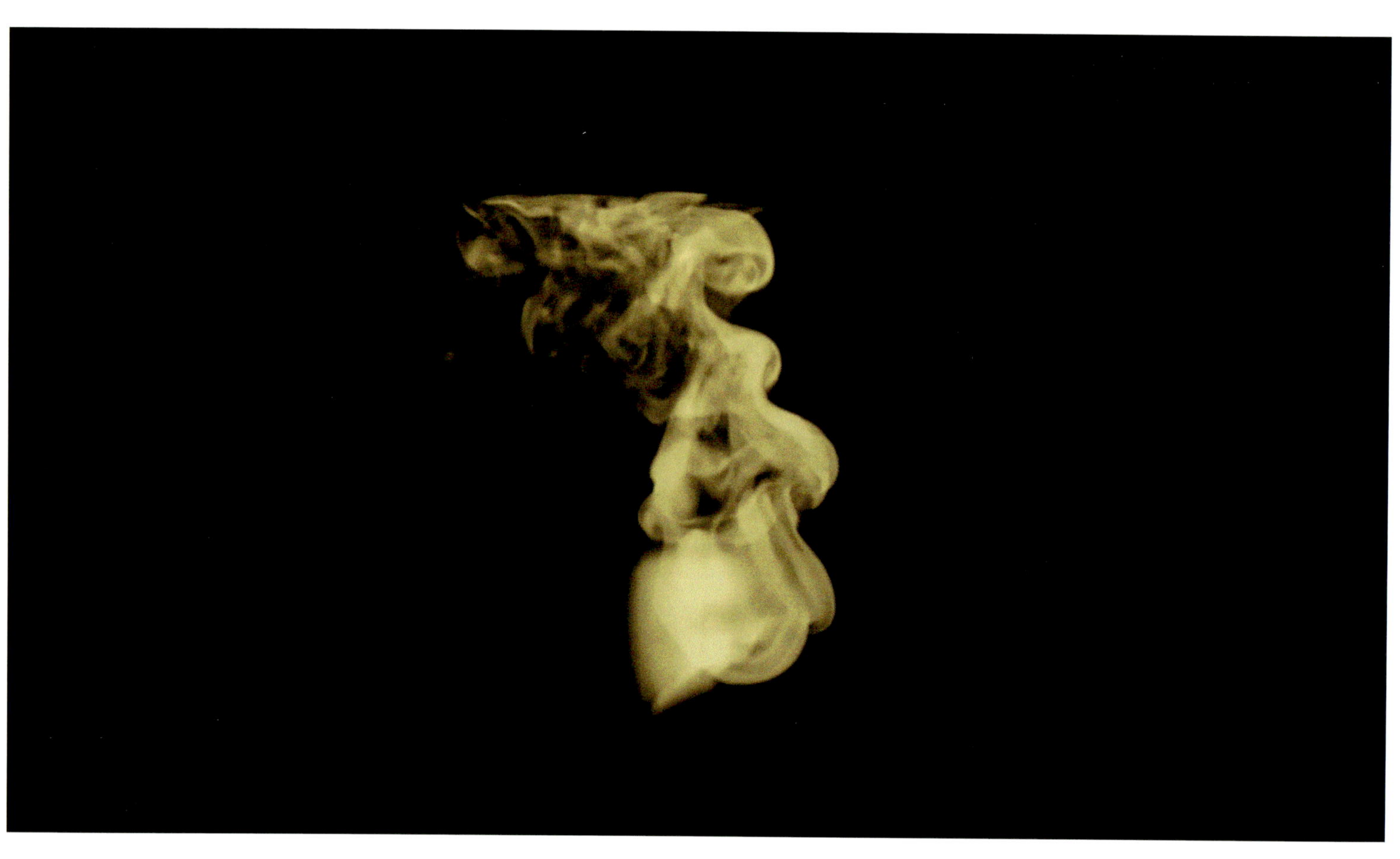

↑
Still from *Archive of Feelings (January 1, 2023, United States of America) #142, Memphis*, 2023

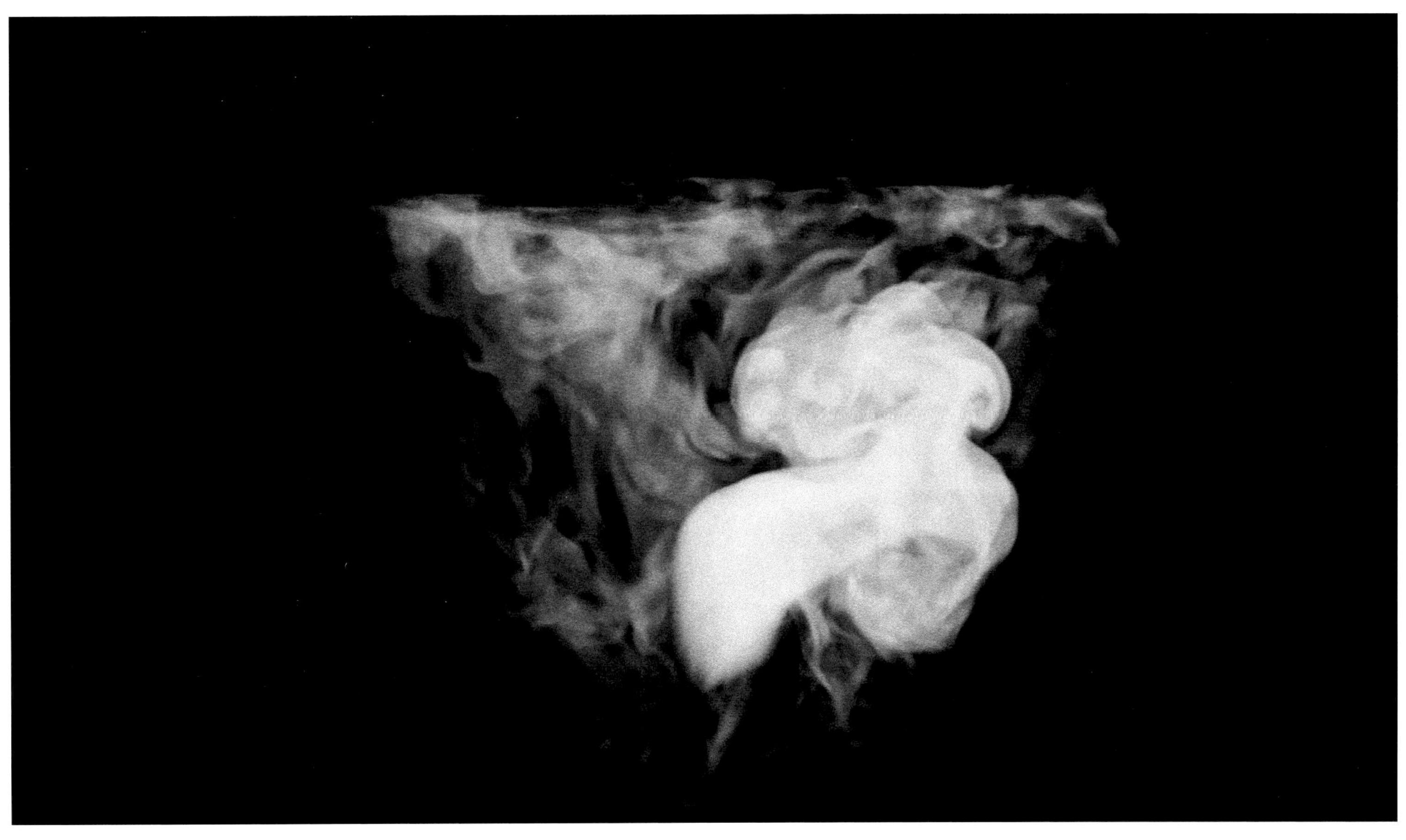

↑
Still from *Archive of Feelings (January 1, 2023, United States of America) #144, New York City*, 2023

Fernanda Viégas Martin Wattenberg

Fernanda Bertini Viégas (b. 1971, São Paulo, Brazil; works in Boston and Cambridge, MA)
Martin Wattenberg (b. 1970, Newton, MA; works in Boston and Cambridge, MA)

Wind Map, 2012
Projection interactive map
Dimensions variable
Courtesy the artists

→
Detail of still from *Wind Map*, 2012

Fernanda Viégas and Martin Wattenberg are important forerunners in the field of data visualization. Having come to the discipline from distinct backgrounds—Viégas via design, Wattenberg via mathematics—their research and projects have significantly shaped the field. On their own and as a team since 2003—with the introduction of *History Flow* (2003), a timely examination of edit histories on Wikipedia—they continue to create works that introduce innovative concepts, forms, and ways of interacting with data. Embracing an open, collaborative practice, their works have introduced interactive and open-source tools for examining a wide range of scientific, social, and artistic questions. Their effort to democratize data visualization practice through open-source means has been persistent, beginning with their work *Many Eyes* (2007),[1] a website where users may upload data, create shared visualizations, and communicate responsively.

Works by Viégas and Wattenberg challenge and blur the perceived divisions between design and art or, within the context of data visualization, the practice of translating data into visual information and the invention of new forms of expression. *Bloom* (2013) is a constantly morphing array of circular blooms informed by live seismic data from the Hayward Fault in California's East Bay.[2] Referred to by Viégas and Wattenberg as a "portrait of the planet's energy," the large-scale projection transforms the earth's natural movements into a mesmerizing array of multihued rings that varyingly resonate outward. Inspired by and dedicated to the late Color Field painter Kenneth Noland, this work reinforces and reinterprets the phenomena of perception for the twenty-first century.

Bloom is also informed by the duo's groundbreaking work of the previous year, *Wind Map* (2012). Although seemingly unrelated to the visual arts, it is as phenomenal a work of art as it is essential to the history of data visualization. Conceived as a personal art project, *Wind Map* culls information from the National Digital Forecast Database, which is maintained by the National Weather Service and available to the public. Viégas and Wattenberg's work continually gathers these forecasts, which are time-stamped and revised each hour, to create a real-time image of the wind landscape over the United States.[3]

Aside from offering the ability to visually comprehend the constant shifts in the wind sweeping across the United States, the most striking aspect of *Wind Map* is the imagery itself. If abstraction is the inverse of information, this work represents the astonishing in-between of these polar forces. The graceful reticulations of white, representing the wind, flowing over the black background reinforce the notion not just of movement but also of landscape, reminding the viewer of the sheer vastness and beauty of the regions depicted, both actual and imagined. As the streaming winds meet and surge in tandem and with increased speed over the Continental Divide, through the Mississippi Valley, and across the hurricane-prone Panhandle, this work stirs our present circumstances, our past memories, and our collective futures. —JJ

1 *Many Eyes* was created at IBM's Visual Communication Lab. See Fernanda B. Viégas, Martin Wattenberg, Frank van Ham, Jesse Kriss, and Matt McKeon, "*Many Eyes*: A Site for Visualization at Internet Scale," *IEEE Transactions on Visualization and Computer Graphics* 13, no. 6 (November–December 2007): 1121–28, doi: 10.1109/TVCG.2007.70577.
2 *Bloom*, created in collaboration with Ken Goldberg and Sanjay Krishnan, was commissioned by the Nevada Museum of Art and appeared as an installation from February 16 to June 16, 2013.
3 Though projected in different ways throughout varying situations and exhibitions, the standard version of *Wind Map* remains in the public domain on their website, http://hint.fm/wind/.

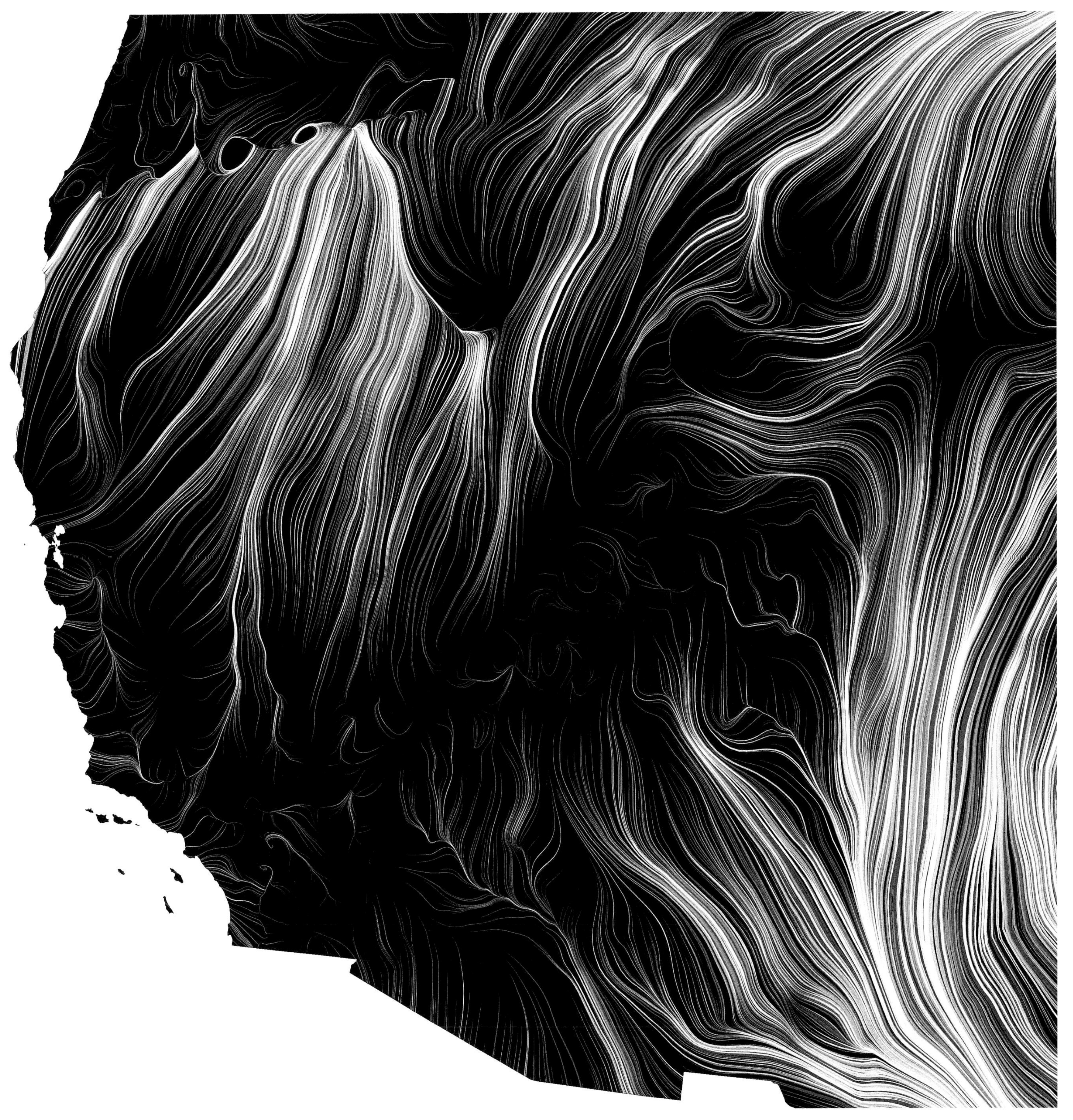

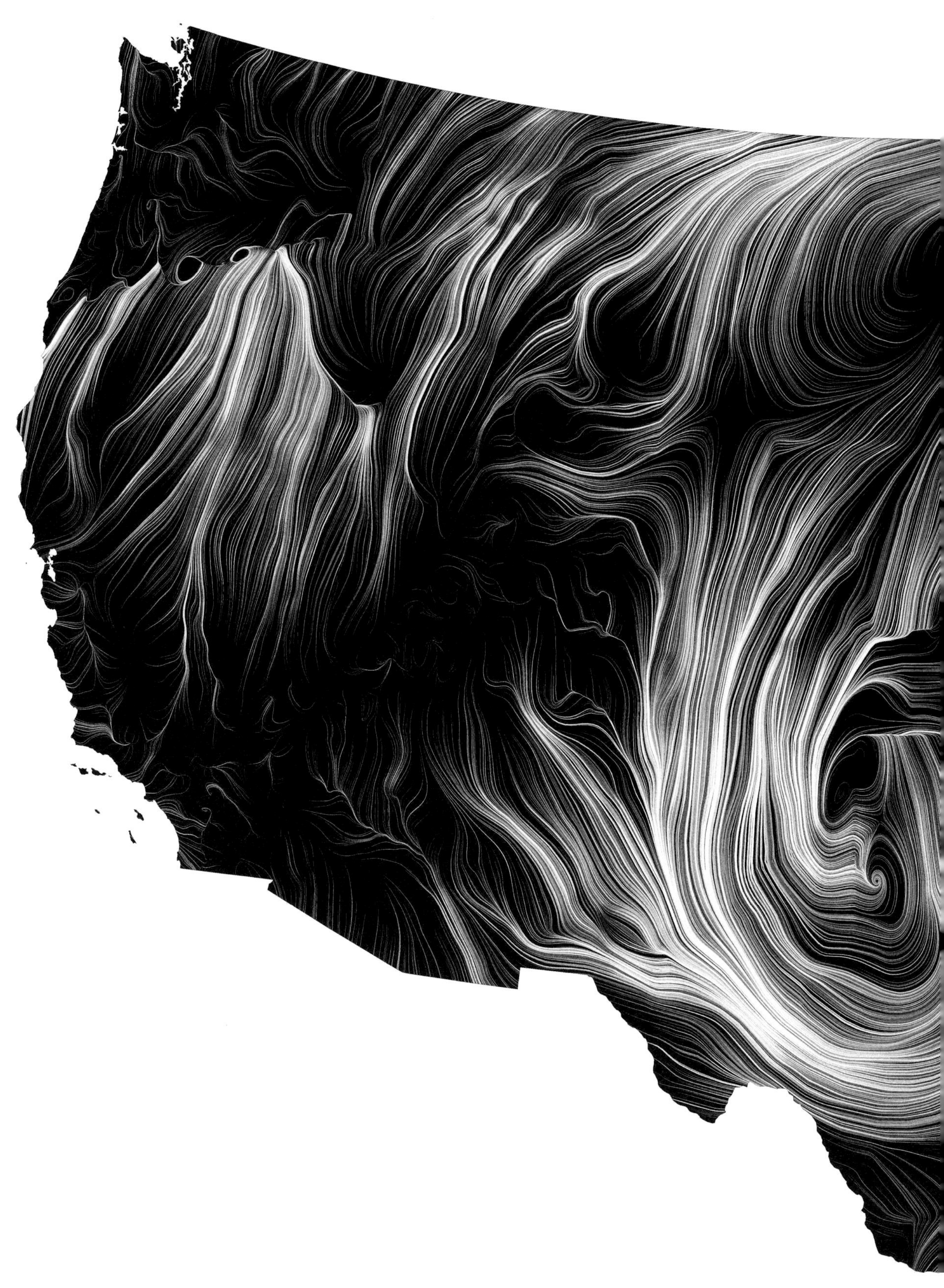

↗
Still from *Wind Map*, 2012

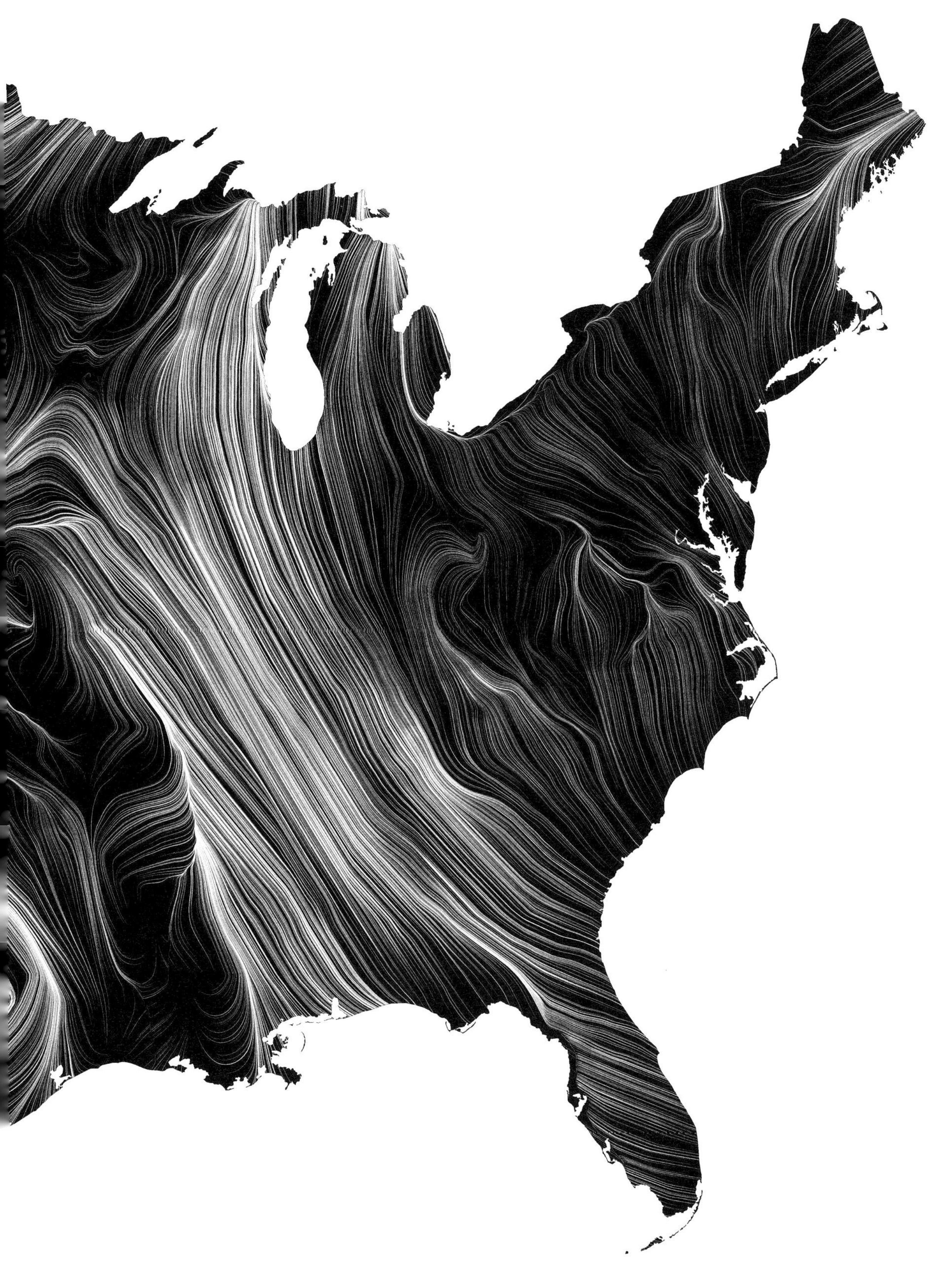

Peggy Weil

b. 1953, Minneapolis; lives and works in Los Angeles

77 Cores, 2024
White mylar digital print
Three panels, 30 × 96 inches each
Courtesy the artist

Dating back to the large camera obscura she built in the 1970s, Peggy Weil has been engaged in the ways of seeing. Today the artist, who works in interactive media, design, and visualization, continues to explore and expand on the realms of perception and to ponder what occurs in realms that are too small, too large, too far away, too deep, or too fast for us to observe. For Weil, this often means collaborating with other artists and with environmental scientists and researchers, who gather samples of the materials they are studying. Through her documentation of these stored records, Weil presents data that the earth holds: hidden under layers of ice, rock, images from so far beneath the surface that they are familiar only to the scientists who study them.[1]

In her project *18 Cores* (2018), Weil explored the earth's history and dwindling resources through her investigation of the geothermal system beneath California's Salton Sea. The artist created a video using eighteen core samples from the Salton Sea Scientific Drilling Project: almost two miles in length, it features a mix of shale, siltstone, and sandstone dating as far back as the Pleistocene era.[2] Projecting the cores side by side in a large-scale installation,[3] Weil creates friction between the vertical movement of each video as it slowly pans down different parts of the sample, offering a feeling of descent and gravity, along with the horizontal movement of viewers as they walk through the presentation, creating a time-based dissonance.

When Weil learned that mile-long Arctic and Antarctic ice cores were stored in one-meter containers at the National Science Foundation Ice Core Facility in Lakewood, Colorado, she felt compelled to, in her own words, "put one back together again." The ice cores—paleo thermometers capturing such environmental evidence as volcanic ash, pollen, and gasses—are, to Weil, "deep space holding very deep time."[4] As such they speak to the notion of the extended landscape, one hidden but revealed upon extraction and examination. In 2018, Weil presented the video *88 CORES A Monument to the Greenland Ice Sheet* (2018) at the Climate Museum in New York City. A partial reconstruction of the drilled ice samples, the video (accompanied by an original score by Celia Hollander) presents a vertical descent into the Greenland ice sheet. The artist's work in *Seeing the Unseeable*, *77 Cores* (2024), reimagines the project; images of seventy-seven ice cores are printed and laid out over twenty-four feet, allowing the viewer to mark time by walking their length.
—FW

1 Peggy Weil, "The Extended Landscape," https://pweilstudio.com/project/underscapes-overscapes/.
2 Weil, "The Extended Landscape," talk given as part of Leonardo's LASER Talks series and the 2022 Fulcrum Festival, Los Angeles, January 31, 2023, https://www.youtube.com/watch?v=8gb0AO6AjKM.
3 *18 Cores* was originally shown on the 360-degree digital screen of the Media Art Nexus (MAN) multimedia platform at Nanyang Technological University in Singapore. MAN is a curated exhibition platform for digitally based art and media.
4 Weil, "The Extended Landscape" talk.

→
Detail of *77 Cores*, 2024

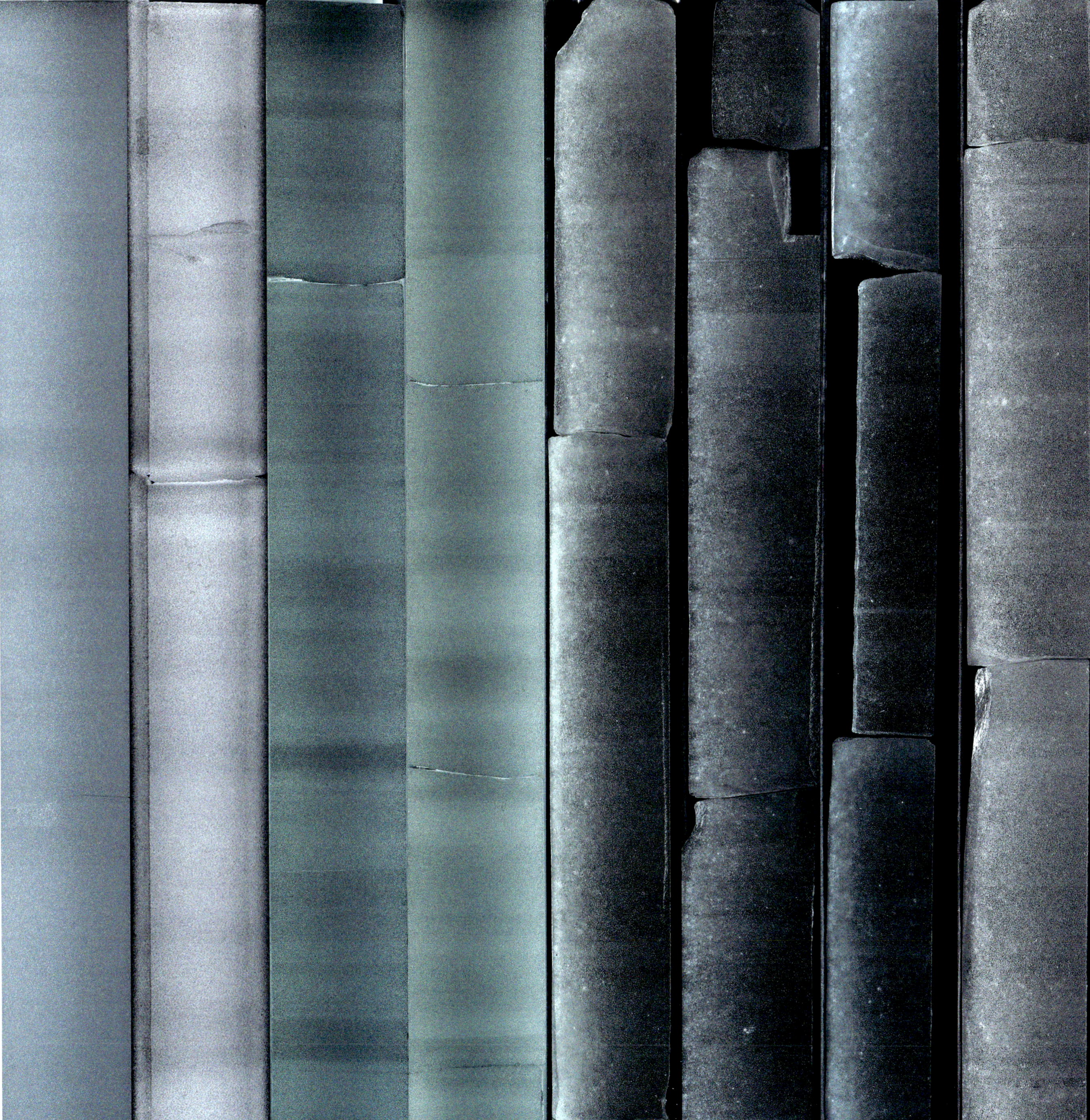

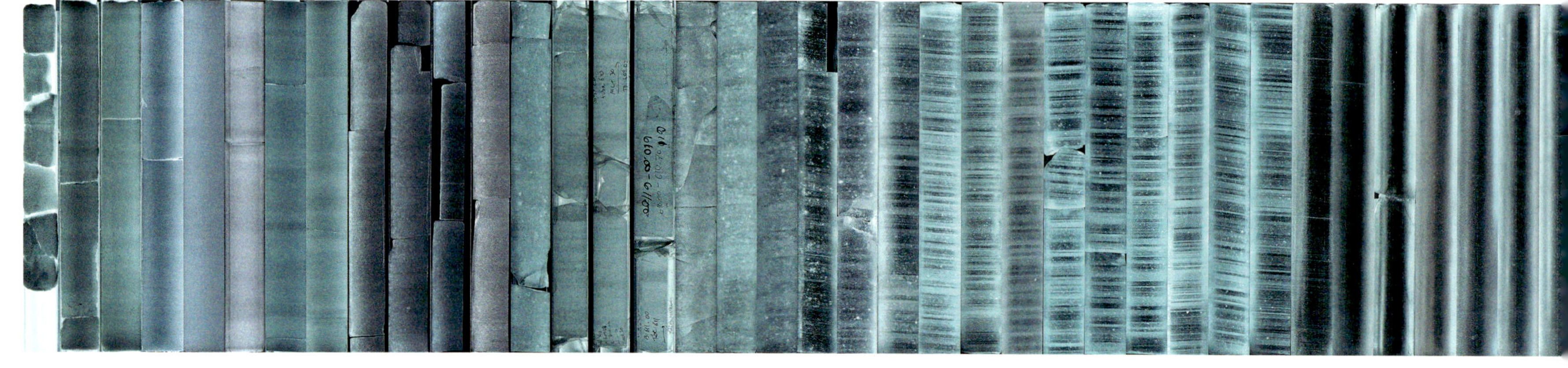

↑
77 Cores, 2024

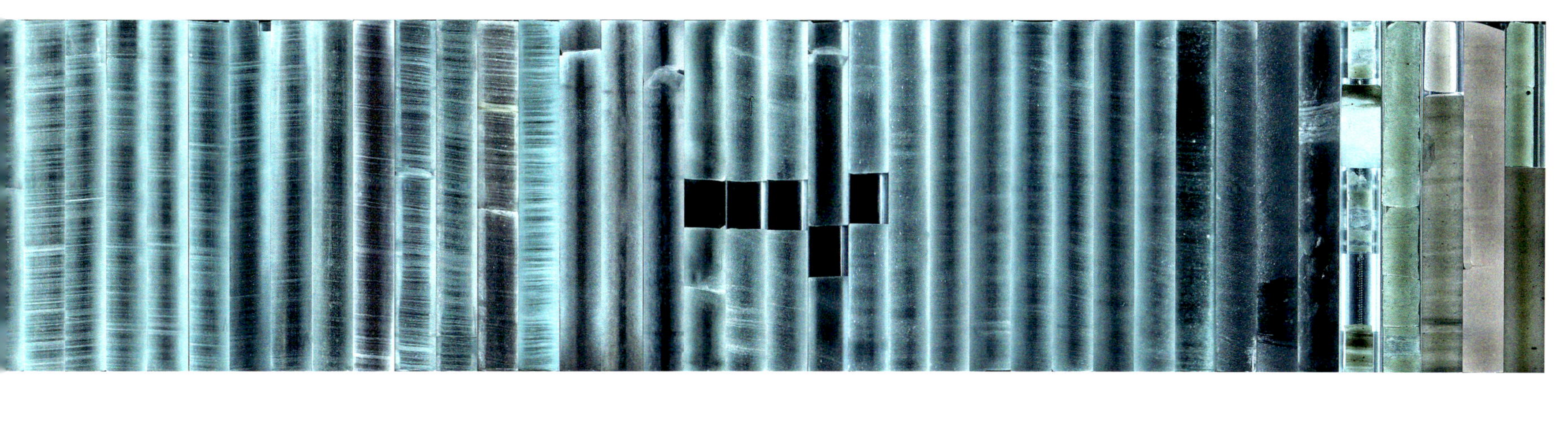

Christine Wertheim Margaret Wertheim and the Institute For Figuring

Christine Wertheim (b. 1958, Brisbane, Australia; lives and works in Los Angeles)
Margaret Wertheim (b. 1958, Brisbane, Australia; lives and works in Los Angeles)
Institute For Figuring (founded 2003, Los Angeles)

Pod Worlds from the *Crochet Coral Reef Project*, 2005–present
Yarn, plastic, beads, wire, sand, and rocks
Courtesy the artists and the Institute For Figuring

Artist twin sisters Margaret (who is also a science writer) and Christine Wertheim (also a college professor) cofounded the Institute For Figuring (IFF) in 2003 as a practice to engage audiences with the aesthetic dimensions of science and mathematics.[1] Through the IFF the sisters have created the *Crochet Coral Reef Project* (2005–present), a continually evolving, global-scale work that addresses environmental threats through craft and community engagement while also proposing that handiwork and critical art go hand in hand.

Historically practiced as a female craft, crochet can be also seen as a kind of materialized data, for the maker uses their hands to create spatially complex configurations following algorithmic stitch patterns. The scope of the coral reef project—from the *micro-* to the *macro*-scopic—stems from the notion of "embodied knowledge,"[2] wherein material things are acknowledged as incarnations of ideas and concepts usually presented by symbolic means, such as equations. Calla lilies, kale, and sea slugs, for instance, all embody hyperbolic geometry—which Margaret describes as "distinguishing itself in swoops and curves."[3] "The *Crochet Coral Reef Project* is like an open experiment in applied evolution,"[4] she explains, referring not only to the acts of crocheting novel coral forms, but also the work's ongoing evolution through each new community-made reef. The Wertheims' project extends pioneering work by Dr. Daina Taimina, who, in 1993, showed how to make models of hyperbolic surfaces using crochet. By deviating from Taimina's pure algorithm, the sisters have been exploring a complex taxonomy of crochet "species"—each one a data point in a wider geometric landscape.

Their *Crochet Coral Reef* has now been expanded to communities worldwide. The artists not only harness their own powers of craftmaking, they have worked with over thirty thousand contributors in fifty-two cities, tapping into a fertile vein of female energy—less than 0.1% of participants have been male—and channeling it into discussions about math, climate change, code, craft, and gender.

In 2007, three small crochet reefs were shown at the Andy Warhol Museum in Pittsburgh as part of *6 Billion Perps Held Hostage! Artists Address Global Warming*, one of the first major exhibitions to focus on climate change. Then invited to do a solo show at the Chicago Cultural Center, the sisters also worked with local communities there to create the first "satellite reef." To directly address causes of climate change, the Wertheims source discarded materials ranging from yarn and electronics to found plastic toys and "thread" made from plastic bags cut into strands.[5] In 2006, Christine Wertheim began crocheting corals from old VHS tape, especially sci-fi classics like *The Matrix* (1999). In the beautiful and disarming work *Pod World: Plastic Fantastic Too* (2015), the "sand" on which the coral pieces sit was gleaned from plastic trash washed up on the beaches of Hawaii from the Great Pacific Garbage Patch. The Wertheims' dedication through their work is raising awareness not only about global warming and the overconsumption of plastics but also the wonders of science and mathematics. —FW

1 "About: Institute For Figuring," *Crochet Coral Reef* website, https://crochetcoralreef.org/about/institute-for-figuring/.
2 Margaret Wertheim, keynote talk given at the 2019 Ecsite Conference, Copenhagen, June 7, 2019, posted on YouTube June 18, 2019, https://www.youtube.com/watch?v=blmrnLWYCoE.
3 Margaret Wertheim, "Making and Knowing: The Vernacular Science of the Crochet Coral Reef," p. 93 in this volume.
4 Wertheim, keynote talk.
5 "Community Artist Talk: Crochet Coral Reef with Margaret Wertheim," webinar presented by the North Carolina Museum of Art, Raleigh, August 11, 2021, https://www.youtube.com/watch?v=ERSsqQEep1Y.

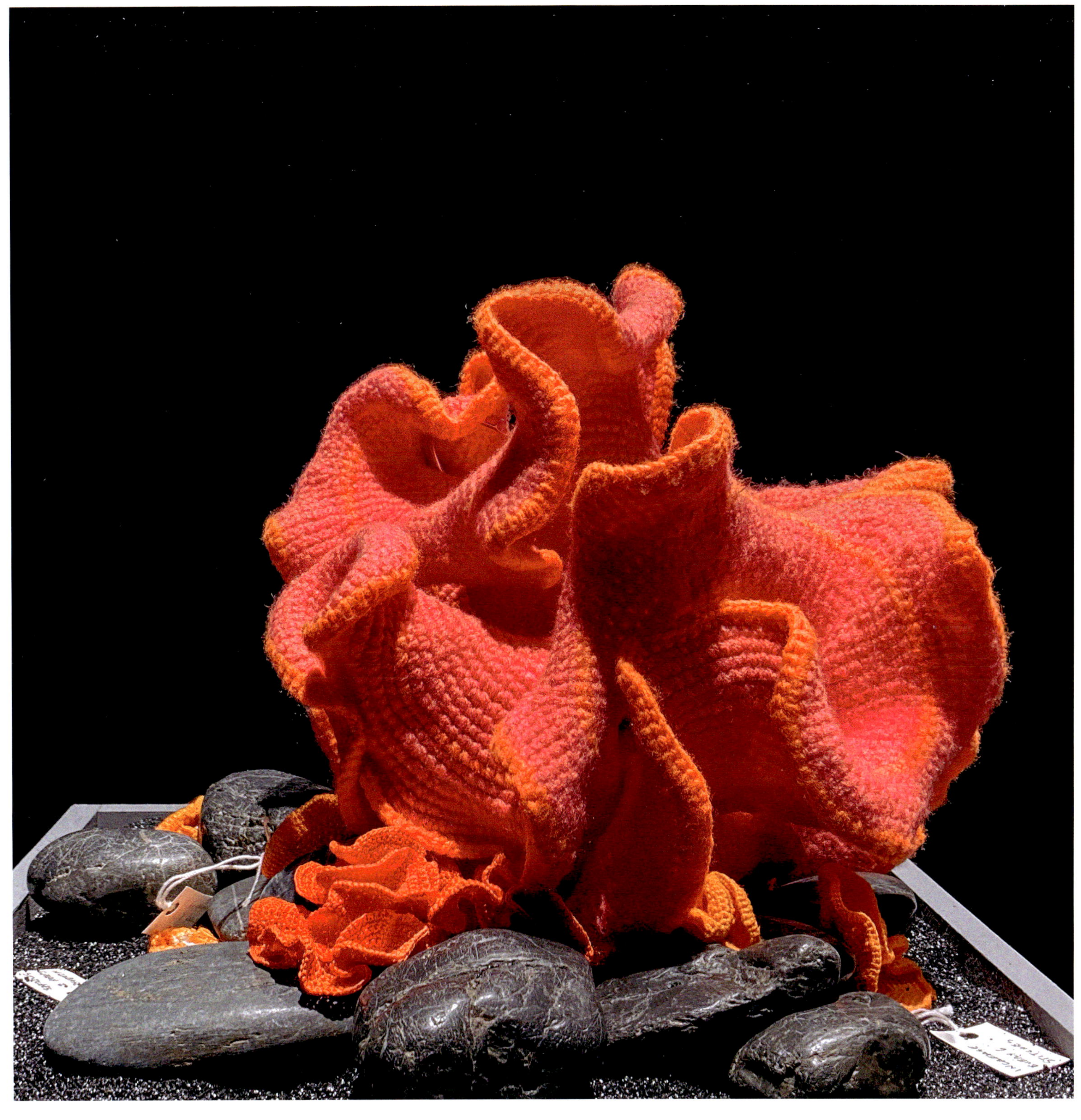

↑
Pod World: Hyperbolic, 2006–19, corals by Christine Wertheim, Margaret Wertheim, and Heather McCarren for the *Crochet Coral Reef Project*, 2005–present

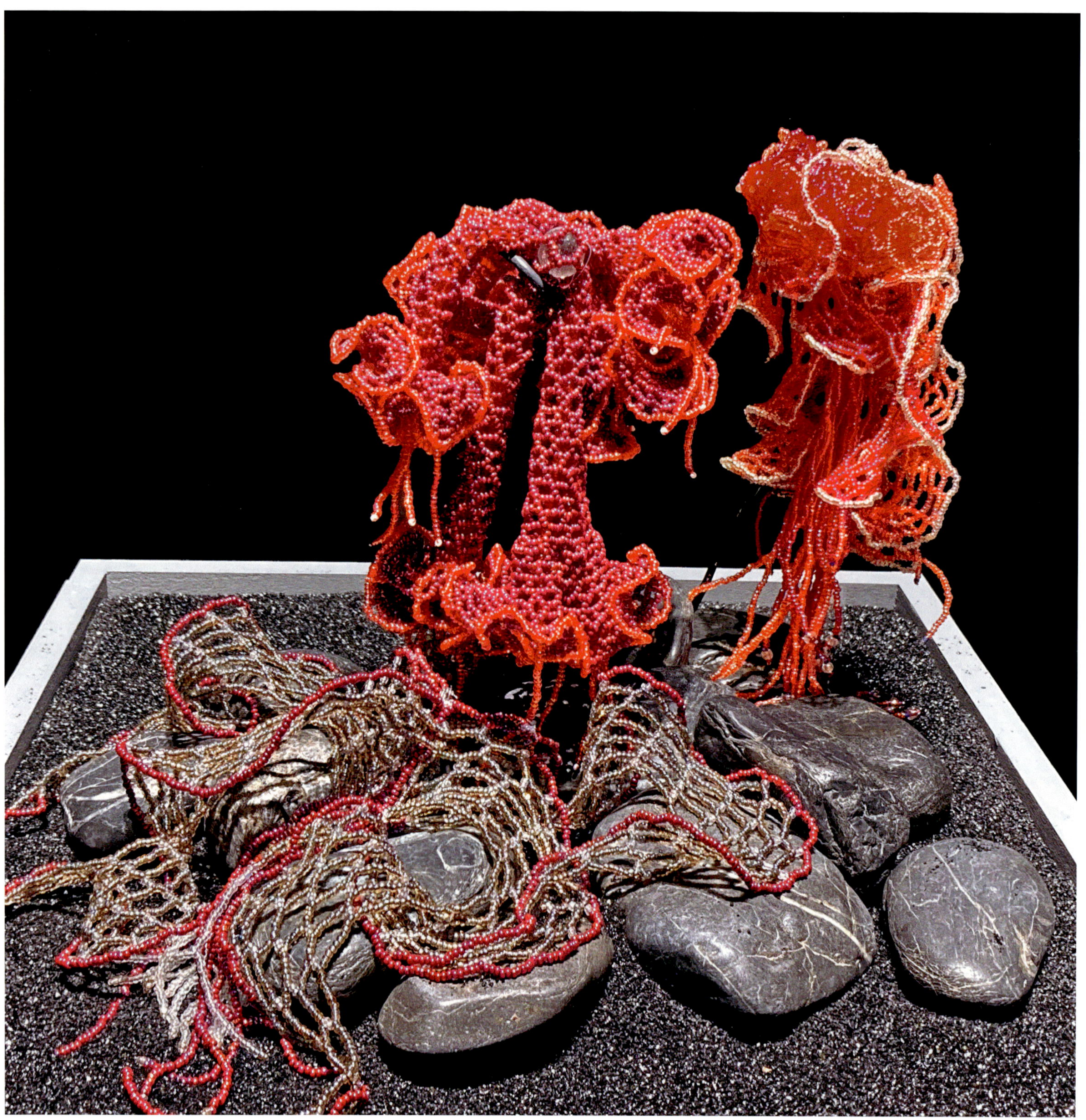

↑
Pod World: Beaded Jellyfish, 2007–9, jellyfish by Vonda N. McIntyre
for the *Crochet Coral Reef Project*, 2005–present

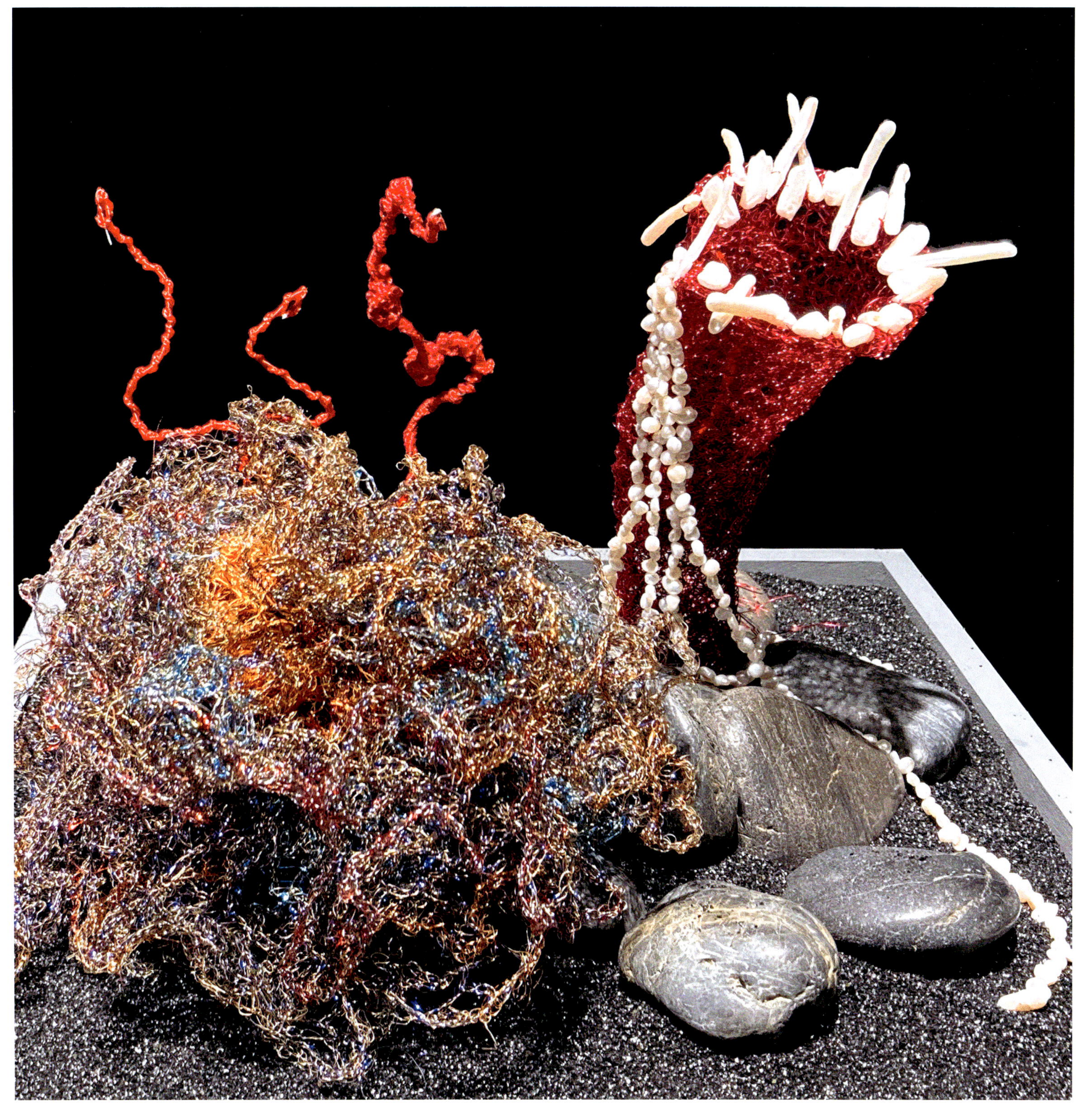

↑
Pod World: Wire, 2007–24, corals by Lucia LaVilla-Havelin and unknown Chicago "reefer" and spires by Margaret Wertheim for the *Crochet Coral Reef Project*, 2005–present

DATA

IS TOO

FOR US NOT

REINTE

ITS POWER

T

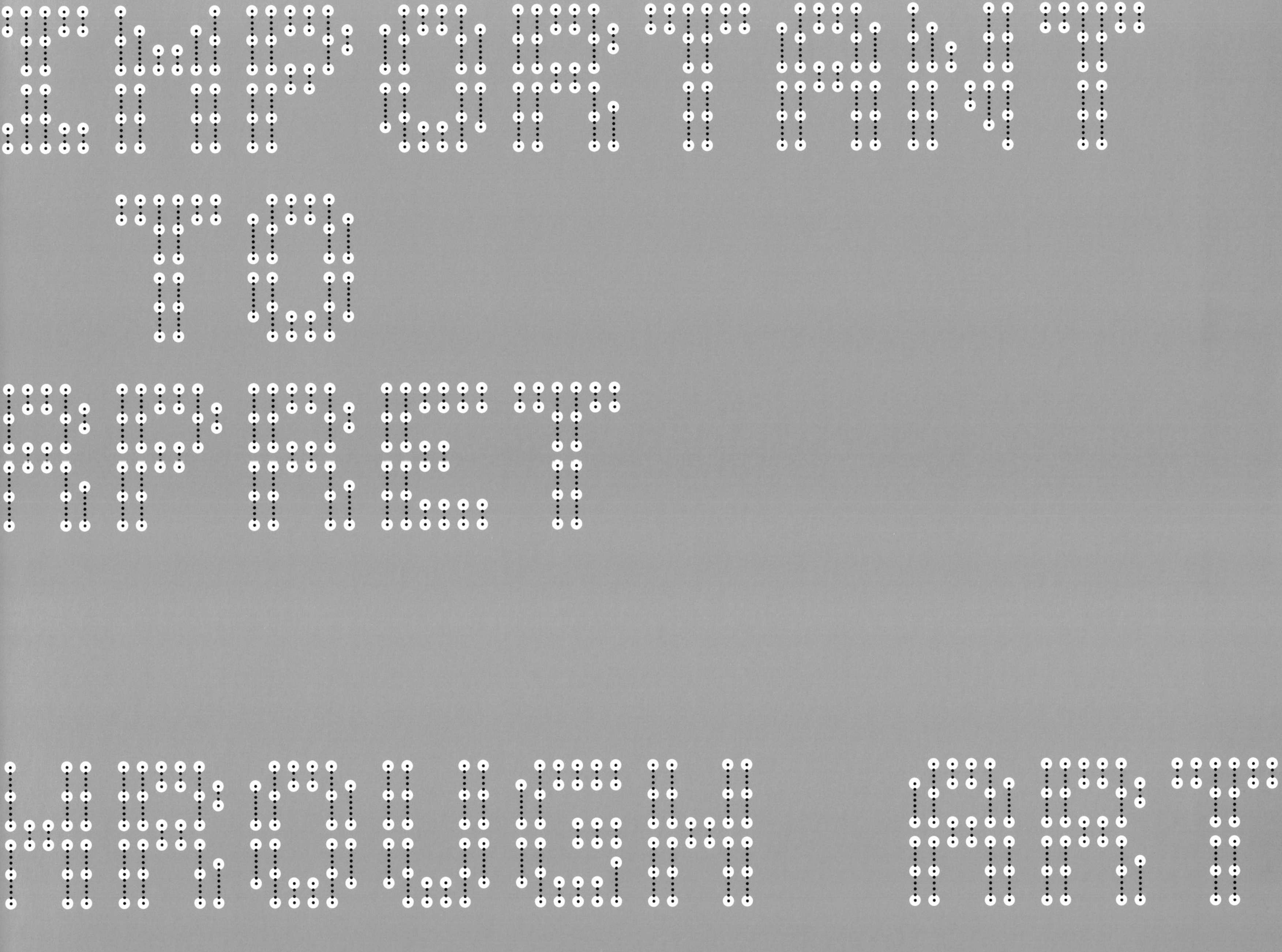

JASON FORREST

Exhibition Checklist
Bibliography
Photo Credits
Typography

Exhibition Checklist

Refik Anadol

California Landscapes: Generative Studies (A), 2023
AI data painting
3840 × 2160 pixels, 16 minutes
Courtesy RAS – Refik Anadol Studio
pp. 32 left, 103, 104 center and right

California Landscapes: Generative Studies (B), 2023
AI data painting
3840 × 2160 pixels, 16 minutes
Courtesy RAS – Refik Anadol Studio
pp. 33 left, 104 left, 105 top right and all bottom

California Landscapes: Generative Studies (C), 2023
AI data painting
3840 × 2160 pixels, 16 minutes
Courtesy RAS – Refik Anadol Studio
pp. 33 right, 105 top left and center

Data to Discovery: Santiago Lombeyda and Hillary Mushkin

3DDNA (3D Genome Structure Map and Analysis), 2016–24
With Jeff Brewer (software engineer) and Ethan Mcfarlin (assistant videographer). Created with 3DDNA interactive data visualization software (2016) and developed by NASA Jet Propulsion Lab/Caltech/ArtCenter Data to Discovery Program and Guttman Lab, Caltech. D2D directors: Scott Davidoff, Maggie Hendrie, Santiago Lombeyda, Hillary Mushkin. D2D visualization team: Peter Polack (software engineer), Aprameya Mysore (designer), Shixie Shi (designer). Collaborators: Mitch Guttman (professor of biology and bioengineering, Caltech), Noah Ollikainen (Guttman Lab postdoctoral scholar)
Data visualization video
3:06 minutes
Courtesy Data to Discovery with Guttman Lab
pp. 31 right, 107–8

GRVIN (Grain Assemblies Visualization and Analysis), 2018–24
With Jeff Brewer (software engineer) and Ethan Mcfarlin (assistant videographer). Created with GRVIN interactive data visualization software (2018) and developed by NASA Jet Propulsion Lab/Caltech/ArtCenter Data to Discovery Program and Andrade Lab, Caltech. D2D directors: Scott Davidoff, Maggie Hendrie, Santiago Lombeyda, Hillary Mushkin. D2D visualization team: Jeff Brewer (software engineer), Adrian Galvin (designer), Pooja Nair (designer). Collaborators: Jose Andrade (professor of mechanical and civil engineering, Caltech), Utkarsh Mital (Andrade Lab postdoctoral scholar)
Data visualization video
1:52 minutes
Courtesy Data to Discovery and Andrade Lab
p. 109

Laurie Frick

Moodjam Intense, 2024
Abet Laminati samples on ACM panel
86 × 86 inches
Courtesy the artist
pp. 40 left, 112

Moodjam Mild, 2024
Abet Laminati samples on ACM panel
86 × 86 inches
Courtesy the artist
pp. 40 right, 111, 113

George Legrady

Phantom Waves Series: Bristle Anistrophy, 2020–21
ChromaLuxe dye-sublimation print on aluminum
30 × 40 inches
Courtesy the artist
pp. 53, 117 top right

Phantom Waves Series: Cascade, 2020–21
ChromaLuxe dye-sublimation print on aluminum
30 × 40 inches
Courtesy the artist
pp. 10–11, 52, 116 bottom left

Phantom Waves Series: Cascade Jaggy, 2020–21
ChromaLuxe dye-sublimation print on aluminum
30 × 40 inches
Courtesy the artist
pp. 53, 117 bottom right

Phantom Waves Series: Irregular Oscillation, 2020–21
ChromaLuxe dye-sublimation print on aluminum
30 × 40 inches
Courtesy the artist
pp. 52, 116 top left

Phantom Waves Series: Linear Oscillation, 2020–21
ChromaLuxe dye-sublimation print on aluminum
30 × 40 inches
Courtesy the artist
pp. 52–53, 115 top

Phantom Waves Series: Linear Oscillation 2, 2020–21
ChromaLuxe dye-sublimation print on aluminum
30 × 40 inches
Courtesy the artist
pp. 52, 116 top right

Phantom Waves Series: Mid-Point Synthesis, 2020–21
ChromaLuxe dye-sublimation print on aluminum
30 × 40 inches
Courtesy the artist
pp. 62, 116 bottom right

Phantom Waves Series: Oscillation Grid, 2020–21
ChromaLuxe dye-sublimation print on aluminum
30 × 40 inches
Courtesy the artist
pp. 53, 117 top left

Phantom Waves Series: Triangular Demarcation, 2020–21
ChromaLuxe dye-sublimation print on aluminum
30 × 40 inches
Courtesy the artist
pp. 52–53, 116 bottom, 176

Phantom Waves Series: Wave Fracture 2 Vertical, 2020–21
ChromaLuxe dye-sublimation print on aluminum
30 × 40 inches
Courtesy the artist
pp. 53, 117 bottom left

Rafael Lozano-Hemmer

Hormonium (Text Stream 8), 2022
Custom-generative code and 4k display
Dimensions variable
Courtesy of the Collection of Arkive
pp. 6, 8, 31, 119–21

Giorgia Lupi and Ehren Shorday

Incroci (Crossings), 2022
Black paint on raw canvas
100 paintings, 15 × 14 inches each;
75 × 280 inches overall
Courtesy of Fondazione Merz
pp. 38–39, 123–25

Iñigo Manglano-Ovalle

Lu, Jack and Carrie
(from *The Garden of Delights*), 1998/2017
Archival pigment prints
Triptych: 61 × 24 inches each panel;
61 × 76 inches overall
Courtesy the artist
pp. 35, 127–28

Storm Prototype: Cloud Prototype No. 2, 2006
Fiberglass and titanium alloy
57 1/4 × 96 5/8 × 60 1/2 inches
Courtesy the artist
pp. 34, 86 top, 127

Storm Prototype: Cloud Prototype No. 4, 2006
Fiberglass and titanium alloy
62 × 102 × 57 1/4 inches
Courtesy the artist
pp. 34, 86 top, 127

Sarah Morris

Deviancy is the Essence of Culture [Sound Graph], 2018
Household gloss paint on canvas
48 × 48 inches
Courtesy the artist and Petzel Gallery, New York
pp. 45 left, 131

Property Must Be Seen [Sound Graph], 2020
Household gloss paint on canvas
60 × 60 inches
Courtesy the artist and Petzel Gallery, New York
pp. 44, 132

You Cannot Keep Love [Sound Graph], 2020
Household gloss paint on canvas
60 × 60 inches
Courtesy the artist and Petzel Gallery, New York
pp. 45 right, 133

Mimi Ọnụọha

The Library of Missing Data Sets, 2016
Steel filing cabinet and folders
22 1/2 × 20 × 16 inches
Courtesy the artist
pp. 41 bottom (white), 135 bottom

The Library of Missing Data Sets v 2.0, 2018
Powder-coated steel filing cabinet and folders
22 1/2 × 20 × 16 inches
Courtesy the artist
pp. 41 bottom (tan), 135 top

The Library of Missing Data Sets v 3.0, 2021
Steel filing cabinet and folders
18 1/2 × 15 3/8 × 19 3/4 inches
Courtesy the artist
p. 41 bottom (black)

In Absentia Series, 2019
Risograph print on paper, edition 1 of 3
Six prints, 20 1/4 × 14 1/4 inches each, framed
An Abridged History
This Land Is Your Land, p. 137 right
The Great Impossibility, p. 136 left
This Land Is My Land
It Could Never Be Large Enough, p. 137 left
Geography of Domination, p. 136 right
Courtesy the artist
pp. 41 top, 136–37

Semiconductor:
Ruth Jarman and Joe Gerhardt

Spectral Constellations, 2022
Generative animations on LED mosaics
Three parts: 30 1/4 × 30 1/4 × 4 3/4 inches; 22 5/8 × 30 1/4 × 4 3/4 inches; and 30 1/4 × 22 5/8 × 4 3/4 inches
Courtesy the artists
pp. 2, 42–43, 72–73, 139-41

Hyojung Seo

Singapore Weather Data Drawing: Windspeed, 2022
Video
24 second loop
Courtesy the artist
pp. 30 right, 145

Singapore Weather Data Drawing: Wind Direction, 2022
Video
24 second loop
Courtesy the artist
pp. 30 left, 34, 143, 144

Singapore Weather Data Drawing: Temperature, 2022
Video
24 second loop
Courtesy the artist
pp. 30 center, 144–45

Linnéa Gabriella Spransy

Prime Mover, 2019
Acrylic on canvas
84 × 132 × 3 inches
Courtesy the artist
pp. 34, 37, 86 bottom, 147 bottom, 149

Prime Mover 0, 2023
Acrylic on canvas
84 × 132 × 3 inches
Courtesy the artist
pp. 36, 86 bottom, 147 top, 148

Mika Tajima

Archive of Feelings (January 1, 2023, United States of America) #127, Los Angeles, 2023
Non-fungible token
24 seconds
Courtesy of Mika Tajima, Proof, and Pace Gallery
pp. 50 left, 151

Archive of Feelings (January 1, 2023, United States of America) #142, Memphis, 2023
Non-fungible token
24 seconds
Courtesy of Mika Tajima, Proof, and Pace Gallery
pp. 50 right, 152

Archive of Feelings (January 1, 2023, United States of America) #144, New York City, 2023
Non-fungible token
24 seconds
Courtesy of Mika Tajima, Proof, and Pace Gallery
pp. 51, 153

Fernanda Viégas and Martin Wattenberg

Wind Map, 2012
Projection interactive map
Dimensions variable
Courtesy the artists
pp. 4, 49, 155–57

Peggy Weil

77 Cores, 2024
White mylar digital print
Three panels, 30 × 96 inches each
Courtesy the artist
pp. 27–28, 159–61

Christine Wertheim, Margaret Wertheim, and Institute For Figuring

From the *Crochet Coral Reef Project* by Christine and Margaret Wertheim and the Institute For Figuring, 2005–present
Courtesy the artists and Institute For Figuring

Pod World: Hyperbolic, 2006–19
Coral pieces by Christine Wertheim, Margaret Wertheim, and Heather McCarren with Victorian black glass coral
15 × 15 × 15 inches
pp. 47 left, 163

Pod World: Beaded Jellyfish, 2007–9
Beaded jellyfish by feminist sci-fi writer Vonda N. McIntyre
15 × 15 × 15 inches
pp. 46 center, 164

Pod World: Wire, 2007–24
Wire corals by Lucia LaVilla-Havelin and unknown Chicago "reefer," with red spires by Margaret Wertheim
15 × 15 × 15 inches
pp. 46 right, 165

Pod World: Beaded, 2008–24
Beaded corals by Sue von Ohlsen, Sarah Simons, and Rebecca Peapples, with gold spires by Christine Wertheim
15 × 15 × 15 inches
p. 46 left

Pod World: Black and White, 2009–24
The Matrix videotape coral by Christine Wertheim, wire sea creatures by Anita Bruce, and white plasticized-thread coral by Christine Wertheim made with yarn gleaned from Noah Purifoy's site in Joshua Tree (with permission of the artist)
15 × 15 × 15 inches
p. 48 left

Pod World: Plastic Fantastic Too, 2015
Plastic corals by Christine Wertheim and Kathleen Greco, with plastic debris from the Great Pacific Garbage Patch collected on Kamilo Beach (Hawaii) by Captain Charles Moore
15 × 15 × 15 inches
pp. 47 center, 90

Pod World: Eye Jellies, 2022
Plastic crochet jellyfish by Margaret Wertheim, with discarded eye medication capsules used by the artist
15 × 15 × 15 inches
pp. 47 right, 99

Bibliography

Articles

Aviles, Mary. "A Guided Virtual Tour of 'Data Visualization and the Modern Imagination.'" *Nightingale: Journal of the Data Visualization Society*, October 2, 2020. https://medium.com/nightingale/a-virtual-guided-tour-of-data-visualization-and-the-modern-imagination-1c7a1c2c0bc7.

Barabási, Albert-László. "Why the World Needs 'Dataism,' the New Art Movement That Helps Us Understand How Our World Is Shaped by Big Data." Artnet.com, September 23, 2022. https://news.artnet.com/art-world-archives/introducing-dataism-2181005.

Bridle, James. "The New Aesthetic and its Politics." *Booktwo* (blog), June 12, 2013. http://booktwo.org/notebook/new-aesthetic-politics/.

Cannella, Cristina. "Subjective Data." *Cooper Hewitt* (blog of the Cooper Hewitt, Smithsonian Design Museum, New York), December 15, 2016. https://www.cooperhewitt.org/2016/12/15/subjective-data/.

Ezera, Anete. "Meet 6 Artists Who Have Swept Data Art into the Digital Age." Infogram blog, July 25, 2016. https://infogram.com/blog/meet-6-artists-who-have-swept-data-art-into-the-digital-age/.

Forrest, Jason. "New York Alive! Blending Performance and Data Art." *Nightingale: Journal of the Data Visualization Society*, March 16, 2021. https://nightingaledvs.com/new-york-alive-blending-performance-and-data-art-for-a-whole-lot-of-fun/.

Glisson, James. "Frederick Hammersley's Art Against the Machine." *Huntington Frontiers* (blog of The Huntington, San Marino, CA), May 12, 2016. https://huntington.org/frontiers/frederick-hammersleys-art-against-machine.

Haridy, Rich. "Art in the age of ones and zeros: Turning big data into art." *New Atlas* (email newsletter), June 7, 2017. https://newatlas.com/art-ones-and-zeros-data-visualization/49926/.

Harmon, Amy. "A Revolution at 50; Twist and Shout! The Double Helix Replicates Itself in Popular Culture." *The New York Times*, February 25, 2003.

Hart, Hugh. "*Decode* Exhibition Points Way to Data-Driven Art." *Wired Magazine*, January 25, 2018. https://www.wired.com/2010/01/decode-exhibition-points-way-to-data-based-future-art/.

Knaack, Nina. "The Artists Who Rewired Web2." *Right Click Save*, July 6, 2023. https://www.rightclicksave.com/article/the-artists-who-rewired-web2.

Lepore, Jill. "Data-Driven." *The New Yorker*, April 3, 2023.

Lupi, Giorgia. "Data Humanism: The Revolutionary Future of Data Visualization." *PrintMag*, January 30, 2017. https://www.printmag.com/article/data-humanism-future-of-data-visualization/.

Mansky, Jackie. "W.E.B. Du Bois' Visionary Infographics Come Together for the First Time in Full Color." *Smithsonian Magazine*, November 15, 2018. https://www.smithsonianmag.com/history/first-time-together-and-color-book-displays-web-du-bois-visionary-infographics-180970826/.

Min, Sey. "Data visualization design and the art of depicting reality." *Inside/Out* (MoMA/MoMA PS1 blog), December 10, 2015. https://www.moma.org/explore/inside_out/2015/12/10/data-visualization-design-and-the-art-of-depicting-reality/.

Ọnụọha, Mimi. "What Is Missing Is Still There." *Nichons-Nous Dans L'Internet*, no. 7 (April 2018): 111–13.

Ríos, Doreen A. "Un acercamiento curatorial a la visualización de datos." *[Anti]materia*, 2017. https://anti-materia.org/visualizacion-de-datos.

Steyerl, Hito. "A Sea of Data: Apophenia and Pattern (Mis-Recognition)." *e-flux Journal*, no. 72 (April 2016). https://www.e-flux.com/journal/72/60480/a-sea-of-data-apophenia-and-pattern-mis-recognition/.

Urist, Jacoba. "From Paint to Pixels." *The Atlantic*, May 14, 2015. https://www.theatlantic.com/entertainment/archive/2015/05/the-rise-of-the-data-artist/392399/.

Vankin, Deborah. "Why everyone is talking about Refik Anadol's AI-generated 'living paintings.'" *Los Angeles Times*, February 18, 2023.

Wattenberg, Martin, and Fernanda Viégas. "Design and Redesign." In *Malofiej 22: Premios Internacionales de Infografía*. Pamplona, Spain: Society of Newspaper Design, 2014. Reprinted in *Medium*, March 27, 2015. https://medium.com/@hint_fm/design-and-redesign-4ab77206cf9#.fyuo8psb2.

Books

Brier, Jessica D., ed. *On the grid: Ways of seeing in print*. Exh. cat. Poughkeepsie, NY: Frances Lehman Loeb Art Center; and New York: Scala Arts Publishers, 2022.

Cairo, Alberto. *The Functional Art: An Introduction to Information Graphics and Visualization*. Berkeley, CA: New Riders Publishing, 2013.

Criado Perez, Caroline. *Invisible Women: Exposing Data Bias in a World Designed for Men*. London: Vintage, 2020.

D'Ignazio, Catherine, and Lauren F. Klein. *Data Feminism*. Cambridge, MA: The MIT Press, 2020.

Jones, Caroline A., and Peter Galison, eds. *Picturing Science, Producing Art*. 1998; reprint, Hoboken, NJ: Taylor and Francis, 2014.

Jones, Leslie, ed. *Coded: Art Enters the Computer Age, 1952–1982*. Exh. cat. Los Angeles: Los Angeles County Museum of Art; and New York: DelMonico Books • D.A.P., 2023.

Frieling, Rudolf, ed. *Rafael Lozano-Hemmer: Unstable Presence*. San Francisco: San Francisco Museum of Modern Art; and Munich, Germany: Delmonico Books/Prestel, 2020.

Lupi, Giorgia, and Stephanie Posavec. *Dear Data: A Friendship in 52 Weeks of Postcards*. New York: Princeton Architectural Press, 2016.

McCandless, David. *Information Is Beautiful*. 2009; new edition, London: William Collins, 2012.

Steele, Julie, and Noah Iliinsky. *Beautiful Visualization: Looking at Data Through the Eyes of Experts*. Sebastopol, CA: O'Reilly Media, 2010.

Thorp, Jer. *Living in Data: A Citizen's Guide to a Better Information Future*. New York: MCD Books, 2021.

Wurman, Richard Saul. *Understanding USA*. Newport, RI: TED Conferences, 2000.

Exhibitions

Big Bang Data, Somerset House, London, December 3, 2015–March 20, 2016

Cloud Walkers, Leeum Museum of Art, Seoul, September 2, 2022–January 8, 2023

Coded: Art Enters the Computer Age, 1952–1982, Los Angeles County Museum of Art, February 12–July 2, 2023

DataViz: Information as Art, Beall Center for Art + Technology, University of California, Irvine, October 4, 2012–January 26, 2013

Decode: Digital Design Sensations, Victoria & Albert Museum, London, December 8, 2009–April 2010

Hito Steyerl: A Sea of Data, National Museum of Modern and Contemporary Art, Korea, Seoul, April 29–September 18, 2022

Drift: In Sync with the Earth, Hyundai Card Storage Gallery, Seoul, December 8, 2022–April 16, 2023

Living Data, Korean Media Arts Festival, New York, 2019

Programmed: Rules, Codes, and Choreographies in Art, 1965–2018, Whitney Museum of American Art, New York, September 28, 2018–April 14, 2019

The Art of Data: Making Sense of the World, Bletchley Park, Milton Keynes, UK, April 2022

Uncanny Valley: Being Human in the Age of AI, de Young, San Francisco, February 22, 2020–June 27, 2021

Vertiginous Data, National Museum of Modern and Contemporary Art, Korea, Seoul, March 23–July 28, 2019

Photo Credits

Copyright © Refik Anadol Studio, pp. 103–5
Copyright © Mel Bochner, courtesy Marc Selwyn Fine Art, p. 68
Copyright © and courtesy Ron Eglash, p. 94
Copyright © and courtesy Laurie Frick, pp. 107–9
Photos: Brian Forrest, pp. 27–28, 30–53, 125, 127, 143
Getty Research Institute, Los Angeles, copyright © Artists Rights Society (ARS), New York, New York / VG Bild-Kunst, Bonn, p. 66
Copyright © Hans Haacke / Artists Rights Society (ARS), New York / VG Bild-Kunst, Bonn, photo: Dario Lasagni, courtesy New Museum, p. 69
Copyright © Institute For Figuring, pp. 91–92
Copyright © Institute of Natural Sciences, p. 59
Courtesy of Ray Kass, The Mountain Lake Workshop, Virginia, p. 85
Courtesy Kunstmuseum Den Haag, pp. 78–79
Copyright © and courtesy George Legrady, pp. 10–11, 52–53, 115–17, 176
Copyright © 2024 The LeWitt Estate / Artists Rights Society (ARS), New York, courtesy Art Resource, p. 83
Copyright © Hillary Mushkin and Santiago Lombeyda, courtesy Santiago Lombeyda, Hillary Mushkin, NASA Jet Propulsion Laboratory / Caltech / ArtCenter Data to Discovery, pp. 107–9
Copyright © Rafael Lozano-Hemmer, courtesy Antimodular Studio, pp. 4, 6, 119–21; West Kowloon Cultural District, p. 121
Copyright © Giorgia Lupi and Ehren Shorday, pp. 123–25
Copyright © Iñigo Manglano-Ovalle, pp. 86 (top), 128–29
Copyright © Sarah Morris, courtesy of the artist and Petzel Gallery, New York, pp. 131–33
Copyright © 1991 Hans Namuth Estate, courtesy of Center for Creative Photography, University of Arizona, p. 80
NASA/JPL-Caltech/GSSR/NRAO/GB, p. 76
Copyright © Mimi Ọnụọha, photo: Brandon Schulman, p. 135 (bottom); photo: Emile Askey, pp. 135 (top), 136–37
Copyright © Estate of Pablo Picasso / Artists Rights Society (ARS), New York, courtesy Art Resource, p. 64
Photos: Juan Posada for ArtCenter, pp. 123–24
Copyright © 2024 Dorothea Rockburne / Artists Rights Society (ARS), New York, p. 84
Copyright © Semiconductor, pp. 2, 72–73, 140–41
Copyright © 2022 Hyojung Seo, All rights reserved., pp. 30, 34 (right), 143–45
Copyright © 2024 Linnéa Gabrielle Spransy, All rights reserved., pp. 86 (bottom), 147 (bottom), 148; photo: Alex Neuss, pp. 147 (top), 149
Copyright © 2023 Mika Tajima, courtesy of Mika Tajima, Proof, and Pace Gallery, pp. 151–53
Copyright © and courtesy Fernanda Bertini Viégas and Martin Wattenberg, pp. 4, 49, 155–57
Copyright © and courtesy Peggy Weil, pp. 159–61
Copyright © 2023 *Crochet Coral Reef* by Christine Wertheim and Margaret Wertheim and the Institute For Figuring, photos: Stephen Nowlin, pp. 99, 163–65
Wikipedia Commons, pp. 60, 61, 63, 97 bottom

Typography

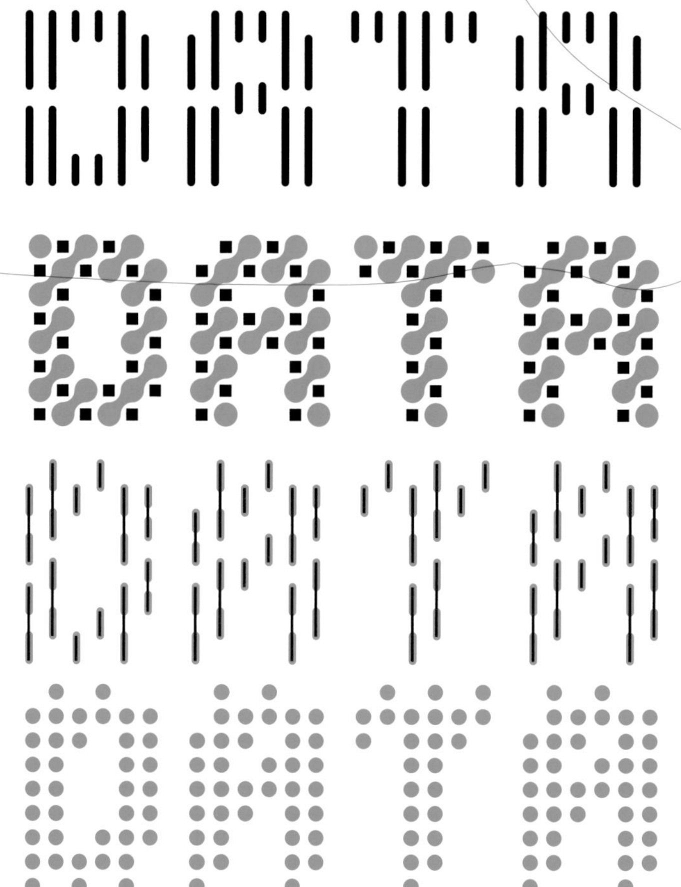

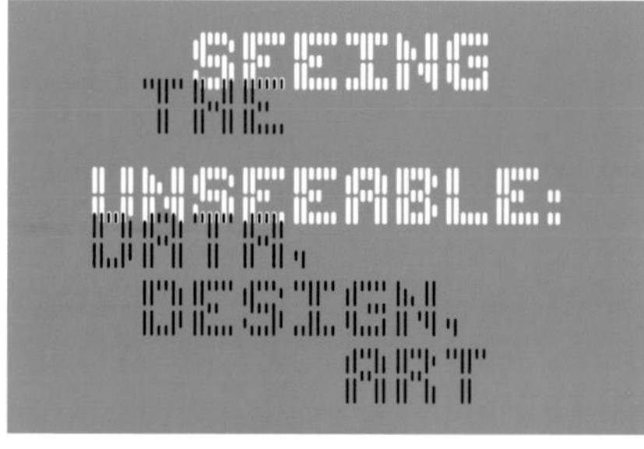

←
Initially derived from markings on the Ishango bone, the exhibition identity features a generative system, where programmed typography responds to changing parameters, creating myriad permutations.

Published in conjunction with the exhibition *Seeing the Unseeable: Data, Design, Art,* curated by Julie Joyce, Stephen Nowlin, and Hyesoo Christina Valentine and presented at the Alyce de Roulet Williamson Gallery, ArtCenter College of Design, Pasadena, California, September 19, 2024–February 15, 2025.

The exhibition and publication are made possible through major support from the Getty as part of the PST ART initiative, *Art & Science Collide.*

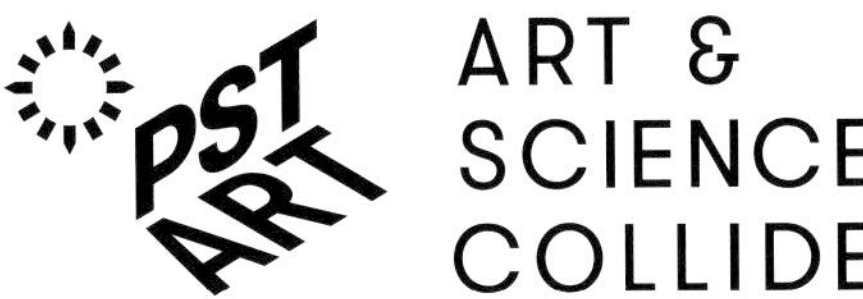

Presented by 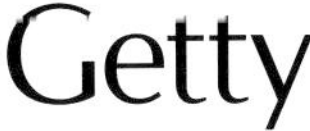

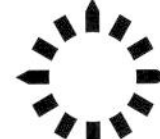

ArtCenter Exhibitions participated in the PST ART Climate Impact Program, a groundbreaking integration of climate action, community building, and data reporting. Learn more at pst.art/climate.

Library of Congress Control Number: 2025901362

ISBN: 978-3-7774-4510-6

The Deutsche Nationalbibliothek lists this publication in the Deutsche Nationalbibliografie; detailed bibliographic data are available on the Internet at http://dnb.ddb.de.

Published by
ArtCenter College of Design
1700 Lida Street
Pasadena, California 91103
artcenter.edu/exhibitions

in association with
Hirmer Verlag
Bayerstrasse 57-59
80335 Munich
Germany
hirmerpubliishers.com

Design and production: Brad Bartlett
Copy editing: Jane Hyun
Pre-press: Reproline Mediateam, Munich
Printing: Printer Trento s.r.l.

Hirmer Publishers
Senior Editor: Elisabeth Rochau-Shalem
Project Manager: Rainer Arnold

ArtCenter Exhibitions
Julie Joyce, Director, ArtCenter Galleries, and Vice President, Exhibitions
Christina Valentine, Associate Director, ArtCenter Galleries, and Curator, Exhibitions
Marco Rios, Lead Preparator
Erik Trammel, Coordinator
Francie Wong, Project Coordinator
Preparators: Tony Ban-Jo, Francisco Casanova, Leo Eguiarte, Curtis Noel, Heddar Sherazi, Angeles Portilla
Gallery Attendants: Ren Bennett, Lizeth Gonzalez, Bianca Kumpis, Aaron Reeves
Getty Marrow Interns: Madison Davis (2023), Juliana Favela (2021), Loran Murray (2024), Samantha Stefanoff (2022)
My Masterpieces Teaching Artists: Jackie Amézquita, Johnnie Pérez

Advisory Committee
Yoon Chung Han, Santiago Lombeyda, Pietro Perona, George Djorgovski, Maggie Hendrie, Dan Goods, Michael Greene, and Jane McFadden

Lenders to the Exhibition
Arkive, Data to Discovery, Fondazione Merz, Laurie Frick, George Legrady, Rafael Lozano-Hemmer, Giorgia Lupi and Ehren Shorday, Iñigo Manglano-Ovalle, Sarah Morris, Mimi Ọnụọha, Pace Gallery, Petzel Gallery, Proof, RAS—Refik Anadol Studio, Semiconductor, Hyojung Seo, Linnéa Gabriella Spransy, Mika Tajima, Fernanda Viégas and Martin Wattenberg, Peggy Weil, and Christine Wertheim, Margaret Wertheim, and the Institute For Figuring

Printed in Italy

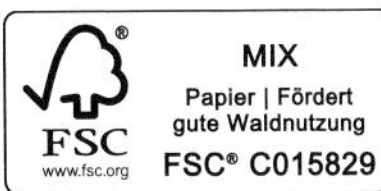

Page 2: Semiconductor, detail of *Spectral Constellations*, 2022
Page 4: Fernanda Viégas and Martin Wattenberg, detail of *Wind Map*, 2012
Pages 6 and 8: Rafael Lozano-Hemmer, details of *Hormonium (Text Stream 8)*, 2022
Pages 10–11: George Legrady, detail of *Phantom Waves Series: Cascade Jaggy*, 2020–21
Pages 72–73: Semiconductor, detail of *Spectral Constellations*, 2022
Page 176: George Legrady, detail of *Phantom Waves Series: Triangular Demarcation*, 2020–21